EUROPEAN MONOGRAPHS

Free Movement of Persons Within the European Community

by

Friedl Weiss
and
Frank Wooldridge

KLUWER LAW INTERNATIONAL
THE HAGUE – LONDON – NEW YORK

Published by:
Kluwer Law International
P.O. Box 85889, 2508 CN The Hague, The Netherlands
sales@kli.wkap.nl
http://www.kluwerlaw.com

Sold and distributed in North, Central and South America by
Kluwer Law International
101 Philip Drive, Norwell, MA 02061, USA
kluwerlaw@wkap.com

Sold and distributed in all other countries by
Kluwer Law International
Distibution Centre, P.O. Box 322, 3300 AH Dordrecht, The Netherlands
kluwerlaw@wkap.com

Library of Congress Cataloging-in-Publication Data is available.

Printed on acid-free paper

ISBN: 90-411-1708-3

Printed and bound in Great Britain by MPG Books Limited, Bodmin, Cornwall.

TABLE OF CONTENTS

Acknowledgments

The authors would like to thank a number of persons for the invaluable help which they have given us when writing this book. We in particular extend our appreciation to Rosemary Richards, who has shown herself to be a dependable and patient research assistant at the Law Faculty of the University of Amsterdam.

In addition we have had a good deal of generous help and competent advice from Suzanne Thorpe, Associate Director for Faculty, Research and Instructional Services at the Law Library of the Law School of the University of Minnesota for which we are extremely grateful.

Futhermore, we have been privileged to have benefited from the skilful services of Linda Wilbram of the Law School of the University of Notre Dame and Susan Hunt of the Law Department of the London School of Economics and Political Science whose cheerful and cooperative approach to the production of the manuscript has assisted us greatly and has helped to reinforce our efforts.

Last but not least we would like to thank our close relations and friends for their tolerance of the fact that we have been necessarily preoccupied with the research for, and the writing of, the book.

Amsterdam,   **Friedl Weiss and Frank Wooldridge**
London,
Minneapolis

October 2001

Preface

The present work attempts a comprehensive overview of European Community law relating to the free movement of persons. The two authors have researched and lectured extensively in this field and have made a number of academic contributions in particular areas within, or related to, its general scope.

The book is intended to be useful for legal practitioners, Community officials, post-graduate and under-graduate students as well as for the wider public interested in the process of European integration.

An attempt has been made to state the law as of 1 June 2001, where possible. The book places its main emphasis on the free movement of persons, although it briefly considers certain relevant matters concerning companies including their freedom of establishment. It deals with a number of diverse subjects including visas, the free movement of workers, posted workers, the harmonization of professional qualifications, freedom to provide and receive services, European citizenship, and agreements between the European Community and other states concerning free movement.

It also puts considerable emphasis on the rights of third country nationals, and gives a detailed account of the importance and somewhat controversial EURODAC regulation enacted in the year 2000.

In addition to making reference to the relevant provisions of the European Community Treaty, as amended by subsequent treaties including the Treaties of Amsterdam and Nice, it takes considerable account of all relevant secondary legislation and sometimes soft law, for example draft treaties, resolutions, and draft legislation.

Freedom of movement of persons is of fundamental economic significance in an economic union or common market, and however imperfectly realized, millions of individuals have already taken advantage of it.

An attempt has also been made to consider what obstacles remain to this freedom and what future developments might take place in this area of Community law.

The writers have collaborated closely in writing this book which, it is hoped, will generally be found to be a useful tool by those who use it.

Abbreviations

AC	Appeal Cases
AG	Advocate General
AJIL	American Journal of International Law
All ER (EC)	All England Law Reports (European Cases)
BOC	British Overseas Citizens
Bull EC	Bulletin of the European Communities
Bull EC Supp.	Bulletin of the European Communities Supplement
CA	English Court of Appeal
CEE	Charges of equivalent effect
CEEC	Central and Eastern European Countries
CSCE	Conference on Security and Cooperation in Europe
CFI	Court of First Instance
CFSP	Common Foreign and Security Policy
CMLR	Common Market Law Reports
CML Rev.	Common Market Law Review
Co. Law	The Company Lawyer
COM	European Commission
DC	Developing Countries
Dec.	Decision
Dir.	Directive
EAEC	European Atomic Energy Community
EBL Rev.	European Business Law Review
EC	European Community
EC Treaty	European Community Treaty
ECHR	European Convention of Human Rights
ECJ	European Court of Justice
ECR	European Court Reports
ECSC	European Coal and Steel Community
ECU	European Currency Unit(s)
EEA	European Economic Area
EEC	European Economic Community
EEIG	European Economic Interest Grouping
EFTA	European Free Trade Association
EGV	Entscheide der Gerichts- und Verwaltungsbehörden
EL Rev.	European Law Review
EP	European Parliament

EU	European Union
EURES	European Employment Services
GATS	General Agreement on Trade in Services
GDP	Gross Domestic Product
ICJ	International Court of Justice
IGC	Intergovernmental Conference
ILM	International Legal Materials
ISD	Investment Services Directive
JBL	Journal of Business Law
J.Bus.L.	Journal of Business Law
JO	Journal Officiel de la Communauté Européenne (the French version of the OJ)
LDC	Least-developed Countries
MFN	Most-Favoured Nation
n.y.r.	not yet reported
OECD	Organisation for Economic Co-operation and Development
OJ	Official Journal of the European Communities
OJ Spec. EC	Official Journal of the European Communities Special European Communities
OUP	Oxford University Press
PCA	Partnership and Cooperation Agreement
QB	Queen's Bench Reports
Reg.	Regulation
RMC	Revue du Marché Commun
RTDE	Revue trimestrielle du droit européen
SEA	Single European Act
SIS	Schengen Information System
SLIM	Simpler Legislation for the Internal Market
SPUC	Society for the Protection of Unborn Children Ireland Ltd
TEU	Treaty on European Union
UCITS	Undertakings for Collective Investment in Transferable Securities
UK	United Kingdom
UN	United Nations
UNECTEF	Union nationale des entraîneurs et cadres techniques professionnels du football
UNHCR	United Nations High Commissioner for Refugees
UNYCE	United New Yorkers for Choice in Education
WTO	World Trade Organization
YBEL	Yearbook of European Law
ZHR	Zeitschrift für Handelsrecht

Table of Cases

EUROPEAN COURT OF JUSTICE AND COURT OF FIRST INSTANCE

A. Alphabetical Order

The Court of Justice of the European Communities – Judgments of the Court

Opinion of the Court of Justice of the European Communities

Opinions of the Advocate General

CASES FROM OTHER JURISDICTIONS

European Court of Human Rights

International Court of Justice

National Case Law

Austria

France

Germany

Brunner, Manfred Brunner and others v. The European Union Treaty, Case 2
    B v. R 2134/92 and 2159/92, Judgment of 13 October, 1993, [1994] 1
    CMLR 57 – p. 25, 106
L.G. Marburg [1994] RIW 63 – p. 106
Oberlandesgericht Düsseldorf [1984] WM – p. 153

United Kingdom

Regina (Javed) v. Secretary of State for the Home Department and Another,
    Regina (Zulfiqar Ali) v. Same, Regina (Abid Ali) v.Same, Court of Appeal,
    17 May 2001, "The Times", 24 May 2001 – p. 199
Adan v. Secretary of State for the Home Department, Judgment of 30
    November, 1999, 1 AC 293, 305 B-C UK – p. 185
Astrid Proll (alias Anna Puttick) v. Entry Clearance Officer Düsseldorf,
    Judgment of 12 April, 1988, [1988] 2 CMLR 387 – p. 149, 153
Horvath v. Secretary of State for the Home Department, [2000] 3 All ER 577
    – p. 185
R.v. Human Fertilisation and Embryology Authority ex parte DB, Judgment
    of 6 February, 1997, [1997] 2 CMLR 591 – p. 123
R.v. Secretary of State for the Home Department, [2000] 2 All ER 1086, 18
    May 2000 (CA)
R.v. Secretary of State for the Home Department, ex parte Adan and Aitsegur
    (HL), [1999] 4 All ER 774 – p. 185, 199
R.v. Secretary of State for the Home Department, ex parte Vitale, [1996] All
    ER (EC) 461 – p. 162
Secretary of State v. Remilien, [1999] All ER (EC) 650 CA – p. 52
The Queen v. Secretary of State for the Home Department, ex parte Sandhu,
    Judgment on 28 May, 1982, [1982] 2 CMLR 553 – p. 52

Table of Treaties, European Legislative Instruments, Proposals for Legislative Instruments, Other Acts, and National Legislation

FREE MOVEMENT OF PERSONS WITHIN THE EUROPEAN COMMUNITY

European Community Bilateral Agreements with Non-Member Countries
1 *European Countries*
1.1 *Countries in Transition*

Bulgaria, OJ 1994 L 358/3
  Article 45(1) – p. 223
  Article 59 – p. 229, 230

Czech Republic, OJ 1994 L 360
  Article 45 – p. 226
  Article 59

Poland, OJ 1993 L 348/2
  Article 1(2) – p. 201
  Article 31(1) – p. 223, 224
  Article 37(1) – p. 223, 227
  Article 41(1) – p. 223
  Article 41(2) – p. 225
  Article 43 – p. 225
  Article 44 – p. 225, 226
  Article 44(1) – p. 223, 225, 226, 227
  Article 44(2) – p. 225
  Article 44(3) – p. 222, 225, 226, 227
  Article 45(1) – p. 229
  Article 52 – p. 227
  Article 52(2) – p. 228
  Article 53 – p. 228
  Article 53(1) – p. 228, 229
  Article 55(2) – p. 228
  Article 58(1) – p. 227, 228, 229, 230, 234, 235
  Joint Declaration annexed to Final Act – p. 223, 227, 229

Russia, OJ 1997 L 327/1
  Article 23 – p. 230, 231
  Article 23(1) – p. 231
  Article 23(2) – p. 231
  Article 24 – p. 231
  Article 25 – p. 231
  Article 26 – p. 231
  Article 27 – p. 232
  Article 28 – p. 232, 233
  Article 28(1) – p. 232
  Article 28(2) – p. 232
  Article 28(3) – p. 232
  Article 29 – p. 232
  Article 30 – p. 232

European Parliament and Council Directives

Commission Directives

DECISIONS OF REPRESENTATIVES OF GOVERNMENTS

COUNCIL OF THE EUROPEAN UNION – JOINT ACTIONS

COUNCIL OF THE EUROPEAN UNION – JOINT POSITIONS

OTHER NON-BINDING ACTS OF COMMUNITY ORGANS

FREE MOVEMENT OF PERSONS WITHIN THE EUROPEAN COMMUNITY

Report of High Level Panel

Resolutions of the Council

National Legislation

France

Germany

Ireland

FREE MOVEMENT OF PERSONS WITHIN THE EUROPEAN COMMUNITY

1 Introduction

I. NOTE ON HISTORICAL AND SOCIO-ECONOMIC CONTEXTUAL MATTERS

Historically, human migration, the movement of labour and peoples, transformed patterns of work and employment as well as a range of social and cultural relations. While human migration is perhaps the most ubiquitous form of globalization, it has had a particularly long history in the form of cross-border migration of labour in Europe. Recent studies suggest that while the economic impact of historical patterns of migration on the labour market and the broader economy are difficult to establish, that on the welfare state may actually be positive.[1] At the same time, the spectacular increase in global and regional migrations due to the movement of labour, tourism, asylum seekers, students, family reunions etc., have also exposed the permeable nature of national borders as well the limited capacity of sovereign nation-states independently to secure their own borders in an effective manner and to stem the flow of illegal immigrants. This has prompted attempts to co-ordinate relevant national policies based on contemporary bureaucratization and documentation of citizenship, mainly by means of passport and visa controls, and common immigration and asylum criteria. However, in view of some of the abominable past practices of European states, such as the forced expulsions of the Jews and the Huguenots, contemporary European liberal democratic states must proceed cautiously. Indeed, immigration policies cannot be conceived and executed in isolation from labour market policies, and the intrusiveness of border controls must be examined against the backgrounds of domestic civil rights and international human rights obligations. A combination of historical legacies, and the need for balancing different domestic policies with international obligations probably explains why the European Union's efforts at collective refugee and migration regulations through the Schengen and Dublin agreements and other instruments have been both complex and limited so far. Nonetheless, it has also been observed that while production and investment have become more globalized, with the encouragement of governments and international organisations, the same authorities,

---

1. See David Held, Anthony McGrew, David Goldblatt and Jonathan Perraton, 'People on the Move', in *Global Transformations: Politics, Economics and Culture* (Polity Press, Cambridge, 1999), chapter 6, pp. 283–5, 295, 313, 322–4; views by economists on immigration differ considerably, see Bob Sutcliffe, 'Freedom to move in the age of globalization', in Dean Baker, Gerald Epstein and Robert Pollin (eds.), *Globalization and Progressive Economic Policy* (Cambridge University Press, 1998), pp. 325–336, at 327.

1

politicians and the media have become more hostile to the international movement of people, driven in part by public concerns about the perceived economic
impacts of immigration.[2] However, it is also argued that a progressive viewpoint
on immigration should not be based upon economic consequences but on rights
and freedoms.[3]

In the European Union governmental prohibitions are not the main constraint
on labour mobility. Although citizens of EU Member States enjoy the right to
live and work anywhere within the EU, it is a well known fact that internal
migration has not been very significant despite variations in living standards. It
would appear, therefore, that only severe economic or political disadvantages
can overcome the bonds of kinship, language, domestic investment and cultural
familiarity.[4]

Some, therefore, have argued that it is the attainment of the European projects
per se – those of European nationhood and of Economic and Monetary Union
– which has motored European integration.[5] However, the present writers believe
that an understanding of the legal foundations of all European projects, that of
non-discriminatory rights and freedoms of movement, is essential, and supportive
of the forging of a new European identity beyond the traditional nation-state.

II. SIGNIFICANCE OF FREEDOM OF MOVEMENT OF PERSONS

Article 39 EC gives workers the right of free movement between Member States.
A similar right is conferred on the self-employed by Article 43 EC, which provides
for the right of establishment. Furthermore, Article 49 EC grants the right to
provide services across borders. These two freedoms are applicable to companies
as well as to natural persons. All the EC Treaty provisions which have been
cited have been held by the Court of Justice to have direct effect, and to be
capable of being invoked by individuals before national courts. Like the prohibition of quantitative restrictions on trade in goods between Member States
provided for by Article 28 EC, one of the twin pillars of the free movement of
goods, and like the free movement of capital and payments enshrined in Article
56 EC, the former provisions are concerned with the free movement of factors
of production within the common market. Such free movement is thought to be
characteristic of a common market, which economically has certain of the
features of one state. According to classical economic theory, it is thought to
result in the most economically efficient use of these factors at their most
economically efficient situation.

There are many reasons why the above ideal should not be fully realised in
practice, for example because individuals lack adequate information; or linguistic

---

2. Bob Sutcliffe, *op. cit.*, at 326.
3. *Ibid.*, p. 328.
4. Malcolm Walters, *Globalization* (Routledge, London and New York), p. 89.
5. See Martin Albrow, *The Global Age: State and Society Beyond Modernity* (Polity Press,
Cambridge, 1996), p. 200.

skills; or are inhibited from movement by cultural barriers; or because despite harmonisation and mutual recognition, certain professions are not open to them; or because there are limitations on employment in the public authorities of the Member States; or because occupational pension schemes are not transferable. Companies, like individuals may also encounter obstacles to freedom of movement, for example discriminatory tax provisions in certain Member States. Certain of the impediments to free movement may be removed by the enactment of new Community secondary legislation, or by action by the Commission and by the European Court. However, this would not always appear possible.

The provisions of the EC Treaty relating to freedom of movement of persons are supplemented by a considerable body of Community secondary legislation, which is fully considered in the following chapters. The introduction of the idea of European citizenship according to which all persons having the nationality of a Member State are citizens of the European Union represents a tendency towards viewing the individual in a wider context than an economic one. Article 18(1) EC (formerly Article 8a EC) stipulates that every citizen of the Union shall have the right to move and reside freely within the territory of the Member States, subject to the limitations and conditions laid down in the Treaty and the measures adopted to give it effect.[6] Nationals of the Member States are citizens of the Union. Articles 19–21 EC contain other provisions relating to European citizenship and although the concept has so far been interpreted cautiously by the European Court, it is obviously one which is capable of significant development in the future.

III. THE PRINCIPLES OF NON-DISCRIMINATION AND PROPORTIONALITY

Articles 39, 43 and 49 EC all prohibit discrimination on the grounds of nationality against migrant workers, self-employed persons, and suppliers and recipients of services. This prohibition is reinforced by that contained in Article 12 EC, which stipulates that within the scope of application of the EC Treaty, and without prejudice to any special provision contained therein, any discrimination on the ground of nationality is forbidden. The prohibition of discrimination has been held to include direct as well as covert or indirect discrimination. Thus,

---

6. Article 18(1) EC (ex Art. 8a), together with Article 14(2) (ex Art. 7a(2) EC) was held in Case C-378/97, *Wijsenbeek* [1999] ECR I-6207, at the time when the relevant events occurred (i.e. 1993, before the entry into force of the Schengen Agreement in 1995 abolishing internal frontier checks, to which both France and the Netherlands, the relevant countries, were parties), not to preclude a Member State from requiring a person, whether or not an EU citizen, upon threat of criminal penalties, to establish his nationality upon entry into the territory of a Member State by an internal frontier of the Community (Rotterdam airport from Strasbourg). This was subject to the proviso that the penalties applicable are comparable to those which apply to similar national infringements and are not disproportionate.

the Court of Justice held in *Südmilch v. Ugliola*[7] that if a Member State protects workers from loss of seniority due to carrying out the obligation to perform national military service, this concession must apply not only to service in its own armed forces, but also to service in those of other Member States. If a Member State[8] were to exclude military service in the armed forces of another Member State, it would be guilty of discrimination on the grounds of nationality. In certain cases, the Court has held that direct or indirect discrimination against workers did not exist because there were objective differences in the relevant situations. Thus the Court has held in a number of cases that there may be objective reasons for differentiating between resident and non-resident workers for the purposes of income tax.[9] These differences involve the source of their income, the possibility of taking account of their ability to pay tax, and their personal and family circumstances. However, in *Royal Bank of Scotland v. Elliniko Dimosio*[10] the Court has recently condemned the differential Greek treatment of companies having their seat in Greece, and those having their seat in another Member State but a permanent establishment in Greece, on the ground that there was no objective difference between the two categories of companies that would justify such differentiation.

Although in some cases the Court has gone further than this,[11] it has not shown a general tendency in the past to interpret Article 39 EC as covering measures which do not distinguish, either in law or in fact, between migrant workers, and those of the host state.[12] Such an approach has been taken by the Court on a more systematic basis in the field of the provision of services (*Säger v. Dennemeyer and Co. Ltd.*).[13] It has also been applied to the exercise of the right of establishment (*Gebhard*),[14] an approach it has recently confirmed in *Centros*,[15] a case concerned with the freedom of a company registered in England and Wales, which did not carry on any business in the United Kingdom, to establish a branch in Denmark. That freedom was somewhat controversially upheld, the Court having found that there had been no improper circumvention of national legislation or fraudulent advantage taken of provisions of Community

---

7. Case 15/69, [1969] ECR 363; [1970] CMLR.
8. See also Case C-330/94, *R. v. IRC ex parte Commerzbank AG* [1993] ECRI-4017; [1993] 3 CMLR 457 in which the Court held that disadvantages imposed on a company on the basis of the fiscal residence were indirectly discriminatory.
9. See Case C-279/93, *Schumacker* [1995] ECR I-225, paras. 31–32; Case C-80/94, *Wielockx* [1995] ECR I-2493, para. 18; and Case C-107/94, *Asscher* [1996] ECR I-3089, para. 41.
10. Case C-311/97, [1999] ECR I-2651.
11. Case C-19/92, *Kraus v. Land Baden-Württemberg* [1993] ECR I-1663; Case C-415/93, *Union Belge des Sociétés de Football Association ASBL v. Bosman* [1995] ECR I-4921.
12. Note in this sense P.J.G. Kapteyn and P. Verloren van Themaat, *Introduction to the Law of the European Communities* (3rd edn, W. Gormley (ed.), Kluwer, 1998), p. 716.
13. Case C-76/90, [1991] ECR I-4221.
14. Case C-55/94, [1995] ECR I-4165.
15. Case C-212/97, [1999] ECR I-1459.

law; and that the national measure taken by Denmark (refusal to register the branch) could not be justified.

In paragraph 34 of its judgment, the Court stipulated that according to its case law,[16] national measures liable to hinder or make less attractive the exercise of fundamental freedoms guaranteed by the Treaty must fulfil four conditions: they must be applied in a non-discriminatory manner; they must be justified by imperative requirements in the general interest; they must be suitable for maintaining the objective which they pursue; and they must not go beyond what is necessary in order to attain it. The latter three requirements seem similar to the elements involved in the German concept of proportionality ('Verhältnismäßigkeit'), which has much influenced Community law.[17] The Court held that the second of these requirements was not necessary such as to attain the objective of protecting creditors which it purported to pursue, since if the company concerned had conducted business in the United Kingdom, its branch would have been registered in Denmark, even though Danish creditors might have been equally exposed to risk. Furthermore, the Court found that the measure imposed was disproportionate. It held that it was possible for the Danish government to adopt measures which were less restrictive, or which interfered less with fundamental freedoms by, for example, making it possible in law for public creditors to obtain the necessary guarantees. Thus a Member State might enact measures to prevent or penalise fraud.[18] The use of the doctrine of proportionality in this case is interesting and is paralleled by many other cases relating to the free movement of persons.[19]

IV. THE INSTITUTIONAL FRAMEWORK

The Court, the Commission, the Council and the European Parliament exercise their usual competencies in relation to secondary legislation (regulations and directives) governing the free movement of workers and in relation to directives made in governing the mutual recognition of diplomas, certificates and other evidence of formal qualifications, and those issued for the purpose of co-ordinating the provisions laid down by law, regulation or administrative action concerning the take-up and pursuit of activities as self employed persons. The same is true of directives made to liberalise specific services. The Court's function in relation to such secondary legislation is principally one of determining its interpretation and validity; as far as the relevant Treaty provisions are concerned, its function is principally one of interpretation.

---

16. The Court cited the four conditions mentioned in *Kraus* and *Gebhard*, but did not mention their use in *Säger v. Dennemeyer* or *Bosman*. It was the first time that the Court had employed this formula in the context of the establishment of companies.

17. J. Schwarze, *European Administrative Law* (Sweet and Maxwell, 1992), pp. 685–6.

18. The decision in *Centros* calls into question certain protective provisions in national systems of law, for example the Dutch legal regime for pseudo-foreign companies.

19. Note for example *Gebhard*, *Kraus* and *Säger v. Dennemeyer* already cited.

In general, the Council is required to act by a qualified majority in the relevant area, but in some cases unanimity is required. A qualified majority is obtained when there are at least 62 votes out of a possible 87 for a particular proposal: the votes of each Member State are weighted. These rules will change when the Treaty of Nice enters into force. A unanimous decision in the Council throughout the complex co-decision procedure laid down by Article 251 EC is necessary in the field of social security[20] and also in relation to decisions on directives the implementation of which involves in at least one Member State, the amendment of the existing principles laid down by law governing the professions with respect to the training and access of natural persons.[21] The co-decision procedure usually involves the Council acting by a qualified majority as opposed to unanimity. This type of co-decision procedure is applicable to the making of rules designed to prohibit discrimination on the grounds of nationality.[22] It is also applicable to legislation on the free movement of workers,[23] and to directives on freedom of establishment[24] but not to legislation concerned with the liberalisation of specific services, in relation to which Parliament only has to be consulted.[25] The Economic and Social Committee has to be consulted in relation to the making of all these three types of secondary legislation.

The Amsterdam Treaty transfers materials formerly governed by the Third Pillar (the special title on Justice and Home Affairs in the Maastricht Treaty on European Union)[26] into the new Title IV of the EC Treaty (Visas, Asylum, Immigration, and other Policies related to the Free Movement of Persons). As is explained below the new Title will form a basis for legislation aimed at ensuring, within a period of five years, the total abolition of controls on persons, whatever their nationality, when traversing the internal frontiers of the Union.[27] Furthermore, legal grounds are provided for the 'flanking' measures needed to make internal free movement work, on such matters as external border controls, asylum and immigration.

---

20. Article 42 EC.
21. Article 47(2) EC. A detailed account of the co-decision procedure appears in S. Weatherill and P. Beaumont, *EU Law* (3rd edn, Penguin Books 1999), pp. 133–9.
22. Article 12(2) EC.
23. Article 40 EC.
24. Article 44(1) EC.
25. Article 52(1) EC.
26. The Maastricht Treaty established two pillars of European Union activity which were differentiated from the EC; these were the Common Foreign and Security Policy and Justice and Home Affairs. These matters were dealt with outside the scope of EC laws and generally decisions therein required unanimity in the Council of Ministers or European Council. The other Community institutions were generally granted at best a minor role under these pillars.
27. The membership and territory of the Union is, of course, the same as that of the EC. The Treaty of Amsterdam on the European Union includes a consolidated treaty on the European Union as well as the EC, Euratom, and Coal and Steel Community.

As is emphasised below, the Court, Commission and Parliament were not granted a significant role under the Second and Third Pillars of the EC Maastricht Treaty. Their role is to some extent diminished under the relevant provisions of the EC Treaty (Articles 61–69) included therein by the Amsterdam Treaty.[28] Furthermore, during the five year transitional period following the entry into force of the Amsterdam Treaty in 1999, the Council is required to act unanimously under Title IV,[29] and the Commission's normal sole right of initiative (which exists under the other provisions considered beneath the present sub heading) is duplicated by one granted to each Member State. The co-decision procedure is replaced by a simple need to consult Parliament. Article 67(2), contains provisions under which the present procedure may change after the expiry of the five year period. The Council is required to act on proposals from the Commission, which must examine any request by a Member State that it submit a proposal to it. The Council, acting unanimously after consulting the European Parliament, is empowered to decide to submit all or parts of Title IV to the co-decision procedure involving both the Council and Parliament, and to adapt the special provisions mentioned below concerning the Court of Justice.

These controversial provisions are contained in Article 68 EC, the first paragraph of which provides for a restricted form of the preliminary reference procedure. Questions of interpretation of Title IV or the validity of secondary legislation based on Title IV may be referred only by a court or tribunal of a Member State against whose decisions there is no judicial remedy under national law, if that court or tribunal thinks that a decision on the question is necessary in order to enable it to give judgment. This provision may have an unfortunate impact on cases involving political asylum, applicants for which will have to exhaust their domestic remedies. Many migrants may lack the resources or the knowledge to take their case to a final court. No such requirement is normally applicable to preliminary references.

The provisions of Article 68(2) have also been subjected to justified criticism. This text stipulates that in any event the Court of Justice shall not have jurisdiction to rule on any measure or decision taken pursuant to Article 62(1)[30] relating to the maintenance of law and order and the safeguarding of internal security. It is not entirely clear what is meant by the maintenance of law and order and the safeguarding of internal security. In cases alleged to involve such matters,

---

28. The United Kingdom, Denmark and Ireland have secured an 'opt-out' from this part of the Treaty, see protocols B4 and B5 thereto.
29. Article 67 EC. Note however Article 67(3) which provides that measures concerning visas referred to in Articles 62(2)(b)(i) and (iii) shall from the date of entry into force of the Treaty of Amsterdam be adopted by the Council acting by a qualified majority on a proposal from the Commission and after consulting the European Parliament.
30. Five types of measures are envisaged by Article 62(1), including measures in the fields of administrative cooperation and police and judicial cooperation.

individual liberties may be particularly at risk, and it is hoped that the European Court will give a restrictive interpretation to this provision.[31]

According to Article 68(3), the Council or Commission or a Member State may request the Court of Justice to give a ruling on a question of interpretation of Title IV or of acts of institutions based on it. However, such a ruling shall not apply to judgments of courts and tribunals of the Member States which have become *res judicata*.

V. MATERIAL COVERED IN SUBSEQUENT CHAPTERS

The present work includes a treatment of the establishment of companies as well as that of natural persons. It does not however deal with freedom of movement in the context of the EAEC (European Atomic Energy Community) and ECSC (European Coal and Steel Community) Treaties. Furthermore, because of the availability of specialist works in these fields, it does not deal systematically with the closely related areas of social security and public procurement, or with financial services and the harmonisation of company law.

The Second Chapter deals in outline with the basic legal provisions governing the free movement of persons. It includes an account of the substantive provisions of Title IV of the EC Treaty and a treatment of the Schengen Agreement and the incorporation of the *Schengen acquis* into title IV EC or Title VI TEU; and an account of the exceptions for the United Kingdom, Ireland and Denmark to the provision of Title IV and the incorporation of the *Schengen acquis*[32] under Protocols to the Amsterdam Treaty. Chapter 2 also emphasises the importance of secondary legislation in the relevant fields, and examines proposals to simplify the right of residence. The topic of visas is also considered in this Chapter.

Chapter 3 deals with the movement of workers. It deals amongst other things with the position of posted workers, students, persons seeking employment and nationals of non-Member States. It also considers the rights of migrant workers and their families; and the territorial and personal scope of freedom of movement; and the exception contained in Article 39(4) EC for employment in the public sector.

Freedom of establishment and the free movement of services are dealt with in Chapter 4. This chapter considers a number of matters, including the Courts' use of the requirements of justification and proportionality in relation to regulatory rules, which has been outlined above in relation to *Centros*. Chapter 4 inevitably considers the impact of harmonising legislation. Chapter 5 attempts

---

31. Note in this sense, Weatherill and Beaumont, *op. cit.*, p. 658.
32. The Schengen Agreement provides for the abolition of border controls between certain Member States. In addition to 13 of the 15 EC Member States, Norway and Ireland are parties to this Agreement. The *Schengen acquis* comprise the Schengen Agreement itself of 1985; the Implementing Convention of 1990; the various Accession Protocols and Agreements; the decisions and declarations adopted by the Executive Committee as well as acts adopted by organs on which the Committee has conferred decision making powers.

to consider the most important cases concerning the provision of services, and also endeavors to show how the relevant cases in this area treat the provision of services in a similar way to the other freedoms, although certain exceptions occur in the area of the free movement of goods.

The sixth chapter considers the conferment of the right of residence on certain additional categories of persons; i.e. persons of independent means and persons who have ceased occupational activities. The seventh Chapter deals with certain limitations on the free movement of persons based on public policy, public security and public health. Chapter 8 deals with European citizenship, and attempts an historical approach whilst mentioning the relevant case law, including *Sala*.[33]

Chapter 9 deals with the increasingly important topic of the rights of third country nationals in the EU. It is estimated that there may be as many as twelve million persons residing in the EU, and the incorporation of part IV of title three into the EC Treaty may perhaps eventually herald a substantial increase in the rights of such persons. It has thus recently been proposed that long-term residents from third countries who reside legally should have something like a common status in the Member States. Certain proposals relating to immigration and asylum are examined in this chapter.

The final chapter is concerned with the impact of international agreements on free movement and necessarily considers the European Economic Area Agreement. It also contains a treatment of the Association Agreements with Morocco and Turkey; the Europe Agreement with Poland; the Partnership Agreements with Russia, and makes some necessary reference to GATS.

---

33. Case C-85/96, *Maria Martinez Sala v. Freistaat Bayern* [1998] ECR I-2691. In this case the Court held that a Spanish national lawfully residing in Bavaria fell within the personal scope of the EC Treaty rules on European Citizenship, and was thus entitled to access to benefits which might have been thought as available to her had she been an employed or self-employed person, and not a mere resident.

2 Basic Legal Provisions Governing the Free Movement of Persons

I. INTRODUCTION

The present chapter outlines the basic legal rules governing the free movement of natural and legal persons who are nationals of a Member State, or which (in the case of companies or firms) are formed in accordance with the law of a Member State and which have their registered office, central administration, or principal place of business within the Community.[1] It also considers the position of persons who are not Community nationals, especially in the context of Title IV of the EC Treaty and the Schengen Agreements. Freedom of movement within the Community may be enjoyed by nationals in third countries in accordance with the provisions of relevant agreements (e.g. EC Association, Cooperation, or other kinds of international agreements with third countries), or because such nationals are family members of EC nationals, or because they are employees of EC service providers. It seems apparent that Articles 14(2) and 18(1) EC, which give rights of free movement and residence to citizens, do not have the effect of removing all the border controls that may be imposed on the free movement of EC nationals or the nationals of third states. According to Article 14(1) EC, the Community was supposed to adopt measures aimed at establishing an internal market by the end of 1992. Article 14(2) EC provides that such market shall comprise an area without internal frontiers, in which the free movement of goods, persons, services and capital is ensured in accordance with the provisions of the Treaty. A Declaration attached to the Single European Act of 1986 purports to state that the deadline has no legal effect. However, the status of such declarations is questionable, and it has been argued that they have no legal effect. Nevertheless, the continuance of certain border controls seems justified on the basis of the reasoning in *Wijsenbeek* which is considered below. The position may well be different as far as the parties to the Schengen Agreement are concerned.

Under the EC Treaty, the free movement of persons comprises their freedom to move to another Member State in order to take up employment there; their freedom to establish themselves in other Member States under the same conditions as nationals of such states; and their freedom to provide or receive services on an equal footing to nationals, in a Member State other than their own.

---

1. Article 48 EC. The company or firm must show that its business activity constitutes a continuous and effective link with the economy of an EC Member State in order to benefit from freedom of establishment it only has its office within the Community: General Programme on Freedom of Establishment [1962] J.O. 22, 36.

The first part of this chapter deals primarily with the free movement of persons and services under the EC Treaty provisions, as subsequently amended. It will only make brief reference to the position under the ECSC and EAEC treaties. The second part mentions the relevant provisions originally contained in the Maastricht Treaty on European Union concerning European citizenship and the Justice and Home Affairs pillar, whilst the third part gives consideration to the special rules contained in Title IV of Part III of the EC Treaty incorporated therein by the Amsterdam Treaty. The provisions of this Title are often of an unusual and indeed controversial nature, and deal with a considerable number of matters formerly dealt with in the "Third Pillar" to the Maastricht Treaty on European Union on Justice and Home Affairs, which is also considered in outline. The fourth part deals with the question of border controls and the Schengen Agreement. The Amsterdam Treaty contains a timetable for the enactment of legislation removing border controls,[2] and it seems unlikely that the relevant provisions of Articles 14(2) or 18(1) EC will be found to require the removal of such controls by the Court of Justice in any action brought before it concerning this matter.[3] The fifth part of this chapter deals with the incorporation of the *Schengen acquis* into Part III, Title IV EC or Title VI TEU.[4] The next part considers the detailed exceptions from Title IV EC for the United Kingdom, Ireland and Denmark under Protocols B4 and B5.[5] These exceptions may well have an inevitable tendency to fragment the constitutional unity of the Community.

The final part of this chapter will mention in brief outline the report of the High Level Panel on the Free Movement of Persons, and some consequences of this Report. The Panel was chaired by Mrs Simone Veil, and reported to the Commission in 1997. It prepared a number of measures intended to ensure that more people can take advantage of the free movement of persons.[6]

Mention will be made of relevant Community secondary legislation in this chapter, wherever necessary.

II. RELEVANT PROVISIONS OF THE EUROPEAN COMMUNITY TREATIES

1. ECSC and EAEC Treaties

Article 69 ECSC contained certain basic provisions for the free movement of persons which were taken over and developed in the EC Treaty. According to

---

2. Protocol 3 on the application of certain aspects of the Treaty to the United Kingdom and Ireland gives the United Kingdom the right to maintain its border controls. Ireland is also given a similar right, for so long as the Common Travel Area between the United Kingdom and Ireland persists.
3. Note in the same sense Weatherill and Beaumont, *EU Law* (3rd edn, Penguin Books 1999), p. 649.
4. This is entitled 'Police and Judicial Cooperation in Criminal Matters'.
5. These are Protocols attached to the Treaty on European Union and the EC Treaty.
6. For subsequent proposals, see Weatherill and Beaumont, *op. cit.*, pp. 625–6.

Article 69(1) ECSC workers who had recognised qualifications in a coalmining or steelmaking occupation were enabled to exercise such an activity in another Member State. Restrictions based upon nationality were required to be removed, subject to limitations imposed by the basic requirements of public policy, public health and public security. Article 69(2) ECSC required the establishment of common definitions of skilled trades and qualifications therefore by Member States, which were also required to determine by common accord the limitations mentioned in Article 69(1) ECSC. They were also required by Article 69(2) to endeavour to work out jobseeker and vacancy matching arrangements on a Community wide basis, and in the case of workers from the coal and steel industries who could no longer be employed there, to facilitate their reemployment. In the case of a shortage of suitable labour to cope with the growth of coal or steel production, the Member States undertook in Article 69(3) ECSC to adjust their immigration rules to the extent necessary to adjust the situation.

Furthermore, Article 69(4) ECSC provided that discrimination in remuneration and working conditions between nationals and migrant workers was to be prohibited, without prejudice to special measures in relation to frontier workers. Member States also undertook to settle among themselves steps to ensure that social security arrangements did not hinder mobility.

The EAEC Treaty which was concluded at the same time as the EC Treaty, contains provisions governing free movement of workers and establishment in Articles 96 and 97 thereof. Article 96(1) provides for the free movement of workers for specialised employment in the nuclear industry. Such employees are also made subject to the limitations based upon public policy, public security and public health. This provision was implemented by a directive of 5 March 1962.[7] As far as social security is concerned the relevant provisions of EC law are applicable. It should be noted that Article 232(2) of the EC Treaty states that the provisions of the EC Treaty are not to derogate from the EAEC Treaty. Thus, it has to be assumed on the basis of this article that the provisions of the EC Treaty are applicable to the extent that the EAEC Treaty does not differ from them.[8]

Article 97 EAEC contains a provision which seems to be directly applicable prohibiting the application of restrictions based upon nationality to natural or legal persons, whether public or private coming within the jurisdiction of a Member State, and wishing to participate in the construction of nuclear facilities of a scientific or industrial nature within the Community.

---

7. See OJ English Spec. Edition 1959–62, p. 226: see also Plender in Vaughan (ed.), *Law of the European Communities* (looseleaf since 1990), paras. 15.43 and 15.46–15.47 and also J. Handoll, *Free Movement of Persons in the EU* (Wiley 1995), pp. 22–29.

8. Note also the provisions of Article 42 of Regulation 1612/68, which provides that whilst that Regulation is not to affect the EAEC Treaty provisions governing eligibility for full employment in the field of nuclear energy, nor any measures taken pursuant to that Treaty, it applies to categories to of workers and members of their families, insofar as their legal position is not affected by EAEC Treaty measures.

2. Free movement of persons under the EC Treaty provisions

In the discussion of the relevant provisions of the EC Treaty which takes place below, account is of course taken of the amendments thereto made by the Single European Act, the Treaty of Maastricht and the Treaty of Amsterdam. These latter two Treaties also merit some separate discussion.

The transitional measures which have been necessitated by the accession of new states do not receive detailed consideration as they now appear to have lapsed, with the exception of the declaration contained in each of the Acts of Accession governing difficulties which may arise for the social situation in one or more Member States from the free movement of workers. In the event of such difficulties such states may bring the matter before the institutions of the Community in order to obtain a solution to the problem in accordance with the Treaties, and measures adopted in accordance therewith.[9]

(1) Title 1 of the Treaty on European Union

The above Title[10] contains certain provisions relating to the free movement of persons which are more fully developed in Title IV of Part III of the EC Treaty, which is dealt with below. It stipulates that one of the objectives of the Union is its maintenance and development of an area of freedom, security and justice, in which the free movement of persons is assured in conjunction with appropriate measures in relation to external border controls, immigration, asylum and the prevention and combating of crime. These provisions are considered under the heading "Title IV of Part III of the EC Treaty".

(2) Impact of principle contained in Part I of the EC Treaty

The preamble of the EC Treaty contains nothing which is directly relevant to the free movement of persons.[11] Article 2 EC emphasises that tasks of the

---

9. Denmark, Ireland and the United Kingdom acceded to the EC Treaty with effect from 1 January 1973; Greece as from 1 January 1980, Portugal and Spain with effect from 1 January 1985; and Austria, Finland and Sweden with effect from 1 January 1995. There are a number of new candidates for membership. The 1994 Act of Accession with Austria, Finland and Sweden contains a Joint Declaration by the existing Member States and Austria governing difficulties relating to the free movement of workers which may result from the Accession of Austria.

10. The Treaty on European Union (Amsterdam Treaty) is in essence made up of four different Treaties, the Treaty on European Union, and the EC (European Community), ECSC (European Coal and Steel Community) and EAEC (European Atomic Energy Community) Treaties. The latter treaties form Titles II, III and IV of the consolidated Treaty on European Union (Amsterdam Treaty) respectively. Title I of that Treaty is entitled Common Provisions, whilst Title V is entitled Common Foreign and Security Policy, and Title VI, Police and Judicial Cooperation in Criminal Matters.

11. See however Handoll, *op. cit.*, pp. 15–16.

Community include the establishment of a common market (which is generally assumed to involve the mobility of factors of production). Article 3(c) EC provides that the activities of the Community shall include an internal market, characterised by the abolition, as between Member States, of obstacles to the free movement of goods, persons, services and capital. Article 3(d) includes among the activities measures concerning the entry and movement of persons, as provided in Title IV, whilst Article 3(h) also includes the approximation of laws of the Member States to the extent required for the functioning of the common market.[12]

Like Articles 3(d) and 3(h), Article 5 EC may be of particular importance when secondary legislation (regulations and directives) is made in connection with the free movement of persons. Article 5 EC is concerned with the limited attribution of powers, subsidiarity and proportionality (in a narrower sense than that in which the term is used in chapter 1). According to Article 5(1) EC, the Community shall act within the limits of the powers conferred on it by the Treaty, and of the objectives assigned to it therein. The controversial principle of subsidiarity (which derives from the Maastricht Treaty) is enshrined in Article 5(2) EC. This text provides that in areas which do not fall within its exclusive competence, the Community shall take action, in accordance with the principle of subsidiarity only if, and insofar as the objects of the proposed action cannot be sufficiently achieved by the Member States and can therefore, by reason of the scale or effects of the proposed action, be better achieved by the Community. The principle of subsidiarity is reinforced by the principle of proportionality (in the narrow sense, which excludes the suitability of the action) which is enshrined in Article 5(3) EC, and which provides that any action by the Community must not go beyond what is necessary to achieve the objectives of the Treaty. Protocol C7 on the application of the principles of subsidiarity and proportionality which was annexed to the EC Treaty by the Amsterdam Treaty on European Union, attempts to define the criteria for applying these principles, which should hopefully result in a greater consistency in their application by the Commission, Council, Parliament and the Court of Justice.[13]

It seems however that the criteria laid down in Protocol 30 for determining whether Community action is necessary do not help sufficiently to clarify the impact of the principle of subsidarity. According to these criteria, Community action is to be preferred over national action where (a) the issue has transnational aspects which cannot be satisfactorily regulated by other Member States; (b) actions by Member States alone or lack of Community action would conflict with the requirements of the Treaty, such as the need to correct distortions of competition, or the internal market requirements; (c) action at Community level

---

12. According to Article 6 EC, environmental protection requirements must be integrated into the definition and implementation of the Community policies and activities referred to in Article 3, in particular with a view to protecting sustainable development.
13. There is also some useful material in the Commission Communication on the Principle of Subsidiarity, Bull. EC 10-1992, 1/6.

would produce clear benefits by reason of its scale and effects. It is not clear whether the relevant criteria are intended to be cumulative or alternatives, and those criteria sometimes appear to involve political as well as legal questions.[14]

It appears that the Community does not have exclusive powers in all matters relating to the free movement of persons, although the Commission has contended in the communication already referred to that it may have such powers in the course of time.[15] The principle of subsidiarity is only applicable where there is no such exclusive competence.

Article 10 EC may sometimes be of importance in relation to the free movement of persons and services. German writers sometimes treat this provision as encapsulating the idea of federal fidelity (*Bundestreue*). It stipulates that Member States are required to take all appropriate measures, whether general or particular, to ensure fulfilment of the obligations arising out of the EC Treaty or resulting from actions taken by the Community institutions, and that they shall abstain from any measure which could jeopardise the attainment of its objectives. However, in the case of *Corsica Ferries Italia*,[16] the Court stated that Article 10 was worded so generally that these can be no question of applying it autonomously.

In the above case, the Court also made mention of the general principle of non-discrimination on the ground of nationality contained in Article 12 EC. It held that this Article applies independently only to situations governed by Community law in respect of which the Treaty lays down no specific prohibition of discrimination. However, Article 12 has been applied independently where it has been the only principle of Community law which was capable of being applied in a number of cases.[17]

(3)   The effect of Articles 14(2) and 18(1) EC

The contents of Article 14 have been set out above. Article 18(1) provides that every citizen of the Union shall have the right to move and reside within the territory of the Member States, subject to the limitations and conditions laid down by the Treaty, and by the measures adopted to give it effect. It is thought that (although this is not entirely decisive) the conditional nature of these provisions militates against their being given direct effect.[18] Furthermore, it also

---

14. Note in this sense J. Steiner and L. Woods, *Textbook on EC Law* (6th edn, Blackstone Press, 1998), p. 36. The writers anticipate that frequent litigation may be necessary to clarify the meaning of those criteria. See also Weatherill and Beaumont, *op. cit.*, pp. 27–32.
15. It clearly does not have them in relation to immigration or asylum, or to the field of criminal law.
16. Case C-18/93, [1994] ECR I-1783. The case invoked a system of differential tariffs for providing services within Italian law.
17. Note for example Joined Cases C-92/92 and 326/92, *Phil Collins* [1993] ECR I-5145.
18. The fact that a provision contains an obligation to enact implementing measures does not necessarily mean that the obligation is dependent on such measures for its execution and effect: note for example Case 43/75, *Defrenne v. Sabena* [1976] ECR 432. The fact that

appears surprising that if Articles 14(2) and 18(1) have direct effect and impose a clear and unconditional obligation, the right of free movement and residence could be limited, as it has been done by the three directives on the right of residence which have been adopted on the basis of the EC Treaty, i.e. Directives 90/364, 90/365 and 93/96.[19] In addition, it would be surprising if, being that the Amsterdam Treaty has made provision for a timetable for the removal of controls when crossing internal borders,[20] the dismantling of such controls already followed from Articles 14(2) and 18(1) EC.

The ECJ did not find it necessary to decide whether the latter articles had direct effect in *Wijsenbeek*.[21] The Commission submitted in this case that Article 8a had direct effect, but in the absence of specific Community rules concerning controls at the Community's external borders, the requirement to produce a valid passport or identity card at internal frontiers provided for in Article 3(1) of Directive 68/360 was not an abusive one.

The Court held in *Wijsenbeek* that at the time when the events in question in the main proceedings occurred, there were no common rules or harmonised laws of the Member States on controls at external frontiers and immigration, visa and asylum policy. Thus, even if under Articles 7a (ex Article 14) and 8a (ex Article 18) EC, nationals of the Member States did have an unconditional right to move freely within the territory of the Member States, the latter retained the right to carry on identity checks at the internal frontiers of the Community, requiring persons to present a valid identity card or passport, in order to be able to establish whether the person concerned is the national of a Member State, thus having the right to move freely within the Member States, or a

---

Articles 14(1) and 18(2) EC provide for implementing measures does not necessarily detract from the possible direct effect of these provisions: note in this sense D. O'Keefe and M. Horspool, *European Citizenship and the Free Movement of Persons, Essays in Honour of G.J. Hand* (Sweet and Maxwell, 1996), pp. 145 at p. 162. The question of the direct effect of Article 18(2) was not considered by the ECJ in Case C-192/99, *R. v. Secretary of State for the Home Department, ex parte Manjit Kaur* because the Court found Kaur not to have had British nationality and therefore not to have any rights under Community law.

19. OJ 1990 L180/26 and L180/28; OJ 1993 L270/1 respectively. These directives grant the rights of residence only to those who have their own means of support and who have health insurance.

20. Note Article 62 EC, which provides that the Council, acting in accordance with the procedure referred to in Article 67 EC shall within a period of five years after the entry into force of the Treaty of Amsterdam, adopt measures with a view to ensuring compliance with Article 14 EC, the absence of any control on persons whether EU citizens or nationals of other countries when crossing internal borders.

21. Case C-378/97, [1999] ECR I-6207. Such a determination was also unnecessary in Case C-297/92, *INPS v. Baglieri* [1993] ECR I-5221. In this case the Court found that the expiry of the period mentioned in what is now Article 14(1) EC did not result in Member States being automatically obliged to admit voluntary affiliation to their social security systems of persons subjected to obligatory assurance in another Member State.

national of a non-Member State, not having that right. The approach taken by the Court to the relevant provisions of the EC Treaty seems consonant with common sense, and will continue to apply to the extent that such common rules and harmonised laws on external frontier controls and immigration, visa and asylum policy are lacking. Certain amendments will be made to Article 18 when the Treaty of Nice enters into force. Article 18(2) will be reworded so as to stipulate that if action by the Community should prove necessary to achieve freedom of movement and residence of citizens of the Union within the territories of the Member States and the Treaty has not provided the necessary powers, the Council may adopt provisions with a view to facilitating the exercise of the rights provided for by Article 18(1) by means of the co-decision procedure contained in Article 251 EC. However, according to new Article 18(3), Article 18(2) does not apply to provisions on passports, identity cards, residence permits or any other such documents, or to provisions on social security or social protection.

(4)   Part III, Title VI, Chapters 1–3 EC

Chapter I: Articles 39–42 EC

The detailed provisions of the above three chapters, which appear under the general heading Community policies, will be examined in outline only. Articles 39–42 EC are concerned with the free movement of workers. Article 39(1) EC provides that freedom of movement of workers shall be secured within the Community, whilst Article 39(2) EC stipulates that such freedom shall entail the abolition of any discrimination based on nationality between workers of the Member States as regards employment, remuneration and conditions of work and employment. The rights provided for in Article 39(3) are spelt out in detail in the first part of Regulation 1612/68,[22] as amended, which deals with eligibility for employment, equality of treatment within employment, and workers' families. The Commission has proposed that the ambit of this Regulation should be extended to cover a wider range of persons, and that Directive 68/360[23] which governs the conditions of entry and residence of workers and their families, should be correspondingly amended.

Article 39(3) EC stipulates that freedom of movement shall entail the rights subject to limitation justified on grounds of public policy, public security or public health: (a) to accept offers of employment actually made; (b) to move freely within the territory of a Member State; (c) to stay in a Member State for the purposes of employment in accordance with the legal and other provisions governing the employment of nationals of that state; (d) to remain in the territory of a Member State after having been employed.

The abolition of restrictions on the freedom of movement and residence of

---

22. OJ 1968 L 157/2.
23. 1968 2 OJ Spec. Edition 483.

workers and their families, as has already been indicated, is dealt with in Directive 68/360. The corresponding directive relating to the movement and residence of persons benefiting from freedom of establishment and providing or receiving services in a Member State other than their own is Directive 73/148. The right to remain in a Member State after having been employed there is dealt with in Commission Regulation 1251/70.[24] As is pointed out in the Report of the High Level Panel on the free movement of persons, the present sectoral approach to residence rights has some unfortunate consequences, and it might be better if it could be replaced by consolidating legislation, perhaps eventually treating all European citizens equally. It is noteworthy that self-employed persons who have ceased their activity, and persons in receipt of social assistance are not protected from expulsion at present. The permitted derogations to the rights contained in Article 39(3) EC are dealt with in Directive 64/221.[25] According to Article 39(4) EC, the provisions of Article 39 EC are inapplicable to employment in the public service.

Article 40 enables the Council, in accordance with the co-decision procedure provided for by Article 251 EC and after consulting the Economic and Social Committee, to issue directives or make regulations setting out the measures required to bring about freedom of movement for workers. This provision has been used as a partial legal basis for the specific and general mutual recognition directives.[26] Article 50 EC provides that Member States shall, within the context of a joint programme, encourage the exchange of young workers. The adoption of measures coordinating national social security systems is provided for in Article 42 EC. The main objective of such measures is to endeavour to remove one of the most important obstacles to the free movement of workers. The most important implementing measure is Regulation 1408/71, which has been amended on several occasions.[27]

---

24. OJ 1980 L142/26.
25. 1963–4 OJ Spec. Edition 117. This directive applies to all who come within the free movement provisions of the EC Treaty whether employed or self-employed, together with their families. It is also applicable to persons of independent means who come within Directive 90/365/EC (OJ 1990 L130/26), retired persons who come within Directive 90/364/EC (OJ 1990 L180/28), and to students who come within Directive 93/96 (OJ 1993 L317/59). However, it is only applicable to restrictions on the free movement and residence of natural as opposed to legal persons.
26. Note, in this sense, Handoll, *op. cit.*, p. 27. The two general directives are considered in a later chapter, and comprise Council Directive 89/48 on a general system for the recognition of higher education diplomas awarded on the completion of professional education and training of at least three years duration (OJ 1989 L9/16) and Council Directive 92/51 on a general system for the recognition of professional education and training to supplement Directive 89/48 (OJ 1992, L209/25) recently amended by Directive 97/38 (OJ 1997, L184/31).
27. OJ English Special Edition 1971 (II) 416.

Chapter II: Articles 43–48

According to Article 43(1) EC within the framework of the provisions mentioned below, restrictions on the free establishment of nationals of a Member State in the territory of another Member State shall be prohibited. This prohibition also applies to restrictions on the setting up of agencies, branches and subsidiaries by nationals of any Member State established in the territory of any Member State (the so called right of secondary establishment). The distinction between the exercise of the right of establishment and the provision of services has been held by the ECJ to be based not only on the duration of the provision of the services, but also on its regularity, periodicity or continuity.[28] A provider of services may set up some kind of infrastructure, for example, an office, chambers of consulting rooms, in the host Member State for the purpose of providing services there, without necessarily being deemed to exercise the right of establishment.

By Article 43(2) EC, the right of establishment includes the right to make up and pursue activities as self-employed persons, and to set up and manage undertakings, in particular companies or firms within the meaning of the second paragraph of Article 48 EC, under the conditions laid down for its own nationals by the law of the country of establishment, subject to the provisions of the chapter regarding capital. Article 48(2) EC defines the phrase "companies or firms" as companies or firms constituted under civil or commercial law, including cooperative societies and other legal persons governed by public or private law, save for those which are not profit making. It is clear from Article 48(1) EC that such entities are to be treated in the same way as natural persons who are nationals of the Member States if they are formed in accordance with the laws of a Member State, and have their registered office, central administration or principal place of business within the Community. As already pointed out, if a company has only its registered office within the Community, it is required to show that its business activity forms a continuous and effective link with the economy of a Member State in order to benefit from freedom of establishment.

Article 44(1) EC stipulates that in order to obtain freedom of establishment as regards a particular activity, the Council shall, acting in accordance with the co-decision procedure provided for by Article 251 EC and after consulting the Economic and Social Committee, proceed by way of directives.[29] By Article 44(2) EC, the Council and Commission are required to take note of certain specific obligations in carrying out the duties imposed on them by the preceding provisions in particular, Article 44(2)(g) stipulates that such duties shall be carried out by coordinating to the necessary extent the safeguards which, for

---

28. See Case C-55/94, *Gebhard* [1995] ECR I-4165.

29. A number of such directives have been made: note, for example, Council Directive 73/148 (OJ 1973 L173/14) on the abolition of restrictions on freedom of movement and residence in the Community on nationals of Member States with regard to establishment and provision of services.

the protection of the interests of members and others, are required by Member States of companies and firms within the meaning of Article 48(2), with a view to making such safeguards equivalent throughout the Community. A number of harmonising directives have been based upon this provision, and are considered in the chapter on the harmonisation of company law.

Article 45(1) EC on the harmonisation of company law which may be compared with Article 55 EC stipulates that the provisions of the present chapter shall not apply, so far as any given Member State is concerned, to activities which in that state are concerned, even occasionally with the exercise of official authority. The provisions of Article 45(2) EC have not yet been implemented. This text stipulates that the Council may, acting by qualified majority on a proposal from the Commission, rule that the provisions of the present chapter shall not apply to certain activities.

Article 46(1) EC provides that the provisions of chapter two (on establishment) and measures taken in pursuance thereof shall not prejudice the applicability of provisions laid down by law, regulation or administrative action providing for special treatment for foreign nationals on grounds of public policy, public security and public health. The issue of directives for the coordination of the above provisions is envisaged by Article 46(2). As already pointed out, Directive 64/221 provides for such coordination; it is also applicable to those who provide or receive services within the Community in a Member State other than their own. As already indicated, it is not applicable to legal persons.

Article 57(1) EC makes provision for the adoption of directives for the mutual recognition of diplomas, certificates and other evidence of formal qualifications in accordance with the co-decision procedure. The purpose of such directives is to make the right of establishment available to the self employed. The mutual recognition of diplomas has been agreed upon in a number of professions, such as doctors,[30] veterinary surgeons,[31] dentists,[32] nurses,[33] midwives,[34] hairdressers,[35] architects[36] and others. As indicated above the Council has issued two general system directives on the recognition of professional education and training. Further amendments to these directives appear possible. It was found necessary to enact these directives, which are in part based upon Article 47(1) EC, because of the slow and inadequate progress which was made with an approach based upon individual professions. Directives based upon Article 47(1) EC are sometimes called "recognition directives", whilst those based upon Article 47(2) EC are often called "coordination directives". The latter provision empow-

---

30. See Council Directive 93/16 (OJ 1993 L165/1), as amended.
31. See Council Directive 78/1026 (OJ 1978 L362/1), as amended.
32. See Council Directive 78/686 (OJ 1978 L223/1), as amended.
33. See Council Directive 77/452 (OJ 1977 L176/1), as amended.
34. See Council Directive 80/156 (OJ 1980, L33/1), as amended.
35. See Council Directive 82/489 (OJ 1982 L218/4), as amended.
36. See Council Directive 85/384 (OJ 1985 L223/13), as amended.

ers the Council to adopt directives coordinating the provisions laid down by law, regulation or administrative action concerning the taking up and pursuit of activities as self-employed persons.

The Council is required to act unanimously throughout the various stages of the co-decision procedure if the implementation of a directive will involve in at least one Member State amendment of the existing principles laid down by law governing the professions with respect to training and access for natural persons. A number of directives have been made on the basis of Article 47(2) EC; one may cite for example the Second Banking Directive.[37] Article 47(3) EC provides that in the case of the medical and allied and pharmaceutical professions, the progressive abolition of restrictions shall be dependent upon coordination of the conditions for their exercise in the various Member States.

Chapter III: Articles 49–55 EC

According to Article 49(1) EC, within the framework of the following provisions, restrictions on freedom to provide services within the Community shall be prohibited in respect of nationals of Member States who are established in a state of the Community other than that of the person for whom the services are intended. It should be noted that the service provider is required to be established within the Community, as well as being a national of a Member State. The same limitation does not, however, apply to recipients of services, who also benefit from Articles 49 and 50 EC. The Council may, in accordance with Article 49(2) EC acting by a qualified majority on a proposal from the Commission extend the provisions governing services to nationals of a third country who provide services and are established within the Community. This facility has never been used.[38] Articles 49 and 50 apply to legal as well as natural persons: this is made clear by Articles 48 and 55 EC.

The relevant case law covers four situations governing the cross-border provision of services to which Articles 49 and 50 EC have been applied.[39] The first of these is where the provider of the service moves from one Member State to another to provide it. The second is where the recipient instead of the provider moves, the third is where neither party moves, the service being provided by means of mail or telecommunications. The final situation is where both the provider and the recipient of the service move to a third Member State such that the service may be provided there. One may cite for example the situation of holidaymakers on a European coach trip.

It has long been held that the prohibition contained in Article 59 EC goes

---

37. Council Directive 89/646 (OJ 1989 L386/1), as amended.
38. However, a proposal for a Directive based on Article 49(2) was recently made by the Commission: see COM (1999) 3 final. It would apply to third country nationals established within the Community.
39. See Kapteyn and Verloren van Themaat, *Introduction to the Law of the European Communities* (3rd edn, Gormley (ed.), Kluwer, 1998), p. 752.

further than the prohibition of direct or indirect discrimination, and it is now clear that it is applicable to non-discriminatory national measures, which form an obstacle to the freedom to provide services.[40] The rules on services have been given a wide scope. Thus, for example it has been held that they enable a service provider to use its own employees in the provision of services.[41] In certain recent cases, the Court has extended the scope of Article 49 EC, by viewing the rules on services in an objective manner, taking no account of the subjective situation of the parties to the transaction, and concentrating instead on the movement of services and any hindrances thereto.[42]

According to Article 50 EC, services shall be considered as "services" within the meaning of the Treaty if they are normally provided for remuneration, insofar as they are not governed by the provisions relating to freedom of movement for goods, capital, and persons. Services shall in particular include activities of an industrial and commercial character; the activities of craftsmen; and the activities of the professions. Article 50 EC, like Articles 39 and 42 EC, has direct effects.[43] Finally, Article 50 EC also provides that, without prejudice to the chapter concerning establishment, the person providing a service may in order to do so, temporarily pursue his activity in the state in which the service is provided, under the same conditions as are imposed by that state on its own nationals.

It has been held by the Court to follow from sentence 1 of Article 50(2) EC that gratuitous services, for example state funded services within the educational, social and cultural fields do not come within Article 49 EC.[44] The wording of the former sentence suggests that the provisions on services have a subordinate character, as they are applicable only where the other rules do not apply. There is a considerable case law defining the ambit of the respective freedoms. The most difficult of the distinctions is that between the freedom to provide services and freedom of establishment, which was fully considered in *Gebhard*[45] which has been referred to above. The delineation of the boundary between the freedom to provide services and the free movement of goods may also give rise to difficulties, especially by reason of the fact that services are often incorporated in or connected with goods.[46]

---

40. This is clearly stated in Case C-76/90, *Säger v. Dennemeyer* [1991] ECR I-4221, as well as in Case C-275/92, *HM Customs and Excise v. Schindler* [1994] ECR I-1039.
41. Note, for example, Case C-113/89, *Rush Portuguesa Lala v. Office national d'immigration* [1990] ECR I-1417. The temporal detachment of workers for the provision of services is dealt with in Directive 96/71/EC of the EP and Council, OJ 1997 L18. See also Case C-272/94, *Guiot* [1996] ECR I-1905.
42. Note in particular Case C-158/96, *Kohll* [1998] ECR I-1931, and see V. Hatzopoulos, 'Recent Developments of the Case Law of the ECJ in the Field of Services,' (2000) 37 CML Rev., pp. 59–60.
43. Note for example, Case C-33/74, *Van Binsbergen* [1974] ECR 1299.
44. Case 263/84, *Belgium v. Humbel* [1988] ECR 5365.
45. Case C-55/94, [1995] ECR I-4165.
46. See Hatzopoulos, *op. cit.*, pp. 45, 51–2.

Article 50 third sentence EC must not be treated as implying that all domestic legislation applicable to nationals of a Member State, and usually applied to the permanent activities of undertakings established there, can be similarly applied to the provisions of services there by undertakings established in another Member State.[47]

By Article 51(1) EC, freedom to provide services in the field of transport shall be covered by the provisions of the Title relating to transport: these are Articles 70–80 EC. Article 51(2) EC provides that the liberalisation of insurance services connected with movements of capital shall be affected in step with the liberalisation of the movement of capital.

Article 52(1) EC provides for a rather different procedure than does Article 47(2) EC, which corresponds to it in the field of establishment. According to the former provision, in order to achieve the liberalisation of a specific service, the Council shall, acting on a proposal from the Commission and after consulting the Economic and Social Committee and the European Parliament, issue directives acting by a qualified majority. By Article 52(2) EC, as far as the former directives are concerned, priority shall as a general rule be given to those services which directly affect production costs, or the liberalisation of which helps trade in goods. Article 53(1) EC provides that the Member States declare that willingness to undertake the liberalisation of their service beyond the extent required by the directives issued pursuant to Article 52(1) EC, if their general economic situation and the situation of the economic sector concerned so permit. Article 52(2) EC empowers the Commission to make recommendations to the Member States concerned. The principle of non-discrimination is enshrined in Article 54 EC, which provides that so long as restrictions on freedom to provide services have not been abolished, the Member State shall apply such restrictions without distinction on grounds of nationality to all persons coming "within the meaning of the first paragraph of Article 49". As already indicated above, Article 49(1) EC has been held to go beyond the prohibition of direct or indirect discrimination, and the same would appear true of Article 54 EC.

The provisions on services sometimes appear a little fragmentary, but they are completed by Article 54 EC, which provides that the provisions of Articles 45–48 EC are also applicable to the matters covered by the chapter on services.

(5) Other relevant EC Treaty provisions

The provisions of Article 230 EC, giving the Court of Justice power to review the legality of acts adopted jointly by the European Parliament and the Council, and acts of the Council and of the Commission, is of obvious importance in the field of free movement of persons and services, as in other areas of Community law. The same may be said of the provisions of Article 234 EC concerning requests by national courts for preliminary rulings concerning the interpretation

---

47. Note in this sense Case 205/84, *Commission v. Germany* [1986] ECR 3755.

of the Treaty, and the validity and interpretation of acts of the institutions of the Community. The special and limitative provisions of Article 68 EC will be noted later on. The provisions of Article 226 EC may also be of importance where a Member State has failed to fulfil its obligations under the free movement provisions. Other provisions of the public law of the EC may also sometimes be of importance.

In addition to the above provisions of the constitutional and administrative law of the EC, certain other provisions of the EC Treaty are of importance in the present field. Thus Article 94 EC which permits the Council, acting unanimously on a proposal from the Commission and after consulting the European Parliament and the Economic and Social Committee to issue directives for the approximation of national measures as directly affect the establishment and functioning of the common market, may form the basis for action in the absence of specific authority given by the free movement provisions.

The complex provisions of Article 95 EC, which permits the adoption of measures for the approximation of national provisions laid down by law, regulation or administrative action having as their effect the establishment and functioning of the internal market, is in principle inapplicable to provisions relating to the free movement of persons. It would seem however, that it might be in the field of services, which does not necessarily involve the free movement of persons.

Article 308 EC has been used as a partial basis for a number of directives on residence,[48] which have extended the groups of persons entitled to free movement under Community law. This article provides that if action by the Community should prove necessary in order to attain in the course of the operation of the common market, one of the objectives of the Community, and this treaty has not provided the necessary powers, the Council shall, acting unanimously on a proposal from the Commission, and after consulting the European Parliament, take the appropriate measures.

The German Constitutional Court expressed its disapproval of the use of Article 308 EC as a sole basis for Community action in *Brunner v. European Union Treaty*,[49] and its use in this sense may be curtailed in the future.

3.   Impact of the Maastricht Treaty

The Maastricht Treaty on European Union incorporated certain provisions on European citizenship into the EC Treaty which underwent only minor changes in accordance with the Amsterdam Treaty on European Union. The provisions concerning European citizenship are fully considered in Chapter 8 below. Apart from its decision in *Maria Martinez Sala*,[50] the Court has shown itself reluctant to give any extensive interpretation to these provisions for the purpose of

---

48. Note for example Council Directive 90/365 on the right of residence for employees and self employed persons who have ceased their occupational activity (OJ 1990 L 180/28).
49. [1994] CMLR 57.
50. Case C-85/96, [1998] ECR I-2691.

enhancing the protection of individuals. Thus, in *Donatella Calfa*,[51] the lifelong expulsion from Greece of a foreign national found guilty of drugs charges was considered by the ECJ under Articles 18, 39, 43 and 49 EC. The Court found that the Greek law violated the latter three articles (free movement of workers, freedom of establishment and freedom to provide services) and said that there was no reason to consider Article 18 EC. It has adopted a similarly restrictive approach in other decisions.

The Maastricht Treaty included the Justice and Home Affairs pillar, under which immigration from outside the Community were dealt with on an intergovernmental basis. Certain measures concerning visas were enacted on the basis of what was then Article 100c EC.[52] A number of measures were also adopted under the Justice and Home Affairs pillar (Article K TEU) but the results of action under this third pillar proved somewhat disappointing. It was not until 1997 that the Dublin Asylum Convention, an instrument adopted under this pillar, came into force. The Europol Convention on the Establishment of a European Police Force was also adopted under this pillar.

Judicial control under the Third Pillar was marked by its general absence, and scrutiny by the European Parliament was minimal. The Court did, however, exercise its jurisdiction to make certain that acts adopted under the cooperation process of the Third Pillar did not encroach upon the powers conferred on the Community by the EC Treaty. Thus, the Joint Action on air transit arrangements adopted under the Justice and Home Affairs pillar was unsuccessfully challenged on the ground that it should have been adopted under Article 100a EC.[53] Other perceived defects with the Third Pillar system before the entry into force of the Amsterdam Treaty on 1 May 1999 included the predominance of unanimous voting, the cumbersome decision making process, the non-exclusive right of initiative of the Commission, and the uncertain legal status of "joint actions" and "joint positions".[54]

4. Alterations made to the EC Treaty by the Treaty of Amsterdam

Much of the material previously included in the Third Pillar has been transplanted into Title IV of Part III of the EC Treaty, and the Third Pillar has been

---

51. Case C-348/96, [1999] ECR I-11.
52. See Regulation 1683/95 [1996] OJ L 164/1 on a uniform format for visas, and Regulation 2317/95 [1996] OJ L 234/1 on determining the third countries whose nationals must possess a visa when crossing the external borders of the Member States. See P. Craig and G. de Burca, *EU Law* (2nd edn, Oxford University Press, 1998), p. 769.
53. Case C-170/96, *Commission v. Council* [1998] ECR I-2763. The Court rather controversially contended that it had jurisdiction to declare third pillar instruments void: see the discussion of this case in Hailbronner, *Immigration and Asylum Law and Policy of the European Union* (Kluwer Law International, 2000), p. 10.
54. Note in this sense, J. Monar, 'Justice and Home Affairs in the Treaty of Amsterdam, Reform at the Price of Fragmentation' (1998) 23 EL Rev. 320. Certain of these defects remain in the revised Third Pillar.

renamed "Provisions on Police and Judicial Cooperation in Criminal Matters". The Third Pillar (Title VI of the TEU) now includes the possibility granted to Member States under Article 35 of the Treaty of European Union to empower the Court to exercise a limited jurisdiction to give preliminary rulings in accordance with Article 35(1) TEU. Member States might accept the jurisdiction of the Court to give such rulings by making a declaration at the time of signature of the Treaty of Amsterdam, or at any time thereafter.[55]

The new title in the EC Treaty is considered below. One of the objectives of the European Union is, according to Article 2 TEU, fourth indent, to maintain and develop the EU as an area of freedom, justice and security. This objective is reflected in the provisions of Article 61 EC and Article 29 TEU. The area is further stated in Article 2 TEU to be one in which the free movement of persons is assured in conjunction with appropriate measures with regard to external border controls, immigration, asylum, and the combating of crime. The new Title has been said by Craig and de Burca to place emphasis on restricting and controlling the entry of nationals of non-Member States into and within the European Union rather than to confer rights and freedoms on them.[56]

III. TITLE IV (ARTICLES 61–69) OF PART III OF THE EC TREATY

1. Substantive legal rules, with special reference to visas

The complexity of the provisions of Articles 61–69 EC may be explained largely on the basis of the differing views of the participants in the negotiations for the Amsterdam Treaty. Title IV covers asylum, immigration, external border controls and judicial cooperation in civil matters and is governed by institutional provisions which are often different from those customary within the Community system. The United Kingdom, Ireland and Denmark enjoy the benefit of "opt outs" from Title IV, and those are considered below, together with the position of these in countries in relation to the *Schengen acquis*.[57]

It may prove difficult to implement the provisions of Title IV, because, with certain exceptions, such implementation will require unanimity during the period of five years from the date of entry into force of the Amsterdam Treaty.[58] In some cases, the duration of the relevant period is not specified.

---

55. Member States may either empower only judicial bodies against whose decisions there is no judicial remedy, or instead all courts and tribunals, to request such rulings. These may be given on the validity and interpretation of framework decisions (which correspond to directives) and decisions, on the interpretation of conventions under Part VI, and on the interpretation of the measures implementing them.

56. *Op. cit.*, p. 664. Very much will, of course, depend on what measures are taken under this Title, and how its provisions are interpreted by the ECJ.

57. See Protocols B2–5 to the Amsterdam Treaty.

58. Article 61(2) EC. Note the minor exceptions for measures connected with visas contained in Article 62(2)(b)(ii) and (iv), where a qualified majority vote in the Council replaces the requirement of an unanimous vote in that body.

Article 61(a) EC requires the Council to adopt measures aimed at assuring the free movement of persons when crossing borders within the Union, in conjunction with flanking measures with respect to external border controls, asylum and immigration, and measures to combat crime in accordance with Article 31(e) of the Treaty on European Union. Article 62(1) EC requires the adoption of measures ensuring the absence of any controls on persons crossing internal borders. The measures outlined in Article 61(a), which have already been mentioned above, take place in accordance with Article 62(2) and (5) and Article 63(1)(a) and 63(2)(a) EC. Article 62(2) EC provides for the adoption of measures on the crossing of the external borders of the Member States, which shall include standards and procedures to be followed by Member States on carrying out checks on such borders, and rules on visas for intended stays of no more than three months.

These rules on visas are required by Article 62(2)(b)(ii) to include a list of third countries whose nationals must be in possession of visas when crossing the borders ("negative list") and of those whose nationals are exempt from that requirement ("positive list"). A list of the former type of countries is contained in Regulation 574/99,[59] which applies to visas granted for an intended stay in one or more Member States for a period of not more than three months, or for the transit through the territory of one or more Member States. The Regulation was adopted under former Article 100c EC, and is inapplicable to airport transits, which are governed by the Joint Action on Air Transit Arrangements of 1996.[60] Regulation 574/99 does not contain any positive list of countries exempt from the visa requirement. However, such a list exists for those states which are parties to the Schengen Implementation Convention of 1990 on the gradual abolition of borders, which receives further consideration below. In fact, there are three Schengen lists, which as well as "positive" list, also include the "negative" and "grey" lists. The Schengen lists, unlike other Schengen provisions concerning visas, have not been attributed to an EU legal basis, as was required by Article 2 of the Schengen Protocol, integrating the *Schengen acquis* into the framework of the European Union. This *acquis* is outlined in Annex to the Protocol and is classified in a Council Decision of 20 May 1999. Because such attribution did not take place, theses lists bind only the Schengen states, which exclude the United Kingdom and Ireland. The Schengen "negative list" is somewhat different from that contained in Regulation 574/99, and can only be amended by a unanimous decision of the parties to the Schengen Convention followed by national legislation.

A proposal exists for a Council Regulation listing the third countries whose nationals must be in possession of visas when crossing the external borders of the EC and those nationals who are exempt from this requirement.[61] The field

---

59. OJ 1999 L 72/2.

60. OJ 1996 L 63/8. Such arrangements are discussed in Hailbronner, *op. cit.*, pp. 138–141.

61. See COM (2000) 27 final for the initial proposal of 26 January 2000, and COM (2000) 577 final/2 for the amended proposal of 1 October 2000. The proposal was enacted as Council Regulation 539/2001, OJ 2001 L 81/1 of 21.3.2001.

of application of the proposed Regulation is similar to that described above in relation to Regulation 574/99. It provides for full harmonisation as regards the third countries whose nationals are subject to the visa requirement, and those whose nationals are exempt from it. The Regulation is inapplicable to the United Kingdom and Ireland, and like Regulation 574/99, it is inapplicable to airport transits.

According to Articles 62(2)(b)(ii)–(iv) EC, the rules are also required to set out the procedure and conditions for issuing visas by Member States, and to provide for a uniform format of visas; and rules on a uniform visa. As far as the Schengen states were concerned, a uniform visa was provided for by Articles 10 and 11 of the Schengen Convention. It was also valid for the whole Schengen area, which came to comprise the majority of the EU states. In accordance with Regulation 1683/95,[62] a uniform format for a Community visa has been introduced, and this has resulted in the replacement of the Schengen visa by the uniform Community visa. However, this Regulation, which was made pursuant to the limited powers conferred on the Community by former Article 100c EC, did not provide for the mutual recognition of visas by Member States, or for the harmonisation of conditions relating to the issue of such visas. Nevertheless, such mutual recognition may possibly have come about by reason of the attribution of the visa-related parts of the *Schengen acquis* to Article 62(2)(b) EC.[63]

The same principle may be true in respect of the harmonisation of certain rules for the grant of the uniform visa, by reason of the incorporation of particular rules contained in the Schengen Implementation Convention concerning conditions of entry into Community law. If this is the case, further harmonisation measures may still be necessary in particular areas.[64]

It would appear that the mutual recognition of visas is also covered by Article 62(3) EC which requires measures to be adopted setting out the conditions under which nationals of third countries have the freedom to travel within the territory of the Member States for a period of not more than three months.[65]

There is nothing in the provisions concerning visas which have been considered above which would appear to derogate from the provisions of national laws governing the rights of entry and residence of nationals of third countries. Article 63(1)(a) and 63(2)(a) and (b) EC empower the Council to take measures on refugees and displaced persons in certain areas.[66]

---

62. Council Regulation 1683/95 (OJ 1995 L 164/1) laying down a uniform format for visas for an intended stay in a Member State or in one or more Member States of not more then three months.

63. Note in particular Articles 5(3) and 10 of the Schengen Implementation Convention, and see Hailbronner, *op. cit.*, p. 142.

64. Note in this sense, Hailbronner, *op. cit.*, p. 147.

65. See Joint Action 97/11 adopted under what was then Article K 3 TEU, [1997] OJ L 7/1.

66. A proposal for a Council Directive has been made on minimum standards for giving temporary protection in the event of a mass influx of displaced persons: see COM (2000) 303 final.

Furthermore, Article 61(b) EC permits other measures, which do not appear, like the measures mentioned above, to be directly related to the free movement of persons, in the fields of asylum, immigration and safeguarding the rights of third country nationals, in accordance with the provisions of Article 63(1), (3) and (4) EC. Article 63(1)(b)–(d) EC enumerates certain kind of measures which may be taken in the fields of asylum and refugees. These measures go further than the determination of which state is responsible for considering an asylum claim by a third country national, which is mentioned in Article 63(1)(a) EC. They involve the adoption of minimum standards on the reception of asylum seekers, minimum standards on the qualification of third country nationals and refugees, and minimum standards in Member States for granting or withdrawing refugee status.[67] Article 63(3) EC provides for measures to be taken on immigration policy within particular areas. These are conditions of entry and residence and standards on procedures for the issue of long-term visas[68] and residence permits, including those for the purpose of family reunion,[69] and illegal immigration and illegal residence including the repatriation of illegal residents.[70] It will of course, take up to five years to enact such measures, and in the intervening time there may be limited opportunities for third country nationals to enter the Community. Furthermore, the new provisions do not grant third country nationals any right to work in the Community. The list of measures contained in Article 63 EC does not seem to be a comprehensive one particularly in the fields of asylum and immigration. Thus, no mention is made of the social integration of asylum seekers. The taking of measures against clandestine immigrants would seem to be covered by Article 63(3)(b) EC, except where such measures involve police and judicial cooperation in criminal matters which has to take place under the intergovernmental framework of Title III of the Treaty on European Union.[71]

---

67. In its Action Plan of 3 December 1998, on the best way to implement the Treaty of Amsterdam, the Council has given priority to improving the implementation of the Dublin Convention and to an agreement on a unified definition of minimum standards for the reception of asylum seekers, with particular attention to the position of children, as well as to the adoption of minimum standards for granting or withdrawing refugee status, see Hailbronner, *op. cit.*, p. 369.

68. See the French initiative for the adoption of a Council Regulation on this matter, OJ 2000 C 200/4, of 13 July 2000.

69. See the Commission's proposed directive, COM (1999) 638 final.

70. There have been two recent French initiatives concerning the repatriation of illegal residents, the first of which was adopted under Article 63(3)(b) EC; and the second under Articles 29(1), 31(e) and 34(2)(c) TEU, see OJ 2000 C 253/1 and OJ 2000 C 253/6.

71. The adoption of measures under this Title (the new "Third Pillar") will usually involve unanimous action. The provisions thereof should lead to increased cooperation between police forces, customs authorities, and other competent bodies of different Member States. The new Third Pillar introduces two legal instruments, decisions and framework decisions, which have a binding character, and assigns a more significant role to the Commission and Parliament than was formerly the case under the Third Pillar. Framework decisions have a similar effect to Community directives.

The adoption of measures in the field of judicial cooperation in civil matters is mentioned in Article 61(c) EC, which refers to Article 65 EC. It is clear from Article 65 EC that such measures must be applicable to civil matters having cross-border service implications. The measures in question must be taken in accordance with Article 67 EC, i.e. by means of a unanimous vote in the Council, but this position will change when the Treaty of Nice comes into force. The actions which may be taken include the improvement and simplification of the system for cross-border service of judicial and extra judicial documents; the recognition and enforcement of decisions in civil and commercial cases including decisions in extra judicial cases; and the promotion of the compatibility of the rules applicable in the Member States concerning the conflict of laws and of jurisdiction. The broad scope of the possible measures requires little emphasis.

In addition Article 61(d) EC requires the Council to take appropriate measures to encourage and strengthen administrative cooperation. Article 66 EC provides that such measures are to ensure cooperation between the relevant departments of the administrations of the Member States in the areas covered by Title IV, and between those departments and the Commission. Article 67 EC is applicable to the enactment of such measures: as from 9 May 2004, these measures will be governed by a Protocol to Article 67 EC.

An important and controversial limitation on the enactment of Community rules is contained in Article 64(1) EC, which provides that Title IV shall not affect the responsibilities incumbent on Member States with respect to the maintenance of law and order and the safeguarding of internal security. It is probable that the judicial review of the invocation of the exception is only available on limited grounds. Article 64(2) EC provides that in the event of one or more Member States being confronted by an emergency situation characterised by a sudden influx of nationals of third countries, the Council may adopt provisional measures of a duration not exceeding six months for the benefit of the Member States concerned. The fact that Article 64(2) EC immediately follows Article 64(1) EC, which is concerned with public order, seems to indicate that it contemplated measures different from those giving temporary protection to displaced persons, which are envisaged in Article 63(2) EC. It is hoped that it may be only rarely necessary to invoke this provision, which is said to operate without prejudice to Article 64(1).[72]

2. Special features of legislative procedure: limited jurisdiction of the Court

The provisions of Article 67 EC have been much criticised because of the requirement of unanimity in the Council, and the merely consultative role of the European Parliament, and also because of the fact that the Commission's right of making proposals is shared with the Member States. This procedure may become more *communitaire* after the expiry of the five-year period, when the

---

72. See in this connection, Hailbronner, *op. cit.*, p. 82.

Council shall, acting on a proposal from the Commission, unanimously take a decision with a view to making all or part of Title IV governed by the co-decision procedure set out in Article 251 EC – which provides for qualified majority voting and gives the European Parliament the final say in the adoption of an act – and adapting the provisions relating to the powers of the Court of Justice. It is by no means clear that it will always be easy to reach such agreement. The provisions of Article 67 EC derive from certain fears expressed by the German government during the negotiating process. It should also be noted that Article 67 EC provides that the Council shall act on proposals from the Commission at the end of the five-year period, but is required to examine any request made by a Member State that the Commission submits a proposal to the Council.

When the Treaty of Nice comes into force, certain amendments will be made to Article 67 EC which is also subject to a Protocol, which contains a Declaration to be included in the Final Act of the conference on Article 67 EC, and which is also significant. The proposed amendments in the foregoing texts envisage a greater use of the co-decision procedure. Article 67(5) EC will provide that the Council shall adopt the measures provided for by Article 65 EC, with the exception of aspects relating to family law, in accordance with the co-decision procedure of Article 251 EC. Furthermore, Article 67(5) EC stipulates that the Council will adopt the measures relating to asylum, refugees and displaced persons provided for by Article 63(2)(a)–(d) and 63(3)(a) by the same procedure. However, this is made subject to the *proviso* that the Council has previously adopted Community legislation defining the common rules and basic principles governing this issue in accordance with Article 67(1) EC, i.e. by unanimity. The latter *proviso* is not clearly expressed, but the relevant rules and principles are presumably intended to relate to asylum, refugees and displaced persons.

It is contemplated by the Protocol and Declaration on Article 67 EC that further changes will be made to this article when the five year period envisaged by the Treaty of Amsterdam has elapsed. The sole article of the Protocol provides that "as from 1 May 2004, the Council shall act by a qualified majority on a proposal from the Commission after consulting the European Parliament in order to adopt the measures referred to in Article 66 of the Treaty establishing the European Community".

The Declaration provides that the High Contracting Parties agree that the Council, in the decision which it is required to take pursuant to the second indent of Article 67(2) EC, will decide as from 1 May 2004, to act in accordance with Article 251 EC in order to adopt measures referred to in Articles 62(3) and 63(3)(b) EC. The former Article concerns measures setting out the conditions under which nationals of third countries shall have freedom to travel in the territory of the Member States during a period not exceeding three months. The latter one concerns measures on illegal immigration and illegal residence, including the repatriation of illegal residents.

The High Contracting Parties also express their agreement in the Declaration that the Council will decide to act in accordance with the procedure referred to in Article 251 EC in order to adopt the measures referred to in Article 62(2)(a) from the date when agreement is reached on the scope of the measures concerning the crossing by persons of the external borders of the Member States. Article 62(2)(a) concerns standards and procedures to be followed by Member States in carrying out checks at their external borders. It is not clear when agreement will be reached on the scope of the relevant measures, and indeed, what would constitute such agreement.

However, the Declaration requires the Council to endeavour to make the Article 251 EC procedure applicable at the date of such agreement, or as soon as possible thereafter, to the other areas covered by Part IV. This provision does not place any binding obligation on the Member States, which may take a considerable time to attain the goal stated therein.

One of the more positive features of the Amsterdam Treaty is that under it, three types of proceedings within Title VI of the Treaty on European Union are made subject to the jurisdiction of the European Court. However, as is clear from Article 35 TEU, the new jurisdiction given to the European Court is subject to certain limitations. The same is true of the new jurisdiction given to the European Court under Title IV of Part III of the EC Treaty. As already indicated in Chapter 1, there are three limitations on the role of the Court in the areas newly communitarised. The first of these, provided for in Article 68(1) EC, restricts the use of the preliminary rulings procedure to national courts and tribunals against whose decisions there is no remedy under Community law. Although one may perhaps comprehend the possible desire to limit the burden of work of the Court in such areas as asylum and immigration, this provision may well give rise to considerable disadvantages for individuals, who may frequently not be in a financial position to afford an appeal to a final national court. This limitation may also restrict the development of Community law by the Court of Justice in exercising its tasks under Article 68(1) EC of giving preliminary rulings on the interpretation of Title IV, or on the validity of interpretation of acts of the institutions based upon that Title. It may not often be faced with such tasks.

Article 68(2) EC provides that the Court shall not have jurisdiction over EC measures taken in view of ensuring the absence of controls of persons when crossing internal borders, if these measures relate to the maintenance of law and order and the safeguarding of internal security. This surprising exemption, which may be compared with the procedures of Article 64(1) EC and Article 2(1) third subparagraph of the Schengen Protocol, and which reflects the preoccupations of the French government that the Court might interfere with national competence over controls for security reasons, is capable of being widely interpreted by national courts. The exclusion of supervision by the Court of Justice under Article 68(2) EC seems hard to justify.

Finally, Article 68(3) EC provides that the Court may be requested by the Council, the Commission or a Member State to give a ruling on the interpretation of Title IV, or any Community act based thereon. If such a ruling is given it has no effect on decisions of national courts or tribunals which have become *res judicata*. Article 68(3) EC does not permit the validity of measures based upon Title IV to be challenged. However, it may be that Member States, the Council, Commission or Parliament can challenge the validity of such acts under the general provisions of Article 230 EC. Article 68 EC is capable of being revised after the lapse of the five-year period: the Council would act by a qualified majority on a proposal of the Commission after consulting the European Parliament.

3. Protocols governing the position of the United Kingdom, Ireland and Denmark

Article 69 EC subjects Title IV to three Protocols. Two of these concern the position of the United Kingdom and Ireland, and the other the position of Denmark. It follows from Article 311 EC that protocols attached to the Treaty form an integral part thereof. These Protocols safeguard the interests of three Member States which adopt a different attitude to the free movement of persons than the remaining ones.

Protocol B3 concerns the application of certain aspects of Article 14 EC to the United Kingdom and Ireland. It provides that the United Kingdom shall remain entitled to exercise at its frontiers such controls on persons as it deems necessary for defined purposes. Nothing in the EC Treaty or the TEU or in any other measure adopted under them shall prejudice the exercise of such controls. Provision is also made to safeguard the Common Travel Area with Ireland. The other Member States remain entitled to exercise at their frontiers or any point of entry into their territory controls on persons seeking to enter from their territory, the United Kingdom or Ireland.

Protocol B4 is on the position of the United Kingdom and Ireland. The need for it follows from the existence of Protocol B3. It grants the United Kingdom and Ireland a complete exemption from the provisions of Title IV and any measure adopted in accordance therewith. These countries do not take part in the voting in the Council on such measures, and the voting rules are adjusted accordingly. However, the United Kingdom or Ireland may opt into certain measures if they notify the Council within three months after a proposal or initiative has been put to it pursuant to Title IV, that they wish to do so, and the Council expresses its approval by a unanimous decision.

Protocol B5 governs the position of Denmark, which is different from that of the United Kingdom and Ireland insofar as Denmark is given a complete exemption from Part IV of Title III EC and measures adopted in accordance therewith, and does not take part in their adoption, the voting rules being adjusted accordingly. Denmark may abandon the concession granted it in the Protocol simply by informing the other Member States, but unlike the United Kingdom and Ireland, may not opt into particular measures under Title IV.

IV. THE SCHENGEN AGREEMENTS

The Schengen Agreement on the gradual abolition of controls at the common frontiers with respect to the movement of nationals of Member States of the EC was signed on 14 June 1985: it was supplemented by the very detailed provisions of the Schengen Implementation Agreement of 19 June 1990. The removal of internal border controls under the Schengen Agreement is compensated for by an extensive range of measures relating to the intensification of police cooperation; judicial cooperation regarding mutual assistance and extradition, and the handing over of criminals; and cooperation in combatting drugs; the creation of the Schengen Information System (SIS), a centralised databank of people and objects; the implementation of unified and stricter border controls, and the coordination of asylum policies. With the entry into force of the Dublin Convention, the Schengen rules on asylum (which are similar to those in the Dublin Convention) became inapplicable. The essence of the Schengen and Dublin Conventions is that only one state is held responsible for processing asylum applications. The Dublin Convention contains a hierarchically ordered catalogue according to which the state which should process the asylum claim is determined.[73]

The Implementation Convention contains a number of rules which are of a controversial nature. One may instance for example the requirement as to reporting. A person may be reported as a person not to be permitted entry to another Schengen state. This generally means that he is a person listed in the Schengen Information System (SIS) as one to be refused entry. This system, which was set up somewhat belatedly, consists of a central databank and materially identical national data files. Categories of data may be stored in the SIS, including data relating to aliens who are reported for the purpose of refusing entry. The fear has been expressed that such reporting occasionally happens for trivial reasons, and that its consequences may be disproportionate.[74]

The key principle in the Implementation Convention is the abolition of checks at the internal borders: however checks appropriate to the situation may be maintained by a Contracting Party for a limited period of time. This provision has often been invoked in practice, sometimes because of fears about criminal activities. Aliens (i.e. non-Community nationals) who have legally entered the territory of a party to the Convention and who hold a uniform visa, are, except where the visa is subject to territorial limitation, permitted to move freely through the territories of all the contracting parties whilst the visa is valid. According to Article 3(1) of the Schengen Agreement, the "external frontiers" may in principle only be crossed at official crossing points and during fixed hours. These external frontiers include those between the Schengen countries and the rest of the Union. The conditions on which a third country national may be admitted for a period of no more than three months are set out in Article 5(1). Controls at the external frontiers involve the checking of travel

---

73. See Hailbronner, *op. cit.*, p. 385. These criteria include a family relationship criteria, the issue of a residence permit, the possession of a valid visa, illegal entry from another country, permission to enter without a visa and finally the first application for asylum.

74. Note in this sense, O'Keefe, 'The Schengen Convention: A Suitable Model for European Integration', (1991) YBEL 185.

documents and other conditions relating to entry, residence, work and departure. They also involve checks on whether an entrant is a threat to the public policy or public security of any of the parties. Checks on goods are also carried out at the Schengen borders.

The Contracting States include all the EU states, apart from the United Kingdom and Ireland. Norway and Iceland are also associated with the implementation and further development of the *Schengen acquis*. These two countries have been admitted into the Schengen group, but without the right to vote.

According to Article 134 of the Schengen Implementation Convention, the provisions of the Schengen Agreement shall apply only insofar as they are compatible with Community law. However, the different issues which have been identified by textwriters as likely to lead to a conflict of competence, such as firearms, have now been resolved in favour of Community competence.

1. Effect of the Amsterdam Treaty on the Schengen System

The Schengen system may now appear to be unnecessary because by signing and ratifying the Amsterdam Treaty, the fifteen Member States have agreed upon the opening of borders, but not according to a single pattern. The Amsterdam Treaty provides a mechanism for the inclusion of the Schengen system in the EU. However, it contains special provisions for the United Kingdom, Denmark and Ireland. Protocol B2, attached to the EC Treaty and the Treaty on European Union (hereinafter "the Schengen Protocol") authorised the signatories of the Schengen Agreements to establish closer cooperation between themselves within the scope of the Schengen Agreements and provided that this cooperation should be conducted within the institutional and legal framework of the European Union.

With the entry into force of the Treaty of Amsterdam, the Schengen Executive Committee established by the Schengen Agreements was replaced by the Council which, acting unanimously, was to take the necessary measures to determine the legal basis for each of the provisions and decisions which constitute the *Schengen acquis*. This *acquis* was somewhat imprecisely defined in an Annex to the Schengen Protocol. Council Decision 1999/435/EC of 20 May 1999,[75] defines the *Schengen acquis* as consisting not only of the Schengen Agreement of 1985, the Implementing Convention of 1990 and a considerable number of accession protocols, but in addition a large number of Executive Committee decisions and a few Central Group decisions.

According to Article 5(1) of the Schengen Protocol, proposals and initiatives building on the *acquis* are subject to the relevant provisions of the Treaties.

The determination of the legal basis for binding acts within the *Schengen acquis* was thought likely to give rise to difficulties, especially in view of the sheer volume of the *acquis*. This *acquis* might be based either upon Part IV of

---

75. OJ 1999 L 176/1.

Title III EC, or Title VI TEU (the new Third Pillar). Certain of the *acquis* did not have to be allocated to any EC or EU basis, because they had been overridden by Community law; or could no longer exist because they were of an institutional nature, and could not survive the integration of the Schengen Agreement into the Union or Community; or because they were merely of historical importance or had no binding character.[76] Article 2 and Annex 8 of Council Decision 1999/435/EC lists the parts of the *acquis* which did not need such allocation.

All the provisions which were required to be given a legal basis obtained one under Council Decision 1999/436/EC,[77] with the exception of those relating to the Schengen Information System. By not deciding anything in relation to these provisions, the Council let them fall automatically under the Third Pillar. Decisions on the removal of internal frontiers, the control of external frontiers and visa policy now come under the relevant articles of Part IV of the EC Treaty. The part of the *Schengen acquis* which relate to visas have been attributed to Article 62(2)(b) EC.

2. The effect of the *Schengen acquis* on the United Kingdom, Denmark, Iceland and Norway

According to Article 4(1) of the Schengen Protocol, the United Kingdom and Ireland are not bound by the *acquis*, but they may at any time request to take part in some or all of the provisions thereof. The United Kingdom government and Ireland have opted into certain parts of the *Schengen acquis*. Thus, that part of the *acquis* which involves police and judicial cooperation in criminal matters and the Schengen Information System now apply to the United Kingdom.[78] Nothing is said in the Schengen Protocol about opting into measures which build on the *acquis*, but it may be that it can take place given such unanimous approval.

The Danish position is complex and is governed in part by Article 3 of the Schengen Protocol, and in part by Article 5 of Protocol B5 on the position of Denmark. According to Article 3 of the Schengen Protocol, following the determination by the Council of the legal basis of the *Schengen acquis*, Denmark shall maintain the same rights and obligations in relation to the other signatories to the Schengen agreement as before the said determination with regard to those parts of the *Schengen acquis* which have their legal basis in Title IV of Part III of the EC Treaty. Presumably the position is the same where parts of the *Schengen acquis* are found to have another Treaty basis. Thus, Article 3(2) provides that where parts of the *acquis* are found to be based upon Title VI

---

76. See paragraph 4 of the preamble to the Council Decision concerning the definition of the *Schengen acquis*, OJ 1999 L 176/1. A full account of the relevant reasons is given in Hailbronner, *op. cit.*, pp. 71–2.

77. OJ 1999 L176/17. See also OJ 2000 L 239/1.

78. Decision 2000/49 of 26 June 1999, OJ 2000 L 15/1.

TEU, Denmark shall have the same rights and obligations as the other signatories.

Article 5 of Protocol B5 provides that within a period of 6 months after the Council has decided on proposals or initiatives to build on the *Schengen acquis* under Title IV, Denmark may decide whether to implement this initiative. The consequences of such an agreement is the creation of an obligation under international law between Denmark and the other Member States. This surprising position may well be explained by political difficulties experienced by the Danish government. By Article 1 of Protocol B5 Denmark may, in accordance with constitutional requirements, inform other Member States that it no longer wishes to avail itself of all or part of this Protocol. In that event, Denmark will apply all relevant measures in force taken within the framework of the European Union.

According to Article 6 of Protocol B2, Iceland and Norway were to be associated with the implementation of the *Schengen acquis* on the basis of the Agreement signed in Luxembourg in 1996. Appropriate procedures were to be agreed to that effect in an agreement to be concluded with those states acting by a unanimous decision of the Member States excluding the United Kingdom and Ireland. Such an agreement was concluded and approved by the Council by Decision 439/EC of 17 May 1999.[79]

3. Fragmentation and future application of the *Schengen acquis*

The new provisions governing the inclusion of the Schengen system in the EU framework have led to considerable complexity, and to a partial fragmentation of the legal order of the EU, partly by reason of the complex opt-outs. The situation with regard to Title IV is rather similar. Article 8 of Protocol B2 may be intended to discourage further fragmentation in the future. It stipulates that the *Schengen acquis* and further measures taken by institutions within its scope must be accepted in full by all future candidates for admission.

4. The Report of the High Level Panel and some subsequent developments

Unlike the provisions of Article 2(1) paragraph 1 of Protocol B2 concerning the determination of the legal basis of the provisions and decisions forming part of the *Schengen acquis* the recommendations contained in the Report of the High Level Panel (the Veil Panel) would seem to remain unimplemented by Member States and the Community institutions to a considerable extent. This is hardly surprising in view of the fact that they are eighty in number; they are intended to ensure that more persons can take advantage of their rights to free movement in the EU. It should be noted that, despite the large number of recommendations that it made, the High Level Panel took the view that, apart from one or two

---

79. OJ 1999 L 176/35. The Decision was on the conclusion of the Agreement with Iceland and Norway concerning the latters' association with the implementation application and development of the *Schengen acquis*.

exceptions, the legislative framework to ensure the free movement of persons is in place, and that the majority of the individual problems can be solved without changes in the recommendations of the High Level Panel in 1998.[80]

The Panel recommend that better information should be made available to raise persons' awareness of their rights. In particular, improvements might take place in the EURES (European Employment Services) network set up by the Commission, which includes two databases, one on job offers, in the participating countries, and one on living and working conditions.[81] In addition, the Panel recommended the rationalisation of the rules concerning residence,[82] and mentioned the unfortunate situation of those who have ceased to work as self-employed persons, and persons in receipt of social assistance, who do not enjoy any right to stay comparable to that granted to former workers under Council Regulation 1251/70/EC or Council Directive 68/360/EC. The Panel recommended that self-employed persons should be given such comparable rights. The Veil Panel also emphasised the position of divorced spouses who were third country nationals, particularly where they had taken up a professional activity, or where there were common children.[83] Such persons might find themselves deprived of the right to stay in the Member State where their spouse was present. The Panel recommended that the provisions of Community law governing the right to remain should be amended so as to grant the divorced spouse who is a third country national right of residence.

The Commission has recently suggested a change of Article 10 of Regulation 1612/68 by giving third country nationals the right of residence in the Member Sates of residence if the marriage is dissolved, provided they have lived in that country in accordance with the provisions of Article 10 for three years.[84] This period of time might be considered too long, and some exceptions may be justified. However, it will obviously deter marriages of convenience.

The Veil Panel also recommended that where a Member State grants rights to its unmarried nationals living together it must grant the same rights to nationals of other Member States,[85] and that a study should be made of practice within the Union.[86]

---

80. Commission Communication to the Council and European Parliament, COM (1998) 403.
81. See page 26 of the Report. The Commission announced the improvement of the *Citizens First* information system after the publication of the Report.
82. Note in particular pages 4, 18 and 21 of the Report.
83. See pp. 74–5 of the Report.
84. Document 598 PCO 394(02) of 12 July 1988. This document contains proposals for changes in Directive 68/360 on the abolition of restrictions on freedom of movement and residence within the Community for workers of Member States and their families. On the same date the Commission issued another proposal suggesting alterations in Regulation 1612/02 on the freedom of movement of workers in the Community: see Document 598 C 394(01).
85. See Case 59/85, *Netherlands v. Reed* [1986] ECR-1288; see also the Commission's proposal for a European Parliament and Council Directive on the rights of citizens of the Union and their family members to move and reside freely within the territories of the Member States of 23 May 2001, COM (2001) 257 final, Article 2(2)(b).
86. See p. 52 of the Report of the High Level Panel.

The High Level Panel has also suggested *inter alia* that there should be a narrower definition of public service posts reserved for a Member State's nationals, more flexible rules to enable the regrouping of families, that social security rights should be modernised; and that there should be greater equality in tax treatment. It has also suggested that a single commissioner should be responsible for the free movement of persons.[87] The recommendation of the High Level Panel are further considered where appropriate in later chapters. Certain of these recommendations have obviously influenced the Commission's recent proposal for a European Parliament and Council Directive on the right of citizens to move and reside freely within the territories of the Member States of 23 May 2001.[88] The proposal lays down the conditions governing the right to move freely and reside freely for Union citizens and their families. It is thus designed to replace a number of legislative instruments on free movement and residence, which are discussed later on in the present work.[89] The proposed directive is also intended to establish a new right of permanent residence for Community nationals and non-national family members. The relevant proposal also adapts Regulation 1251/70[90] and Directive 75/34,[91] which concern the right to remain of persons who have been workers or self-employed persons.

The proposed new Directive would also replace the provisions of Directive 64/221[92] on public policy with new ones, which would have some liberal features, especially in regard to protection against expulsion and the duration of exclusion orders. The enactment of this Directive would extend the right of residence of Union citizens and members of their families in a Member State other than their own without compliance with any formalities from the present period of three months[93] to six months.[94] However such persons would be required to have a valid identity card or passport. If family members were required to have a visa, they would be required to apply for a residence permit before it expired. The proposed Directive would also place non-national family members on an equal footing with nationals after four years residence in a Member State as far as permanent residence are concerned. It would also facilitate the free movement and residence of family members of a Union citizen, and improve the position of children over 21 and the divorced spouses of such citizens.

---

87. There is now a Commission Directorate for Justice and Home Affairs.
88. COM (2001) 257 final.
89. These include Council Directive 86/360/EEC, OJ 1968 L 257/13; Council Directive 73/148/EEC, OJ 1973 L 172/14; Council Directive 90/364/EEC, OJ 1990 L 180/26; Council Directive 90/365/EEC, OJ 1990 L 180/28; Council Directive 93/96/EEC, OJ 1995 L 317/59.
90. OJ 1970 L 142/24.
91. OJ 1975 L 14/10.
92. OJ Special Edition 1964, No. 850/64, p. 117.
93. See Directive 68/360, Article 8(1)(a).
94. After that time registration with the relevant authorities of the Member State might be required.

3 Free Movement of Workers and Related Matters

I. INTRODUCTION

The most important legal provisions governing the free movement of workers are contained in Article 39 EC. The provision stipulates:

1. Freedom of movement of workers shall be secured within the Community.
2. Such freedom of movement shall entail the abolition of any discrimination based upon nationality between workers of the Member States as regards employment, remuneration and other conditions of work and employment.
3. It shall entail, the right subject to limitations justified on grounds of public policy, public security or public health.

   (a) to accept offers of employment actually made;
   (b) to move freely within the territory of Member States for this purpose;
   (c) to stay in a Member State for the purpose of employment in accordance with the provisions governing the employment of nationals of that state laid down by law, regulation or administrative action;
   (d) to remain in the territory of a Member State after having been employed in that state, subject to conditions which shall be embodied in implementing Regulations to be laid down by the Commission.

4. The provisions of this article shall not apply to employment in the public service.

As pointed out in the previous chapter, secondary legislation has been introduced to implement the above principles. It is noteworthy that Article 39 has two implicit limitations. Although it does not expressly limit the benefit of free movement to nationals of Member States, it is clear from the provisions of Directive 68/360 read together with those of the Oporto Agreement on the European Economic Area of 1992 that it does not apply to persons who are not nationals of a Member State of the EC or of the European Free Trade Association (Iceland, Norway and Liechtenstein). Furthermore, it requires the existence of an employment relationship and is inapplicable to persons who are not workers. Article 40 EC which permits the Council to enact secondary legislation setting out the measures required to bring about freedom of movement for workers had similar limitations.

Persons who do not have the required nationality may well be affected by the new Title IV of Part VI of the EC Treaty, which was discussed in the previous chapter in which it was also indicated that certain provisions of the *Schengen acquis* were allocated to this Title, or to Title VI of the TEU. Such *acquis* may be of considerable significance to persons who do not have one of the required nationalities. However, the principal emphasis of the new title may perhaps be restricting, checking and regulating the entry into and movement within the European Union of such non-nationals rather than conferring new rights and freedoms on them.[1]

It is doubtful whether the new status of EU citizenship adds anything significant to the situation of persons who are not pursuing an economic activity, or students within Directive 93/96, employed or self-employed persons who have ceased to work within Directive 90/365, or persons of independent means within Directive 90/364. However, a different approach was taken to this problem in *Maria Martinez Sala v. Freistaat Bayern*[2] but this decision has encountered considerable criticism.[3] In that case the Court of Justice held that a Spanish woman lawfully resident in Bavaria fell within the scope of the EC Treaty provisions on Union citizenship, and thus was entitled to protection from discrimination on grounds of nationality within the material scope of the application of the Treaty. This meant that she was entitled to a child allowance given to German nationals. It is of considerable interest to see whether the Court will maintain its rather doubtful stance in *Maria Martinez Sala* in subsequent decisions. The rules governing EU citizenship are fully considered in a later chapter.

The nationality of a Member State is determined solely by reference to the nationality law of the Member State in question.[4] Germany and the United Kingdom have both made declarations defining who are to be regarded as their nationals. A Declaration on the nationality of a Member State was adopted together with the Maastricht Treaty on European Union. The current definition of United Kingdom nationals for the purpose of EC Law (which definition does not cover British Overseas Citizens), was applied by the Court of First Instance in *Farrugia*,[5] in which it was held that a BOC was not ineligible for a research

---

1. Note in this sense Craig and de Burca, *EU Law: Texts, Cases and Materials*, (2nd edn, Oxford University Press, 1999), p. 664. The same would seem likely to be true of measures taken under Title VI of the TEU.
2. Case C-85/96, [1998] ECR I-2691.
3. See Tomuschat, Case Note in (2000) 37 CMLRev., p. 449. As Tomuschat says, the judgment may be criticised on the grounds that in the circumstances the child raising allowance did not fall within the material scope of Community law (the claimant was neither an employee nor a self-employed person), and that the Court should have discussed whether Mrs Sala's right of residence derived directly from Article 18 EC, and was thus subject to the limitations and conditions laid down in the Treaty, and the measures taken to give it effect. No measures have been taken providing for the acquisition of social entitlements simply on changing the state of residence.
4. See the Declaration concerning the nationality of a Member State adopted together with the Maastricht Treaty on European Union. Note, however, that the extent of the freedom of Member States to define citizenship has been the subject of questions referred by the English High Court to the ECJ in Case C-192/99, *R. v. Secretary of State for Home Department, ex parte Manjit Kaur* [2001] ECR I-1237.
5. Case T-230/94, *Farrugia v. Commission* [1996] ECR II-195. Note also the valuable discussion in A. Evans, *A Textbook of European Union Law*, (Hart Publishing, 1998), pp. 280–1.

fellowship in the United Kingdom by reason of having the nationality of that state. In this case, the applicability of the definition was found consistent with the functional requirements of the EC scheme. It is not clear how the declaration would have been treated if it had not been so consistent.

Article 39 EC, like Article 43 (freedom of establishment) and Article 49 (freedom to provide services) has been held by the Court of Justice to be directly effective.[6] This direct effect does not only take effect between natural or legal persons and the state or its agencies, but also between legal persons and individuals neither of whom belongs to the state or its agencies. This is illustrated by *Walrave and Koch,* and *Bosman,* which are mentioned below. It is not entirely clear however, whether such horizontal direct effect takes place where the employer is an individual who does not have a rule making power, as was the case with the cyclists' association in *Walrave and Koch,* and with the football association in *Bosman.*

Both direct and indirect discrimination on the ground of nationality are forbidden by Article 39 EC. However, indirect discrimination may be justified on objective grounds. Indirect discrimination was in question *in Sotgiu v. Deutsche Bundespost,*[7] which concerned a separation allowance paid to persons working away from their place of residence. A higher allowance was paid to persons working away from their place of residence in Germany than to persons whose residence was outside that country at the time of their first engagement. Thus, although the distinction was based upon residence, it would clearly have distinct effects in accordance with nationality. The Court held that the distinction made, which was indirectly discriminatory, could be justified on objective grounds if the higher allowance paid to workers resident in Germany, but working away from home was granted because such persons might eventually be expected to move their residence to their place of work, but that this could not be expected of persons resident outside Germany. The determination of whether this was the case was left to the national court.

The question as to whether indirect discrimination could be justified has also been of relevance in certain tax cases. Thus, in *P. H. Asscher v. Staatssecretaris van Financiën,*[8] the Court considered whether the imposition of a higher rate of

---

6. See Case 167/73, *Commission v. French Republic* [1974] ECR 359 in which a French rule contained in the Code du Travail Maritime, according to which a three to one ratio for the employment of French as opposed to non-French crew was provided for, was held to be in violation of Article 48(2) EC (now *Association Union Cyclistes Internationales* [1974] ECR 1405) and in Case C-415/93, *Union Royale Belge des Sociétés de Football Association v. Bosman* [1995] ECR I-4921. In Case 2/74, *Reyners v. Belgium* [1974] ECR 631, the Court of Justice held Article 43 EC was directly effective, and in Case 33/74, *Van Binsbergen* [1974] ECR 1299, it also held that Article 49 EC was also directly effective.
7. Case 152/73, [1974] ECR 153.
8. Case C-107/94, [1996] ECR I-3089. Although this case concerned a self-employed person and was decided under Article 43 EC, similar principles would apply to an employed person, to which Article 39 EC was applicable.

taxation upon taxpayers who were not resident in the Netherlands and earned more than 10 per cent of their income elsewhere was unjustified. Asscher, who was the director of two companies, one in Belgium and one in the Netherlands, of which he was the sole shareholder, was a Netherlands national resident in Belgium since 1986. He was taxed on his Belgian income in Belgium, and in the Netherlands on his Netherlands income. The Court upheld his objection to being taxed at the higher rate on a reference being made to it under Article 177 EC (now Article 234 EC).

The Court held that Article 52 EC (now Article 43 EC) was the relevant provision which had to be considered and not, as the referring court considered, Article 48 EC (now Article 39 EC), but reiterated the position which it has often taken that both these provisions are based on the same principles, insofar as discrimination on the grounds of nationality is concerned.

The Court found that the differentiation in treatment between residents and non-residents was not based on any objective difference between their situations. It rejected the contention that it was necessary to prevent non-residents from escaping from double taxation. This argument was found to ignore the fact that under the double taxation agreement in force, Belgium took account of the income earned by Asscher in the Netherlands when determining the rate at which he should be taxed in Belgium.

The Dutch authorities had also contended that the higher tax rate imposed on Asscher could be justified on the ground of ensuring fairness between residents and non residents. The latter were not required to apply contributions to the national social insurance schemes. The Court rejected this submission, holding that either Asscher was liable to pay national insurance contributions in the Netherlands, or he was not. If he was liable, he should have been brought within the protection of that system, and if he were not so liable, he should not be penalised because of his exercising his right not to pay social insurance contributions. The Court also found that the higher tax rate could not be justified on the basis of the need to ensure cohesion of the Dutch tax system.

It has been pointed out by Stanley[9] that the Court's reasoning in Asscher is defective insofar as a distinction based on residence cannot properly be said to operate as covert discrimination on the grounds of nationality when the non-resident is also a national of the Member State in question. As he says, it would have been better if the Court had adopted a similar approach to that which it took in Kraus[10] (the similar approach which it took in Bosman[11] should also be noted), according to which measures, which do not discriminate on grounds of nationality but, which are liable to hinder or render less attractive the exercise by Community nationals of fundamental freedoms guaranteed by the Treaty, can only be justified if it meets an imperative requirement of general interest.

---

9. See his case note in (1997) 34 CMLRev. 713.
10. Case C-19/92, [1993] ECR I-1663.
11. Case C-415/93, [1995] ECR I-4921.

It was held by the European Court of Justice in *Bosman* that Article 48 EC (now Article 39 EC) applies to national measures which restrict the freedom of movement of workers, but which are neither directly nor indirectly discriminatory on the grounds of nationality. In that case the transfer system adopted by both national and transnational football associations was held to be in breach of Article 48 EC (now Article 39 EC). This system required a football club which sought to engage a player whose contract with another club had come to an end to pay that club a substantial transfer fee. This transfer system applied both to transfers from one club to another within a Member State and to players moving between Member States, and was not dependent upon nationality. The Court held that this system, which impeded the free movement of workers, was in breach of Article 48 EC (now Article 39 EC). The Court held that the transfer rules could only be upheld if they pursued a legitimate aim compatible with the Treaty, and were justified by pressing grounds of public interest. It held that even if this were the case, the application of the rules would have to be such as to ensure achievement of the aim in question, and not go beyond what was necessary for that purpose.[12]

More recently in *Terhoeve*,[13] in which the Dutch provisions on income tax and social security were examined under Article 39 EC, the Court held that "provisions which preclude or deter a national of a Member State from leaving his country of origin in order to exercise his freedom of movement constitutes an obstacle to that freedom even if they apply without regard to the nationality of the workers concerned ... It is therefore unnecessary to consider whether there is indeed discrimination on grounds of nationality."[14]

II. THE SCOPE OF FREEDOM OF MOVEMENT OF WORKERS

1. Territorial and personal scope of freedom of movement of workers

The provisions of the EC Treaty governing the free movement of persons (i.e. the free movement of workers and freedom of establishment) and the free movement of services are applicable to Madeira, the Azores and the Canary Islands.[15] However, the Council is empowered to adopt specific measures laying

---

12. The Court of Justice took the view that Belgian rules restricting the transfer of basket ball players constituted an obstacle to the free movement of workers which might go beyond what was necessary for ensuring the regularity of sporting competitions in Case C-176/96, *Lehtonen and Castors Braine ASBL v. FRBSB* [2000] ECR I-2681. The case may be contrasted with Joined Cases C-51/96 and C-191/97, *Deliège* [2000] ECR I-2549.

13. Case C-18/95, [1999] ECR I-345.

14. The Court's decision in this case may be contrasted with that which it gave in Case C-190/98, *Volker Graf v. Filzmoser Maschinenbau GmbH.* [2000] ECR I-493 in which the Court held the relevant provisions of Austrian legislation on compensation for termination of employment had too uncertain an effect to constitute an obstacle to free movement.

15. Article 299(2) EC.

down the conditions of application of the Treaty to those regions. The EC Treaty is applicable to Gibraltar[16] and the Aaland Islands,[17] but Protocol 3 to the Act of Accession of 1972 excludes the Channel Islands and the Isle of Man from the freedom of movement of persons and services.[18] The EC Treaty is inapplicable to the Faroe Islands[19] and to the United Kingdom's Sovereign Base Area in Cyprus.[20] Its provisions governing the free movement of persons is inapplicable to Greenland, which is associated with the Community in accordance with the provisions of Part IV of the EC Treaty.[21]

It should be noted that a worker benefits from free movement under Article 39 EC where the work is done outside the Community, provided that the employment relationship is entered into within the Community.[22] This article has also been held to be applicable to the employment relationship of a Member State national which was entered into and primarily performed in a non-Member State in which the national resided, of at least as far as those elements of the employment relationship to which the law of the Member State of employment was applicable.[23]

As indicated in the previous chapter, the entry, residence, treatment and right to remain of Community workers and their families is dealt with in a considerable body of secondary legislation, which is considered later on in this chapter, and in the case of Directive 64/221/EC, in a later chapter. Much of the terminology contained in Article 39 of the Treaty and in the relevant secondary legislation is undefined, and it was left to the Court of Justice to define what was meant by the term "workers". It is possible to read Article 39 EC as applicable to all workers in the Community, irrespective of their nationality. However, the ECJ has not adopted this interpretation of Article 39 EC, and has instead restricted its ambit to workers who are nationals of the Member States.

The concept of a worker was held in *Levin v. Staatssecretaris van Justitie*[24] to have a Community law content. The Court also held in that case that part-time workers were not excluded from the ambit of Article 39, provided that their work involved genuine and effective activities, which were not pursued on such a small scale that they might be considered as marginal or ancillary. The Court

---

16. Article 299(4) EC.
17. Article 299(5) EC see also Protocol 2 to the Act concerning the conditions of accession of the Republic of Austria, the Republic of Finland, and the Kingdom of Sweden.
18. See also Article 299(6)(c) EC.
19. Article 299(6)(a) EC.
20. Article 299(6)(b) EC.
21. For the position of Andorra, Monaco, San Marino and the Vatican City, see Kapteyn and Verloren van Themaat, *Introduction to the Law of the EC*, (3rd edn, Gormley (ed.), Kluwer Law International, 1998), pp. 703–4, note 768.
22. Case 36/74, *Walrave and Koch v. Association Union Cyclist Internationale* [1974] ECR 1405.
23. See Case C-214/95, *Boukhalfa v. BRD* [1996] ECR I-2253.
24. Case 53/81, [1982] ECR 1035.

did not deal in Levin with the situation in which a part time worker augments his income by means of state benefits. However, in *Kempf v. Staatsecretaris van Justitie*,[25] the Court held that the status of a worker could not be denied to a person whose remuneration fell below national minimum subsistence levels, but which was supplemented by other lawful means of subsistence. A person who receives no reimbursement, but who carries out genuine and effective work in return for services given to him by a commune is treated as a worker within the meaning of Article 39.[26] Nevertheless the pursuit of an activity does not qualify a person as a worker if it is simply a means of rehabilitation for a handicapped person.[27] The position might be different, however, if the sole purpose of the work done was not simply the reintegration of the handicapped person into employment.[28]

A trainee teacher who has simply been giving lessons for a few hours a week may be treated as a worker provided the activities carried on are genuine and effective.[29] Thus, in *Lawrie-Blum*, the Court held that the essential feature of an employment relationship is that for a period of time a person performs services for and under the direction of another in which he receives remuneration. In a rather similar case, *Raulin*,[30] a French national who was employed in the Netherlands on an on-call contract which gave no guarantee as to the hours she would work, and under which she worked for only 60 hours during an eight month period was held to be not precluded from treatment as a worker. A person paid by a share may also be treated as a worker.[31]

Self-employed persons and students are not covered by Article 39. The same is true of job seekers. These categories of persons receive further treatment in the present and in the succeeding chapter.

2. Exception for employment in the public service

According to Article 39(4) EC, the provisions of Article 39 do not apply to employment in the public service. The European Court of Justice has interpreted this exception narrowly, treating it as applicable only to jobs involving the participation in the exercise of powers conferred by public law and involving the exercise of duties designed to safeguard the general interests of the state or local authorities.[32] The Court of Justice has always followed the functional

---

25. Case 139/85, [1986] ECR 1741.
26. Case 196/87, *Steymann v. Staatssecretaris van Justitie* [1988] ECR 6159.
27. Case 344/87, *Bettray v. Staatssecretaris van Justitie* [1989] ECR 1621.
28. Note in this sense Craig and de Burca, *op. cit.*, p. 680.
29. Case 66/85, *Lawrie-Blum v. Land Baden-Württemberg* [1986] ECR 2121.
30. Case C-357/89, *Raulin v. Minister van Onderwijs en Wetenschappen* [1992] ECR I-1027.
31. Case C-3/87, *R. v. MAAF ex parte Agegate Ltd.* [1989] ECR I-4459.
32. See Case 149/79, *Commission v. Belgium* [1980] ECR 3881 in which these cumulative requirements were first stated, and note also Case 307/84, *Commission v. France* [1986] ECR 1725; Case 225/85, *Commission v. Italy* [1987] ECR 2625; and Case C-473/93, *Commission v. Luxembourg* [1996] ECR I-3207. In Case C-283/99, *Commission v. Italy*,

47

interpretation of Article 39(4), and has rejected an institutional one, which has been supported by several Member States. Thus, according to the Court, the application of Article 39(4) is dependent on the nature of the tasks and responsibilities involved in a post, and not on the concept of public service as it exists in the national legislation of the Member States. Thus the majority of posts with Belgian public undertakings and public authorities including those of hospital nurses and railway workers have been held to be outside the scope of the Article 39(4) EC exception. A similar approach was taken to public nursing posts in France.

As the result of certain early decisions of the Court, the Commission adopted a Communication on 18 March 1988 on its activity concerning the application of Article 48(4) EC (now Article 39(4) EC).[33] This communication was primarily concerned with four priority sectors, organisations responsible for managing a commercial service, public health services, public educational establishments and civil research. The Commission found that in all these four sectors, the activities carried out by the state were sufficiently generally removed from the exercise of public authority, and were thus in principle accessible to all Community nationals, Article 48(4) being only applicable in exceptional circumstances. It would appear probable that posts in the judiciary, and senior posts in the police, armed services, and the tax authorities do come within the Article 39(4) EC exception.

It is thought that the Commission should reinforce the sectoral approach which it adopted in its 1988 Communication.[34] The Report of the High Level Panel[35] suggests that the Commission should, acting on the basis of an action carried out in close cooperation with the Member States, specify the criteria for determining whether a post belongs to the activities typical for the state and should define more accurately those sectors which may still be reserved for nationals, and within those sectors, the levels of post above which nationality may continue to be a condition of access. The High Level Panel also recommended that the Commission should endeavour to ensure that the principle of the mutual recognition of qualifications is recognised in the public sector. It found many impediments to freedom of movement between different Member States in this sector.[36] For example the requirements as to the knowledge of the language of the host state were sometimes disproportionately burdensome, diplomas acquired in other Member States were sometimes not given adequate

---

judgment of 31.5.2001, n.y.r., the Court adopted a narrow approach to the intepretation of what are now Articles 45 and 55 EC which provide for exceptions for activities connected with the exercise of official authority, to the right of establishment and freedom to provide services. The Court held that the activities of private security undertakings and of sworn security guards are not normally directly and specifically concerned with the exercise of official authority.

33. [1988] OJ C 72/2.
34. Note in this sense, Report of the High Level Panel, p. 37.
35. *Ibid.*, note 33.
36. See Report of the High Level Panel, pp. 37–40.

recognition, and professional experience gained in another Member State was sometimes disregarded.

3. Rights of movement, entry and residence

Article 39 EC provides for rights of entry and residence for persons entering a Member State for the purpose of accepting offers of employment actually made. It also permits persons to reside in the relevant Member State for the purposes of employment and provides that, subject to an implementing Regulation made by the Commission, (which is considered below), persons who have been employed in a Member State may remain there after such employment has finished. However, Article 39 cannot be invoked by a worker against his own state, when no cross-border element is involved. An individual who has never sought to make use of his or her right to freedom of movement will be unable to rely upon rights under European Community law. Thus, in *Morson and Jhanjan v. Netherlands*,[37] two mothers from Surinam wished to join their children in the Netherlands. They were not entitled to do so under Dutch law, and they thus endeavoured to rely on EC Law, which allows family members to join EC migrants. It was held that they were unable to do so since their children had never exercised their right to freedom of movement within the Community, no factor existed connecting them with Community law.[38] It does not seem that this situation has been altered by reason of the provisions of Article 18(1) EC, which stipulates that every Union citizen shall have the right to move and reside freely within the Member States. The right is said, however, to be subject to the limitations and conditions laid down in the Treaty, and to measures adopted to give it effect.[39]

Persons seeking work have similar rights to persons taking up an offer of a job in another Member State. They enjoy the right of entry into, and the right to move freely, within Member States for the purpose of seeking employment.[40] In addition, they are permitted to reside in a relevant Member State for a reasonable period of time, whilst they are actively seeking work, and have a genuine chance of being employed. The Court held in *Antonissen* that a Member

---

37. Cases 35 and 36/82, [1992] ECR 3723.
38. See also Joined Cases C-64 and 65/96, *Land Nordrhein-Westfalen v. Uecker* [1997] ECR I-3171.
39. The attempt to invoke the concept of citizenship of the EU to broaden the scope of Community law to cover a situation treated as being purely internal to a Member State failed in Joined Cases C-64 and 65/96, *Land Nordrhein-Westfalen v. Uecker* [1997] ECR I-3171.
40. In Case 48/75, *Procureur du Roi v. Royer* [1976] ECR 497, the right of entry granted to nationals of other Member States by Article 3 of Directive 68/360 was held applicable to persons entering in search of work. It may be that the text of the Directive will be clarified in this sense, in accordance with the Commissions proposal of 22 July 1998, which suggests an appropriate amendment of Article 2(1) of the Directive.

State might deport an EC national if he had not found employment within six months, unless he provided evidence that he was continuing in the search for employment, and had a genuine chance of engagement.

The Court of Justice held in *Dimitrios Tsiotras v. Landeshauptstadt Stuttgart*[41] that a Greek national who had been unemployed at the time of Greek accession, and had remained unemployed since that time, had no right to reside in Germany. The Court has also held that a person seeking work has the right to equal access to employment, but no right to equal access to social and tax advantages under Article 7(2) of Regulation 1612/68.[42]

Member States are required to grant the right of residence in their territory to persons who enter that state and take up or find a job there (and their families) who are able to produce the documents set out in Article 4(3) of Directive 68/360/EC. As far as the worker is concerned, these are the document on the basis of which he entered the territory, and a confirmation of engagement from the employer, or a certificate of employment.[43] Such a permit is valid throughout the Member State within which it was granted. It lasts for five years, and is automatically renewable.[44] It may not be withdrawn because of unemployment by reason of temporary incapacity for work, by reason of illness or accident or by that of involuntary unemployment.[45] Gaps in residence not exceeding six consecutive months and absences on military service do not affect the validity of a residence permit.

Article 6(3) of Directive 68/360/EEC provides for temporary residence permits for temporary and seasonal workers who work for more than three months but for less than one year. The residence documents granted to nationals of an EC Member State must be issued and renewed free of charge or on payment of an amount not exceeding the duties and taxes charged for the issue of identity cards to nationals.[46] The proposed amendments to Directive 68/360/EC would improve the residence rights of persons who have a series of fixed term or short term contracts once they had worked twelve out of eighteen months.

Failure to obtain a valid residence permit does not justify the refusal of entry or the deportation, of a worker or his family.[47] A worker (who is not temporary

---

41. Case C-171/91, [1993] ECR I-2975.
42. Case 316/85, *Centre Public v. Lebon* [1987] ECR 2811. The Court might possibly take a different view of such a situation by reason of its decision in *Maria Martinez Sala*, but the latter decision appears inadequately reasoned.
43. See Directive 68/360/EEC, Article 4(1) and (3). A Community national enjoying freedom of movement simply has to produce a valid passport or identity card in order to enter the territory of another Member State. Compliance with this formality will not normally be necessary where both the state of exit and that of entry are parties to the Schengen Agreements.
44. Article 6(1), *ibid.*
45. Article 7(1), *ibid.*
46. Article 9(1), *ibid.*
47. Case 157/79, *R. v. Pieck* [1980] ECR 217.

or seasonal) will be allowed to stay for a normal period of five years, and an additional further year, together with the family. Penalties may be imposed by the authorities of a Member State in the case of failure by workers and their families to comply with the necessary formalities, provided they are not disproportionate. However deportation is never justified as a sanction for such non-compliance.

4. Family members

Members of the family of a worker who exercises his freedom of movement under Article 39 EC are entitled, irrespective of their nationality, to enter and reside with him, and they also have the right to engage in employment.[48] The members of the family of such a person are defined in Article 10(2) of Regulation 1612/68, as the spouse and those of his descendants who are under the age of 21, or who are dependants, and dependants on the ascending line of the worker and his spouse. The status of dependency was held in *Lebon*[49] not to depend upon objective factors indicative of a need for support, but upon the actual provision of support by the worker. The Commission has also prepared an amendment to Article 10 of Regulation 1612/68 of 22 July 1998, according to which the age and dependency criteria would be removed in relation to descendants.[50]

According to Article 10(2) of Regulation 1612/68 of 22 July 1998, Member States shall facilitate the admission of any member of the family not coming within Article 10(1), if dependent on the worker, or living under his roof in the country whence he comes. Such workers, unlike those mentioned in Article 10(1), are not specifically granted the right to pursue an activity as an employed person in the host state by Article 10(2) of Regulation 1612/68, but may be entitled to do so on other grounds.

In order that a family member may install himself with the worker, he is required by Article 10(3) of Regulation 1612/68 to have housing considered as normal for national workers in the region in which he is employed. This requirement may only be made applicable at the initial stage of entry by the family, and it should not be used as a reason for refusing to renew residence if housing

---

48. See Article 11 of Regulation 1612/68. This provision does not specifically permit the spouse or children to engage in self-employment (see Report of the High Level Panel, p. 75). The spouses' access to employment is considered in Case 131/85, *Gül v. Regierungspräsident Düsseldorf* [1986] ECR 1573. The Commission's proposal of 22 July 1998, Document 598 PCO 394(02), suggests that family members should retain the right to employment if the marriage is dissolved, on condition that they have lived in the territory under the terms of Article 10(1) for a period of at least five years. This requirement may seem a little Draconian, but it would probably be only necessary for family members of a Community worker who did not possess the nationality of a Member State to invoke it.
49. Case 316/85, *Centre public d'aide sociale de Courcelles v. Lebon* [1987] ECR 2811.
50. See Document 598 PCO 394(01).

conditions get worse. Such a refusal may contravene Article 8 of the European Convention of Human Rights.

The family of a person who exercises his rights under Article 39 EC will be admitted to another Member State on the production of a passport or an identity card, unless they are not nationals of a Member State, in which case they will be required to get an entry visa or document. According to Article 3(2) of Directive 68/360/EC, Member States shall accord to such persons every facility for obtaining any necessary document. It is understood however, that such states have not always done so in the past.[51] A member of the family who is not a national of a Member State shall, according to Article 4(4), be issued with a residence document which shall have the same validity as that of the worker on whom he is dependent.

The derived right of residence granted to a spouse is not lost when the person exercising his or her right of free movement separates from them.[52] The situation after a divorce takes place remains unclear. In *R. v. Secretary of State for the Home Department, ex parte Sandhu*,[53] the English High Court adopted the view that divorce did not automatically bring an end of the derived right of residence of an Indian national, the husband of a German national resident in this country. However, both the Court of Appeal and the House of Lords found that the husband's rights ended once the wife had returned to Germany. Steiner and Woods,[54] take the view that a spouse's EC rights do not necessarily end on divorce, or when the worker leaves the country which appears to be correct; and is echoed by the High Level Panel adopting a similar approach in its Report. Nevertheless, as the two authors say, the Court of Appeal still interprets the rights of the divorced spouse restrictively.[55]

No problems corresponding to that of the divorced spouse appear to arise for the children of the marriage. Like the workers' other dependent relatives, they remain members of the worker's family after divorce. The Commission has proposed that Article 10 of Regulation 1612/68 should be amended so as to provide that members of the family of a worker who are not nationals of a Member State retain the right of residence in the Member State of residence if the marriage is dissolved, on condition that they have lived in that country for three years in accordance with the provisions of Article 10.[56] The latter draft

---

51. See the Report of the High Level Panel, p. 74 in this sense. The Panel recommends the abolition of this requirement at least in the case of family members.
52. Case 267/83, *Diatta v. Land Berlin* [1985] ECR 567. In this case, the separated spouse was a non-EC (Senegalese national). The Court also held that she was entitled to install herself separately from her husband for the purpose of exercising her rights under Article 11 of Regulation 1612/68.
53. [1982] 2 CMLR 553.
54. *Textbook on EC Law*, (7th edn, Blackstone Press, 2000), pp. 302–3.
55. Note in this sense *Secretary of State v. Remilien* [1999] All ER (EC) 650 CA.
56. See Document 598 PCO 394. The position of such a person is more difficult than that of a national of a Member State who may find it comparatively easy to become a Community

provision presumably entails that a non-national spouse must have lived in the host state as the spouse of a national of another Member State employed in the former state for at least three years. As indicated in the preceding chapter, the adoption of some such provision appears very desirable.

Unmarried partners may exceptionally receive protection and be allowed to reside under the law. The Commission proposal of 22 July 1998 contained a draft provision according to which anyone corresponding to the spouse of a worker under the legislation of the host state could install himself with the worker. In *Netherlands v. Reed*.[57] an unemployed British national came to live with her partner, a British national, in the Netherlands, were he was employed. The Court of Justice held that in the present stage of social development, he could not be treated as a spouse under EC Law. However, the Netherlands had a policy of treating an alien who had a stable relationship with a worker of Dutch nationality as that worker's spouse. The Court (rather subtly) found that this possibility had to be treated as a social advantage under Article 7(2) of Regulation 1612/68, with the consequence that it was available to the long term partner of a British worker.[58]

It should be noted that in the decision *in Kaba v. Secretary of State for the Home Department*[59] the Court did not find it necessary to rule on the question whether the right to remain indefinitely in the national territory is a social advantage. The Court held, perhaps somewhat unconvincingly, that the distinction in the United Kingdom Immigration Rules between the rights of spouses of migrant workers who are nationals of other Member States and spouses of UK nationals and persons settled in the United Kingdom, as far as the residence period before which the right to apply for indefinite leave to remain was concerned, was based on an objective distinction between United Kingdom nationals, and nationals of other Member States, and was not discriminatory. Unmarried partners might sometimes be entitled to entry and residence in accordance with the provisions of Article 8 of the European Convention of Human Rights, which requires respect for privacy and family life.

5. Controls on entry

Systematic frontier checks may not be imposed on persons travelling within the EC who benefit from Directive 68/360. Such persons may only be required to

---

worker in his or her own right. See also Article 18(2) of the Commission proposal of 23.5.2001, COM (2001) 257 final, which would require marriage to have lasted for five years up to the initiation of the divorce or annulment proceedings (including one year in the host state); or that the spouse not being a Union national, whose right of residence depends on their being married to a Union citizen, having been granted custody of the Union citizen's children; or the marriage has been dissolved by reason of particularly difficult circumstances.

57. Case 59/83, [1986] ECR 1283.
58. The Courts' judgment may have had an influence on the work of the High Level Panel and also on the Commission's recent proposal for a Directive COM (2001) 257 final.
59. Case C-356/98, [2000] ECR I-2623.

produce a valid identity card or passport.[60] However, it should be remembered from the discussion of Part IV of the EC Treaty in chapter 2 that the abolition of internal frontier controls on Union citizens or nationals of third countries are to take place in accordance with measures taken by the Council by 1 May 2004.[61] It will be remembered that such measures are to take place in conjunction with directly flanking measures with respect to external border controls, asylum and immigration, and measures to prevent and combat crime.[62] Furthermore, the Council is empowered to adopt other measures in the field of immigration, asylum, and safeguarding the interests of third country nationals;[63] measures in the field of judicial cooperation in civil matters;[64] measures to encourage and strengthen administrative cooperation;[65] and measures in the field of police and judicial cooperation in criminal matters.[66]

It has already been pointed out above that the United Kingdom and Ireland have been permitted to retain their controls on entry.[67]

III. THE PROVISIONS OF PART I OF REGULATION 1612/68

Part I of Regulation 1612/68 gives increased substance to the worker's right to free movement. The remaining two parts thereof have generated comparatively little legal consideration and case law; and it is not thought appropriate to give them further consideration. The first part of the Regulation is made up of three titles, Title I (Articles 1–6) is concerned with eligibility for employment; Title II (Articles 7–9) governs equality of treatment in employment, and has been extended to protect workers' families; Title III (Articles 10–12) is specifically concerned with such families.

1. Eligibility for employment (Title I)

By Article 1 of Regulation 1612/68, the nationals of a Member State have the right to take up employment in another Member State under the same conditions as nationals. The Commission's proposed amendments of 22 July 1998 included a new Article 1a, which would provide that within the scope of this Regulation (which is applicable to workers exercising the right of free movement), all discrimination on grounds of sex, racial or ethnic origin, religion, belief, disability,

---

60. Case 321/87, *Commission v. Belgium* [1989] ECR 997. The requirement for such checks may be inapplicable to parties to the Schengen Agreement.
61. Article 62(1) EC.
62. Article 61(a) EC.
63. Article 61(b) EC.
64. Article 61(c) EC.
65. Article 61(d) EC.
66. Article 61(e) EC.
67. Protocol on the application of certain aspects of Article 14 EC to the United Kingdom and Ireland.

age or sexual orientation is prohibited.[68] Discrimination against workers of other Member States in concluding and performing contracts of employment is prohibited by Article 2. Article 3(1) of Regulation 1612/68 forbids Member States from imposing rules limiting applications for and offer of employment, or subjecting the right of EC nationals to take up and pursue employment to conditions to which nationals of the host state are not subject. This rule is not, however, applicable to conditions related to linguistic knowledge. Thus, in *Groener v. Ministry of Education*,[69] a requirement of Irish law, applicable both to nationals and non-nationals, that teachers in vocational schools should have a sufficient knowledge of Irish was held to be permissible in view of the clear policy of promoting the Irish language, and not to be disproportionate. Such indirectly discriminatory rules must be designed to achieve legitimate ends, and be both necessary and appropriate for that purpose. The reservation of a quota for posts for foreign nationals is contrary to Article 4.[70] Article 5 requires the same assistance from employment offices for EC nationals as is given to home state nationals. Discriminatory medical, vocational or other criteria for recruitment and engagement are prohibited by Article 6.

2. Equality of treatment in employment (Title II)

(1)   Prohibition of discrimination in relation to conditions of employment

Article 7(1) provides that a worker who is a national of a Member State may not, in the territory of another Member State, be treated differently from national workers by reason of his nationality in respect of any conditions of employment and work, in particular as regards remuneration, dismissal, and should he become unemployed, re-instatement or re-employment.

The above provision has a wide ambit, and catches both direct and indirect discrimination. The Commission's proposal of 22 July 1998 suggests that the wording of Article 7(1) should be altered to prohibit the differential treatment of a migrant worker by reason of his nationality in respect of any conditions of employment and work, particularly as regards health, safety and hygiene, remuneration and dismissal or occupational rehabilitation, re-instatement or re-employment should he or she become unemployed or partially unfit for work. These forms of discrimination would seem to be, in general, caught by the present form of Article 7(1).

It follows from Article 7(1), that Member States must grant to Community

---

68. A directive implementing the principle of equal treatment between persons irrespective of racial or ethnic origin has recently been adopted: see Directive 2000/43/EC, OJ L180/22. A further directive, covering other grounds of discrimination, has been enacted recently; see Directive 2000/78/EC, OJ 2000 L303/16.

69. See Case 379/87, [1989] 2 CMLR 3187. Note also Case C-272/92, *Spotti v. Freistaat Bayern* [1983] ECR I-5195, in which the rules in question were found not to be justified.

70. Such a quota was in question in Case 167/73, *Commission v. France* [1974] ECR 359.

workers who have completed their military service in another Member State the same advantages, for example in relation to seniority, as those granted to their own nationals.[71] Furthermore, (although, as the High Level Panel pointed out, this requirement seems frequently to be ignored, especially in the public sector), where prior professional experience determines the professional and salary classification of an employee, account must be taken of experience acquired abroad. In *Schöning-Kougebetopoulou v. Freie und Hansestadt Hamburg*,[72] the Court held that a term in a collective agreement which provided for promotion on grounds of seniority after eight years' employment in any given group with the exclusion of periods of employment in the public service of another Member State was contrary to EC law. It is fairly obvious that migrant workers might find it harder to satisfy the requirement of eight years employment. The draft new Article 7(5) included in the Commission proposal of 22 July 1998, addresses the form of discrimination evidenced in *Schöning*. This new paragraph provides that where working conditions, professional advancement or certain advantages accorded to a worker depend in a Member State, on the occurrence of facts or events, any comparable facts or events which have occurred in another Member State shall entail the same consequences, or confer the same advantages.

(2)   Social advantages

Article 7(2) which provides that migrant workers from Member States shall enjoy the same social and tax advantages as national workers, has been extensively litigated and broadly interpreted by the European Court. Family members have thus been held entitled to invoke Article 7(2),[73] provided that the advantage claimed is of some direct or indirect benefit to the worker,[74] and not simply to the family member. The latter are defined in accordance with Article 10. Thus in *Inzirillo*[75] the Court of Justice held that an Italian worker in France was entitled to a disability allowance for his handicapped adult son. It adopted the view that the dependent adult was covered by Article 10(1) of Regulation 1612/68, and that an allowance for handicapped adults which was awarded by a Member State to its nationals would constitute a social advantage to a national worker.

The limits of the rights to which workers might be entitled under Article 7(2)

---

71. Case 15/69, *Württembergische Milchverwertung-Südmilch AG v. Salvatore Ugliola* [1969] ECR 363.
72. Case C-15/96 [1998] ECR I-47; [1998] 1 CMLR 931; [1998] All ER (EC) 97.
73. It was suggested in the Commission's proposal of 22 July 1998 (Document 598 PCO 394(01)) that members of the family entitled to live in a Member State under Articles 10(1) and (2) of Regulation 1612/68/EEC should be entitled to all financial, tax, social, cultural or other advantages available to nationals.
74. Case 316/85, *Lebon* [1987] ECR 2811.
75. Case 63/76, *Inzirillo* [1976] ECR 2057.

were addressed by the Court of Justice in *Ministère Public v. Even and ONPTS.*[76] The case concerned Even, a French worker in Belgium, who received an early retirement pension, which was made subject to a percentage reduction for each year of early payment. Such a reduction was made in respect of all workers except Belgian nationals who were in receipt of a Second World War service pension granted by an Allied nation. Even was the recipient of a war service pension under French legislation, and he claimed that he was entitled to equality of treatment and that he should thus benefit from an early retirement pension without any deduction.

The Court found that the advantages granted by Article 7(2) to workers who are nationals of other Member States were all those which, whether or not linked to a contract of employment, were generally granted to national workers primarily because of their objective status as workers or by virtue of the mere fact of their residence of the national territory, and the extension of which to workers who are nationals of other Member States therefore seemed suitable to facilitate their mobility within the Community. The Court found that the Belgian benefit, which was based on a system of national recognition for services rendered in wartime, could not be considered as an advantage given to a national worker by reason primarily of his status as a worker, or residence on the national territory, and for that reason it did not comply with the essential characteristics of the social advantages referred to in Article 7(2).

The most important feature of *Even* is its broad definition of the scope of Article 7(2). It may well be that it is difficult to distinguish this decision from *Ugliola,*[77] in which it was held that military service in the forces of another Member State should be taken account of for the purposes of calculating seniority at work.

The *Even* formula has been used in a number of subsequent cases. Thus, in *Reina v. Landeskreditbank Baden-Württemberg*[78] an Italian couple living in Germany where the husband was a worker, were held entitled to claim an interest free childbirth loan, financed by the state, from the defendant German bank. The loan was granted to German nationals to stimulate the birth rate. The defendant bank contended that failure to grant the loan in no way hindered the mobility of workers within the Community, and that as the interest free childbirth loan, which was granted on a discretionary basis, it fell within the area of demographic policy, and was a measure adopted within the field of political rights. The bank also contended that it was proper to take account of

---

76. Case 207/78, [1979] ECR 2019.
77. Case 15/69, [1970] ECR 363. Note the discussion in Craig and de Burca, *op. cit.*, p. 702–3. The writers correctly point out that the distinction between *Ugliola* and *Even* cannot depend on that between wartime service and military service, because the Court ruled in Case C-315/94, *De Vos v. Bielefeld* [1996] ECR I-1417, that the statutory obligation on an employer to continue paying certain pension insurance contributions on behalf of workers absent on military service was not a social advantage within Article 7(2).
78. Case 65/81, [1982] ECR 33.

the fact that many foreign workers return to their countries of origin before the expiry of the period prescribed for the payment of the loan, such that repayment is placed in jeopardy.

The Court refused to accept the bank's apparently cogent arguments. It found that the concept of social advantages included in Article 7(2) also encompassed benefits granted on a discretionary basis, and this included interest free loans granted on childbirth by an institution incorporated under public law to families with a low income for the purpose of stimulating the birthrate.

A special allowance granted to old persons whose income was insufficient was held to fall within the scope of Article 7(2) in *Frascogna*.[79] In this case, the widow of an Italian national was held entitled to such an allowance. It was held that a requirement that relatives in the ascending line of a worker from another Member State should have resided for fifteen years in France was discriminatory, and could not be invoked against her. The Court emphasised that Article 7(2) prohibits any discrimination against the relatives in the ascending line of a worker from another Member State when these relatives have exercised the right granted by Article 10 of Regulation 1612/68 to install themselves with that worker.

Article 7(2) has also been invoked for the purpose of using one's own language in legal proceedings.[80] However, Article 7(2) will be inapplicable if the benefit claimed would not be a social advantage for the state's own nationals. Thus in *Belgian State v. Taghavi*,[81] the Iranian wife of an Italian national residing as a worker in Belgium claimed benefit as a handicapped person. It was shown that entitlement to a benefit for handicapped persons was reserved to Belgian nationals residing in Belgium. It was a personal right, and a person who did not possess the nationality of an EC state could not be entitled to the benefit simply because his or her spouse had Belgian nationality. The Court of Justice held that since the spouse of a Belgian worker who was not himself or herself an EC national could not claim the benefit in question, there was in those circumstances no "social advantages" available to national workers, and Article 7(2) was inapplicable.

The importance of lawful residence in claiming the advantages, granted under Article 7(2) should be noted. Such residence rights may become available under Directive 68/360 or Regulation 1251/70, or under the provisions governing the self-employed. Regulation 1251/70 and the latter provisions are discussed below.

The rights to equality of treatment under Article 7(2) are not available to persons who are in search of work.[82] They are also unavailable to students in

---

79. Case 157/84, *Frascogna v. Caisse des depots et consignations* [1985] ECR I-739.
80. Case 137/84, *Ministère Public v. Mutsch* [1985] ECR 2681. Note also Case C-274/96, *Bickel and Franz* [1999] ECR I-7637, in which the Court held that the requirement of non-discrimination in the use of language could be applied to criminal proceedings against German nationals temporarily staying in Bolzano, Italy.
81. Case C-243/91, [1992] ECR I-4401.
82. Case 316/85, *Lebon* [1987] ECR 2811.

the circumstances mentioned in *Brown*[83] and *Lair*,[84] which are discussed towards the end of this chapter, where it is shown that it is not clear that these cases would be decided by the Court in the same restrictive manner following *Maria Martinez Sala*.

It was recognized, in *Bernini*,[85] that study finance awarded by a Member State to children of migrant workers constitutes a social advantage to a migrant worker as provided for in Article 7(2) of Regulation 1612/68 when the worker continues to support the child. In *Meeusen*[86] the Court held that the dependent child of a national of one Member State who pursued an activity as an employed person in another Member State whilst continuing to reside in the state of which he or she was a national could rely on Article 7(2) in order to obtain study finance under the same conditions as are applicable to children of nationals of the state of employment, without any further requirements as to the child's place of residence. A similar rule was said by by the Court to apply to the dependent child of a national of a Member State who pursues an activity as a self-employed person in another Member State whilst maintaining his residence in the state of which he is a national.

(3)   Indirect discrimination and tax advantages

Indirect discrimination on the basis of residence may be permissible in relation to tax advantages granted to migrant workers where such discrimination is objectively justified, perhaps on the basis of preserving the cohesion of a fiscal system,[87] or the effectiveness of fiscal supervision,[88] or where the situations of the national and the migrant worker are not comparable.[89] In *Bachmann v. Belgium*, a Belgian rule which permitted the deduction from income tax of contributions to health and life insurance policies only if they were paid in Belgium was held to be justified on the ground of the need to protect the cohesion of the tax system, even though it was indirectly discriminatory. This approach permitted tax deductions in respect of insurance contributions to be offset against tax paid by insurers in that country. It is obvious that this would have been impossible if the insurance had been effected in another Member State.

In *Asscher*,[90] the justification allowed in *Bachmann* was narrowly construed. The Court refused to accept the contention that the cohesion of the tax system

---

83. Case 197/86, *Brown v. Secretary of State for Scotland* [1988] ECR 3205.
84. Case 39/86, *Lair v. University of Hannover* [1988] ECR 3161.
85. Case C-3/90, *Bernini v. Minister van Onderwijs en Wetenschappen* [1992] ECR I-1071.
86. Case C-337/97, [1999] ECR I-3289.
87. Case C-204/90, *Bachmann v. Belgium* [1992] ECR I-249; Case C-279/93, *Finanzamt Köln-Altstadt v. Schumacker* [1995] ECR I-225.
88. Case C-250/95, *Futura Participations v. Singer* [1997] ECR I-2471.
89. Case C-279/93, *Finanzamt Köln-Altstadt v. Schumacker* [1993] ECR I-225; Case C-80/94, *Wielockx v. Inspector der Directe Belastingen* [1995] ECR I-2493.
90. Case C-107/94, [1996] ECR I-3089.

justified the imposition of the higher rate of Dutch taxation on Asscher, a director of a Dutch company, who was not liable to pay national insurance contributions. The Court also rejected the arguments that the differentiation in treatment between residents and non-residents was based upon an objective distinction between their situations, or that it was required to ensure fairness between residents and non-residents.[91]

In *Schumacker*, indirect discrimination based on the residence of a worker according to which an EC national employed but not resident in a Member State cannot benefit from personal tax allowances was said by the Court to be justifiable in certain circumstances. Such justification was held to be possible because of the likelihood of distinctions between the position of resident workers and those from other Member States. However, no such distinction was held to be possible by the Court in the case before it. It found that a regime which denied benefits to non-residents granted to residents would be acceptable where the worker earned most of his income, and was therefore taxed, in his state of residence, because the latter state, was in a more favourable position, when determining his overall tax liability, to take account of the personal and family circumstances of the worker. Under such circumstances, the positions of resident and non-resident taxpayers are not comparable. However, in *Schumacker*, the relevant worker, was a Belgian national working in Germany who retained his residence in Belgium but earned at least 90 per cent of his income in Germany, so that the Belgian tax authorities would not have been able to take account of Schumacker's personal and family circumstances, because of his lack of income in that state. The Court thus found that the German tax regime which failed to take account of Schumacker's personal and family circumstances was discriminatory, and contravened EC law.

Following the Court's judgment in *Schumacker* and the related one in *Wielockx*, the German legislature provided that where a Community national had neither permanent residence nor usual abode in Germany, he and his spouse could nevertheless under certain circumstances be treated as subject to tax in Germany on their total income, and on that basis, be entitled to the tax concessions granted to residents to take account of their personal and family circumstances. In *Gschwind v. Finanzamt Aachen-Aussenstadt*[92] the Court held that the conditions laid down for that purpose by the German legislature are compatible

---

91. Article 58(1)(a) EC permits Member States to discriminate in their tax laws between taxpayers who are not in the same position with regard to their residence. However, Article 58(1)(a) is subject to the provisions of Article 58(3) EC, which makes it clear that the measures permitted by Article 58(1)(a) may not constitute a means of arbitrary discrimination or a disguised restriction on the free movement of capital and payments. See Dassesse, 'The TEU, Implications for the Free Movement of Capital', (1992) 6 *Journal of International Banking Law* 238. Note also J. A. Usher, *The Law of Money and Financial Services in the European Community*, (2nd edn, OUP, 2000), pp. 235–8. The writer suggests that a situation governed by another Treaty freedom does not fall within Article 58(1)(a).
92. Case C-391/97, [1999] ECR I-5451.

with Community law, namely that at least 90 per cent of the total income of the non-resident married couple must be subject to tax in Germany, or if that percentage is not reached, that their income from foreign salaries not subject to German tax must not be above a certain maximum. The Court took the view that where these conditions are not satisfied, the state of residence is in a position to take account of the taxpayer's personal and family circumstances, since the tax base there is sufficient for this to be done.

(4)   Vocational schools

The provisions of Article 7(3) of Regulation 1612/68 are fully considered in the part of this chapter which deals with students. Article 7(3) provides that the worker should, by virtue of the same rights and under the same conditions as national workers, have access to training in vocational schools and retraining centers. As shown below, this provision has been interpreted restrictively by the European Court of Justice in two important cases.

(5)   Discriminatory clauses in collective agreements

According to Article 7(4) EC, any clause of a collective or individual agreement or any other collective regulation concerning eligibility for employment, employment remuneration and other conditions of work or dismissal shall be null and void in so far as it lays down or authorizes discriminatory conditions in respect of employees who are nationals of other Member States.[93]

(6)   Trade union rights

According to Article 8 of Regulation 1612/68, "a worker who is a national of a Member State and who is employed in the territory of another Member State shall enjoy equality of treatment in regards members of trade unions and the exercise of rights attaching thereto; he may be excluded from taking part in the management of bodies governed by public law and from holding an office governed by public law." The bodies covered by Article 8 are not only trade union organisations; this text also covers participation in other entities which carry out similar functions.[94] The inclusion of the clause concerning bodies and offices governed by public law appears to have taken place on the insistence of France[95] which was motivated by the fact that in that country, important bodies such as the Economic and Social Council include trade union representatives.

---

93. See Case C-15/96, *Schöning-Kougebetpoulou v. Freie und Hansestadt Hamburg* [1998] ECR I-47; [1998] ECR I-47; [1998] All ER (EC) 97; [1998] 1 CMLR 931.
94. Case C-213/90, *ASTI (Association de Soutien aux Travailleurs Immigrés)* [1991] ECR I-3507.
95. Evans, *op. cit.*, p. 296.

It would seem that Article 8(1) is construed by the Court[96] and the Commission as conforming with the requirements of Article 39(4) EC.

(7) Housing

According the Article 9(1) of Regulation 1612/68, a worker who is a national of a Member State and who is employed in the territory of another Member State shall enjoy all the rights and benefits accorded to national workers in relation to housing, including ownership of the housing he needs. Restrictions on the rights of foreigners to acquire property were held to be contrary to Community law in *Commission v. Greece*.[97] The rights of migrant workers extend to both public and private housing.

3. Families (Title III)

(1) The families of workers

The definition of workers' families contained in Article 10(1) of Regulation 1612/68 has been explained above, as also has the fact that persons within it have the right to install themselves with the migrant worker. The provisions of Article 10(2) and 10(3), which respectively govern the admission of family members not coming within in Article 10(1), and the availability of housing for the families of migrant workers, have likewise been already considered. The same is true of the provisions of Article 11, concerning the rights of family members of migrant workers to take up employment in the host state. This right is also applicable to family members of self-employed person working in a Member State other than that of which he is a national.

Article 12 requires the equal treatment of the children of migrant workers residing in the territory of the host state as far as admission to the states' general educational, apprenticeship and vocational training courses is concerned. This article, which is considered more fully in the section of this chapter dealing with education, applies to university courses as well. The spouses of Community workers may also be entitled to such equal access.[98]

(2) Right to remain after employment

Regulation 1251/70 implements Article 39(4)(a) EC, and grants workers and members of their families, as defined in Article 10 of Regulation 1612/68, the right to remain in a state after the worker has been employed there. Different

---

96. See note 74, *ibid.*
97. Case 305/87, [1989] 1461: note also Case 63/86, *Commission v. Italy* [1988] ECR 29. In the latter case, the Commission's claim was admitted by Italy, and proceedings on this point ended after the amendment of the relevant Italian legislation.
98. Case 152/82, *Forcheri v. Belgium* [1983] ECR 2323.

rules are prescribed for the retirement of the worker, his incapacity and for frontier workers.

Article 2(1) provides that the following persons have the right to remain in the territory of a Member State:

(a) a worker when he has reached the age laid down by law for entitlement to an old age pension in that state and has been employed there for at least twelve months,[99] and has resided continuously there for more than three years:
(b) a worker who having resided continuously in that Member State for more than two years, has ceased to work there as an employed person by reason of a permanent incapacity to work. If the incapacity is the result of an accident at work or an occupational disease entitling him to a pension at work for which an institution of the state is wholly or partially responsible, no condition shall be imposed as to length of residence;
(c) a worker who after three years continuous employment and residence in the territory of that state, works as an employed person in the territory of another Member State, but retains his residence in the territory of another Member State, but retains his residence in the territory of the first state, to which he returns, as a rule, every day or at least once a week.

Periods of time spent working in the territory of another Member State shall be treated as completed in the territory of the state of residence for the purpose of satisfying the employment requirements contained in subparagraphs (1) and (6).[100]

The residence and employment conditions set out in subparagraphs (a) and (b) are inapplicable if the worker's spouse is a national of the relevant Member State or has lost the nationality of that state through marriage to the worker.[101]

According to Article 3 of Regulation 1251/70 members of the worker's family will be entitled to remain permanently in the following circumstances:

(a) if the worker is entitled to remain;
(b) if the worker dies during his working life, before acquiring the right to remain in the relevant state, but
  (i)   the worker resided there for at least two years before his death; or
  (ii) the death resulted from an accident at work or an occupational disease; or
  (iii) the surviving spouse is a national of the state of residence, or last their nationality through marriage to the worker.

Article 5(1) of the Regulation provides that persons entitled to remain must exercise their right within two years of its coming into existence. According to

---

99. According to Article 4(2) periods of involuntary employment recorded at the unemployment office, and absences due to sickness or accidents are treated as period of employment.
100. See Article 2(1).
101. See Article 2(2).

Article 5(2), no formality is required on the part of the person exercising the right to remain, but they are required by Article 6(1) to be issued with a residence permit valid throughout the territory for at least five years, which is automatically renewable. By Article 6(2), periods of non-residence not exceeding six months shall not affect the validity of the residence permit.

Persons exercising their right to remain in a Member State in accordance with Regulation 1251/70 will be entitled to equal treatment, in accordance with Article 7 of Regulation 1612/68. They are thus entitled to the same social and tax advantages as nationals of that state.

(3) Certain other rights of migrant workers

Article 141 EC requiring men and women to have equal pay for equal work, and the Community directives concerning equal pay and equal treatment are applicable to migrant workers. They are also entitled to protection under the European Convention of Human Rights (ECHR). Furthermore, the fundamental rights contained in the Convention and in national constitutions have been treated by the European Court of Justice as forming part of the Community legal order, and as giving rise to general principles of Community law which may prevail over Community secondary legislation and, in appropriate circumstances, national legislation. It is well recognized that general principles of Community law are binding on national authorities when they enforce Community policies and interpret Community law.[102] When such authorities act outside the sphere of Community law, they are not required to respect the general principles of such law. It is sometimes difficult to determine where the limits of Community law are placed for the present purpose.

The latter matter may be illustrated by the interesting case of *Konstantinidis v. Stadt Altensteig*.[103] This case concerned a self-employed Greek masseur working in Germany, who complained that his Community rights were infringed by an official mistranslation of his name, allegedly improperly rendered according to the Latin alphabet. The referring Greek court took the view that there might be an infringement of Konstandinidis's right to personal identity, and discrimination on the grounds of nationality in the context of employment. Advocate General Jacobs took the view that Article 8 of the European Convention of Human Rights, which is concerned with the protection of privacy and family

---

102. Thus, in Case 249/86, *Commission v. Germany* [1989] ECR 1263, which concerned the manner of implementation of Article 10 of Regulation 1612/68, permitting members of a migrant Community worker's family to install themselves with the worker in the host Member State, providing that the worker has available for the family housing considered as normal for national workers in that region. Germany made renewal of a family member's residence permit conditional upon the family living in appropriate housing throughout their time of residence in Germany. This interpretation was held incompatible with the requirements of the respect for family life set out in Article 8 of the ECHR.
103. Case C-168/91, [1993] ECR I-1191.

life, protected the applicant's right to object to improper interference with his name. The Advocate General took the progressive view[104] that a Community national who goes to another Member State as a worker or self-employed person is entitled to assume that, wherever he goes to earn his living in the European Community, he will be treated in accordance with a common code of fundamental values, in particular those laid down in the ECHR. He said that such a person could claim he was a European citizen and could invoke that status to oppose any violation of his fundamental rights. The Advocate General contended whenever a Community national exercises his rights of free movement and travels to another Member State, any infringement of one of his fundamental rights, irrespective of whether it is connected with his work, is a breach of Community law.

The Court refused to accept the Advocate General's viewpoint, and based itself instead upon familiar principles of EC law according to which self-employed people are entitled to exercise their right of establishment in another Member State without being discriminated against on grounds of nationality.

It is arguable that the protection of fundamental rights in the manner contended for by Jacobs AG should encourage labour mobility. However, the Court has not shown itself willing to depart from the conservative approach it took in *Konstandinidis*.[105] Nevertheless, as was pointed out earlier in the present chapter, the Commission made a proposal in July 1998 which would, inter alia, have placed a new provision Article 1a, in Regulation 1612/68, which would prohibit all discrimination on the grounds of sex, race, ethnic origin, religion or conviction, age, disability or sexual orientation when workers are exercising their right to free movement. A Directive has recently been enacted forbidding discrimination on the grounds of race or ethnic origin. The Community Charter of Human Rights, which has been considered at the Nice Intergovernmental Conference, has declaratory force only but could still have "inspirational" effect.

The Commission's proposed amendment to Regulation 1612/68 which is discussed above, bears the obvious influence of Article 13 of the Treaty of Amsterdam. This provision states:
"Without prejudice to the other provisions of the Treaty and within the limits of the powers conferred by it upon the Community, the Council, acting unanimously, on a proposal from the Commission, and after consulting the European Parliament, may take appropriate action to combat discrimination based upon

---

104. Note especially paragraph 83 of his Opinion.
105. Thus Gulmann AG in Case C-2/92, *R. v. MAFF ex parte Bostock* [1994] ECR I-955 expressed his disagreement with the approach taken by Jacobs AG. In Case C-291/96, *Criminal Proceedings Against Grado and Bashir* [1997] ECR I-5531, the Court failed to mention *Konstantinidis*, but held that the position of a national of a Member State in criminal proceedings in another Member State did not involve issues of Community law. It was thus not possible for the Court to determine whether the aliens right to dignity and equality had been respected.

sex or ethnic origin, religion or belief, disability, age or sexual orientation".[106] In recent years, the European Court of Justice has been prepared to condemn discrimination against a transsexual on the ground that discrimination on the basis of gender reassignment was essentially discrimination based on the sex of the person concerned.[107] The Court's judgment was probably influenced by the strong Opinion of Tesauro AG, who emphasised the importance of equality. However, the Court of Justice, unfortunately, showed itself unwilling to extend the same principle to discrimination against homosexuals in a later case.[108] That case was concerned as to whether the plaintiff was entitled to receive travel concessions in respect of her female partner, and it is possible, but by no means certain that the Court might have adopted a less cautious approach if the plaintiff had alleged that she had been refused or dismissed from employment because of her sexual orientation. The Court did say that Article 119 EC (now Article 14 EC) did not cover discrimination on the grounds of sexual orientation, but that Article 13 EC (introduced therein by the Amsterdam Treaty) would allow legislation to be introduced covering such discrimination.[109]

(4) Educational rights available to migrant workers their children and others

a. Introductory remarks

Until the EC Treaty was amended by the Treaty of Maastricht, there was nothing in it covering education. There was, however, a reference to vocational training in what used to be Article 128 EC (now Article 150 EC). This latter provision seems to go a little further than Article 128 EC did. It provides that the Community shall implement a vocational training programme which shall support and supplement the action of the Member States, whilst fully respecting their responsibility for the organization of vocational training. In addition, the Community is given a limited competence in the field of education by Article 149 EC. However, even before the new Treaty provisions were adopted, a considerable body of secondary legislation was adopted recognising that the Community was competent in relation to certain features of education. One may

---

106. A minor amendment to Article 13, by which the Council may adopt incentive measures excluding any harmonisation of the laws and regulations of the Member States, to support action taken by the Member State to contribute to the achievement of the aims referred to in Article 13 in accordance with the co-decision procedure set out in Article 251 EC.
107. Case C-13/94, *P. v. S. and Cornwall County Council* [1996] ECR I-2143.
108. Case C-249/96, *Grant v. South West Trains Ltd.* [1998] ECR I-621.
109. See Council Directive 2000/78/EC of 27 November 2000, establishing a general framework for equal treatment in employment and occupation, OJ 2000 L 303/16. The Directive is applicable to discrimination based on religion or belief, disability, age or sexual orientation in employment or occupation. According to Article 18 of the Directive, Member States are required to adopt the laws, regulations and administrative practices necessary for compliance by 2 December 2003, but they may be granted an additional period of three years in the case of age and disability discrimination.

instance, for example, the old Erasmus Programme on the mobility of students,[110] and the old Comett Programme on cooperation between universities and industry, and in training for technology.[111] Many earlier programmes have now been included in the Socrates[112] scheme, which seeks to carry on the Community's contribution to transnational education programmes. The same is true of the Leonardo da Vinci[113] programme which is an action programme in the field of educational training.

Perhaps, more significantly, educational rights have come to be recognized in Community law in three ways. The first time of these, applicable respectively to children and probably other family members of the workers, and to the workers themselves, are derived respectively from Articles 12, and Articles 7(2) and (3) of Regulation 1612/68. Finally students have been granted rights under provisions of law now contained in Articles 12 and 150 EC. It is felt convenient to deal with all the relevant categories of educational rights covered together; each of the relevant provisions has a slightly different ambit.

b. Children of migrant workers

The children of workers who migrate within the EC are, according to Article 12 of Regulation 1612/68, admitted to courses of general education, apprenticeship and vocational training under the same condition as nationals of that state if those children reside in its territory. Member States are required to encourage all efforts to enable such children to attend these courses under the best possible conditions. Council Directive 77/486/EC[114] on the education of children of migrant workers requires that free tuition should be available, including the teaching of the official language of the host state. Furthermore, it provides that the host state must promote the teaching of the children's mother tongue and culture.

The provisions of Article 12 have been interpreted generously by the European Court in the relation to the type of courses which it covers, and insofar as the requirement of admission to courses has been interpreted generously, so as to cover the payment of grants for maintenance and training. Thus, in *Casagrande*[115] it was held that the German authorities could be required to pay a monthly maintenance grant to the daughter of an Italian working in Germany.

---

110. See Decision 87/327 (OJ 1987 L166/20), as subsequently amended.
111. See Decision 89/27 (OJ 1989 L13/28). This has now been supplanted by the Comett II programme, on which see Joined Cases C-90 and 94/89, *United Kingdom et al v. Council* [1991] ECR I-2757.
112. See Decision 95/819 (OJ 1995 L87/10), as subsequently amended by Decision 98/576 (OJ 1998 L77/1). These decisions were based on Articles 126 and 127 EC (now Articles 149 and 150 EC).
113. See Decision 94/819 (OJ 1994 L340/8), based upon Article 122 EC (now Article 150 EC).
114. [1977] OJ L191/32.
115. Case 9/74, [1974] ECR 773.

As indicated above, the Court has held that the families of workers may be entitled to the same social advantages as national workers under Article 7(2) of Regulation 1612/68, so it would seem that those members of the family who are not covered by Article 12 may invoke Article 7(2) to claim certain educational benefits.

A similar right also applies to children of a Community migrant worker who wish to study in a country other than the host state. Thus in *Di Leo*[116] the daughter of an Italian migrant worker who had been employed in Germany for many years, and who had received her primary and secondary education in Germany, was refused an educational grant because she was pursuing a course in medicine in Italy. This refusal was held to be in violation of Article 12. If the young woman had been a German national, she would have been entitled to a grant to study abroad.

Furthermore, Article 12 has been held capable of being applicable to the situation of the children of a migrant worker who were living in the Netherlands, but whose father had returned to Germany, his state of nationality, *in Echternach and Moritz v. Netherlands Ministry of Education and Science.*[117] Although the parents had returned to Germany, the children wished to continue to pursue their college studies in the Netherlands because their Dutch qualifications would not have been recognized in Germany. They were held entitled to education and support on the same terms as Dutch nationals, in accordance with Article 12 of Regulation 1612/68.

An equally generous approach to the interpretation of Article 12 was taken by the European Court in *Gaal.*[118] In that case it was held that the orphaned child over the age of 21 of a deceased Belgian migrant worker who had been living in Germany and not dependent on his remaining parent was entitled to claim equal treatment with German nationals to finance his status in Scotland. The Court thus treated the term "children" in Article 12 as having a more extensive scope than in Article 10.

c. The position of workers

Article 7(3) of Regulation 1612/68 provides that workers shall have access to training in vocational schools and retraining courses under the same conditions as national workers. Grants and loans are capable of being treated as coming within the requirement of equality of access contained in Article 7(2). This proposition follows from the European Court's decisions in *Brown*[119] and *Lair*[120] However, the phrase "vocational school" in Article 7(3) was more restrictively

---

116. Case C-308/89, [1980] ECR I-4185.
117. Joined Cases 389 and 390/87, [1989] ECR 723.
118. Case C-7/94, *Landesamt für Ausbildungsförderung Nordrhein-Westfalen v. Gaal* [1995] ECR I-1031.
119. Case C-197/86, *Brown v. Secretary of State for Scotland* [1988] ECR 3205.
120. Case 39/86, *Lair v. University of Hannover* [1988] ECR 3161.

interpreted in these cases than was the phrase "vocational training" in Article 128 EC (now Article 150 EC) in such cases as *Gravier*[121]and *Blaizot*[122] where this phrase received a more liberal interpretation. In these two cases, in which a claim for a maintenance was made based upon Article 7(2) and (3), the Court held that the phrase "vocational school" should be applied only to institutions which provide sandwich or apprenticeship courses. Despite this narrow interpretation, the Court held that such a grant might constitute a social advantage under Article 7(2).

However, Member States have often shown themselves concerned by the fact that they may suffer increasing financial burdens because of the claims of migrating students. It was also feared that too liberal an approach by the Court to educational rights might encourage Community nationals to migrate to another Member State, work briefly for a period of time, and then claim to be entitled by Community law to a maintenance grant. These fears have to some extent been allayed by the decisions of the Court in *Brown* and *Lair*.[123]

The first of these cases, *Brown*, concerned a student having dual British and French nationality who had lived with his parents in France for several years before coming to the United Kingdom to take up a place at Cambridge to read engineering. He was sponsored by Ferrantis, and was employed by the company for eight months before he started his course. The Court refused to recognize him as being enabled to a grant because his status as a worker had been acquired solely as the result of his acceptance for admission by Cambridge University. The decision in Brown gives rise to the conclusion that different categories of workers may have somewhat different rights.

In *Lair*, the Court decided in favour of the intending student, a French woman who had moved to Germany, where she had been employed under a number of part time contracts. She decided to pursue a course of study at Hannover University, and was held entitled to a grant as a social advantage under Article 7(2). The Court emphasised that such an entitlement would only arise if a worker voluntarily gave up work if there was some connection between the course which he intended to pursue and his previous work. Such a connection would not, however, be required where the employee was involuntarily employed, and be forced to retrain. The limitations which the Court placed on Article 7(2) and (3) were obviously intended to assuage the concerns of Member States. It also held in Lair that abuses of the student assistance system were not within the ambit of Article 7(2) and (3). It envisaged the possibility of such abuses where a worker entered a Member State for the sole purpose of benefiting from this system after a short period of paid activity.

In *Raulin*[124] the Court had to consider a claim by a French part-time waitress

---

121. Case 293/83, *Gravier v. City of Liège* [1985] ECR 593.
122. Case 24/86, *Blaizot v. City of Liège* [1988] ECR 379.
123. Note in this sense, Weatherill and Beaumont, *op. cit.*, pp. 708–9.
124. Case C-357/89, *Raulin v. Minister von Onderwijs en Wetenschappen* [1992] ECR I-1027.

working on an "on call" contract in the Netherlands for 60 hours, to be given a grant to pursue a course in the plastic arts in that country. The Court held that it was necessary to determine whether the work undertaken was genuine and effective for the purpose of obtaining the status of a worker, and that when addressing itself to this question, the referring national court should take account of the irregular nature and limited duration of the services actually performed under a contract for occasional employment. The very limited number of hours worked might constitute an indication that the activities exercised were purely marginal and ancillary. However, the national court might take account, if appropriate, of the on-call nature of the contract. In *Bernini*,[125]an Italian national paid at a low wage for ten weeks as part of her occupational training was held to be not precluded from being regarded as a worker.

Students tend to be financed by loans rather than grants at the present time, but this fact is unlikely to cause any change in the approach taken by the Court in the cases similar to those mentioned above. However, it has been suggested that the Court might change its approach to such cases as *Brown* and *Lair* because of the willingness shown by it in *Maria Martinez Sala*[126] to find that a national of one Member State lawfully resident in another fell within the scope of the Treaty provisions on Union Citizenship, and enjoyed the protection from discrimination on the grounds of nationality within the material scope of application of the Treaty. Unless they qualify for residence on some other grounds i.e. as persons engaged in economic activities (or who have been so engaged), or as members of the family of a migrant worker, students will have to comply with the requirements of Directive 93/96 on the right of residence of students, which are described below. It is thought doubtful for policy reasons whether the Court will extend the ruling in *Maria Martinez Sala* (which seems of somewhat questionable authority) in the manner indicated. However, it seems questionable whether Member States will display the same generosity in granting residence to nationals of other Member States as the German government did in *Maria Martinez Sala*.[127]

d. Vocational training policy

Persons may claim educational rights under Article 12 and 150 of the EC Treaty although they are not workers or the children (or other members of the family) of workers. In *Forcheri v. Belgium*[128] the Court held that the Italian wife of a Community official of the same nationality working in Brussels was entitled by reason of these two provisions to be enrolled on a social work training course without paying a minerval (enrolment fee) required from students who were not

---

125. Case C-3/90, *Bernini v. Minister van Onderwijs en Wetenschappen* [1992] ECR I-1071.
126. Case C-85/96, [1998] ECR I-2891.
127. Note in this sense Weatherill and Beaumont, *op. cit.*, p. 709.
128. Casse 152/82, *Forcheri v. Belgium* [1983] ECR 2323.

Belgian nationals. A similar approach was taken by the Court in *Gravier*[129] which concerned a French student in Belgium who (in contrast to Forcheri) had no relations there, and who also challenged the requirement to pay the minerval. The imposition of the minerval only on non-national students as a condition of access to vocational training was held to violate Articles 7 and 128 EC, the precursors of Articles 12 and 150 EC. The Court's judgment in these cases can be criticised insofar as it rested upon a somewhat dubious interpretation of Article 128 EC, which provided for a common vocational training policy, but which was not worded in such a clear and unconditional way as to produce direct effects.[130] The Court was prepared to give a broad interpretation to the concept of vocational training in its judgment in *Gravier*, finding that this consisted of any form of education which prepared a person for a profession, trade or employment. In its subsequent decision in *Blaizot*,[131] the Court held that university education could constitute vocational training, unless the course was one designed for individuals to improve their general knowledge, rather than to prepare them for a particular occupation. In *Belgium v. Humbel*,[132] the Court found that a course of general secondary education forming part of a course which, as a whole, appeared to be vocational must itself be treated as vocational if it formed a constituent part of a programme of vocational education.

However, the Court adopted a more cautious approach to the interpretation of the phrase "conditions of access" to vocational education in *Brown* and *Lair*. For fairly obvious policy reasons the Court held that such conditions of access did not involve the provision of maintenance grants. As already indicated, the position is different under Article 7(2) of Regulation 1612/68, which applies to workers.

e. Legislation concerning students

According to the decision of the Court in *Raulin*[133] the principle of non-discrimination based upon former Articles 7 and 128 EC requires that an EC national who had been admitted to a course of training in another Member State should be entitled to reside in that host state for the duration of his course. The question of residence for students who are, not entitled to the right of residence by reason of the fact that they are, or have been engaged in economic activities, or not so entitled because they are the children of workers, is covered by Council Directive 93/96.[134] This Directive also grants the right of residence to a student's spouse and his dependent children, provided that the student assures the relevant

---

129. Case 293/83, *Gravier v. City of Liège* [1985] ECR 593.
130. See Steiner and Woods, *op. cit.*, p. 351. One may entertain similar doubts about the present Article 150 EC, which takes account of the principle of subsidiarity.
131. Case 24/86, *Blaizot v. University of Liège* [1988] ECR 379.
132. Case 263/86, [1988] ECR 5365.
133. Case C-357/89, [1992] ECR I-1027.
134. OJ 1993 L317/59.

national authority by declaration or such alternative means that the student may choose which are at least equivalent, that he has adequate means to avoid becoming a burden on the social assistance system of the host state during their period of residence, and also provided that the student is enrolled in a vocational training course in a recognised institution, and that he is covered by sickness insurance for all rules in the host state.[135]

The right to residence is evidenced by a residence permit, which may be limited to the duration of the course of studies, or to one year, when the course lasts longer. In the latter event, it is renewable annually.[136] The spouse and the dependent children of a national of a Member State entitled to a residence permit within the host state may take up any employed or self-employed activity in that state, even if they are not nationals thereof.[137] Nevertheless, the Directive does not establish any right to the payment of maintenance grants by the host state on behalf of students benefiting from the right of residence.[138]

A Green Paper on transnational mobility was adopted by the Commission on 2 October 1994,[139] which examined the position of persons wishing to move for the purpose of education training and research, and found it to be fairly weak, particularly in view of the fact that students are not covered by the system of protection given to migrant workers under the Social Security Regulation,[140] and also because there is at Community level no system of academic recognition (for students wishing to study in another Member State) of qualifications obtained or study periods spent in a Member State. The Green Paper included a number of recommendations, including the abolition of the principle of territoriality of grants.

Nothing has yet been done to implement any of the recommendations contained in the Green Paper, although the Commission's Green Paper was briefly considered in the Report of the High Level Panel.[141] It has been suggested by Lenaerts[142] that the Community now has power to pass legislation concerning maintenance grants and financing for EC nationals, but it would seem unlikely to do so in the immediate future.

---

135. Council Directive 93/96, Article 1.
136. Article 2(1), *ibid.*
137. Article 2(2), *ibid.*
138. Article 3, *ibid.*
139. COM (95) 462.
140. Regulation 1408/71, OJ 1971 L149/2.
141. Pages 67–68, *ibid.*
142. K. Lenaerts, 'Education in European Community Law after Maastricht', (1994) 31 CML Rev. pp. 15–16.

IV. POSTED WORKERS

1. Introductory remarks

The situation of posted workers has been addressed by the Court of Justice in a number of cases.[143] "Posted workers" are workers employed by an undertaking established in one Member State who are temporarily sent to another Member State to perform services there and who return to their country of origin after the completion of their work. The rather extensive formulation of the host states powers' in *Rush Portuguesa* finds some reflection in the provisions of Article 3 of the Posted Workers Directive.[144] According to paragraph 18 of its judgment in the former case, the Court held that Community law did not prevent Member States from extending their legislation or collective labour agreements to any person who is employed, even temporarily, within their territory, no matter in what country the employer is established. The Court has, however adopted a rather more cautious attitude in later cases.[145]

It is controversial whether Article 39 EC or Regulation 1612/68 apply to posted workers. The general view appears to be that the free movement of workers provisions do not apply to a person who moves to another Member State, not to take up or seek employment, but in pursuit of employment with an undertaking in his own state to which that person will return after completion of the task.[146] Even though the former provisions may not be applicable, it is thought convenient to deal with posted workers in the present chapter.

Certain categories of such workers came within the provisions of Council Directive 96/71/EC concerning the posting of workers in the framework of the provision of services.[147] The Directive was somewhat controversially based upon Articles 57(2) and 66 EC (now Articles 47(2) and 55 EC). The former provision governs the issue of Community directives coordinating the provisions of the

---

143. Note in particular Case C-113/89, *Rush Portuguesa v. Office Nationale d'Immigration* [1990] ECR I-1417 and Case C-43/93, *Vander Elst v. Office des Migrations Internationales* [1994] ECR I-3803. It has been controversially contended that these cases must be interpreted as meaning that Member States no longer enjoy any discretion with regard to the admission of third-country national employees making use of their freedom to provide services, and are bound to issue them with entry visas of the necessary time period. See S. Peers, 'Indirect Rights for Third Country Service Providers Confirmed', (1995) 20 EL Rev. 303, 307.
144. Council Directive 96/71, OJ 1997 L18/1.
145. Note, for example, Case C-272/94, *Criminal Proceedings against Michel Guiot and Climatec SA* [1996] ECR I-1905 at 1920.
146. Note in this sense Case C-43/93, *Vander Elst* [1994] ECR I-3803, at para. 21. See however the different view taken by Van Gerven AG at para. 14 of his Opinion in *Rush Portuguesa*. See also the Court's judgment in Case C-292/89, *R. v. Immigration Appeal Tribunal ex parte Antonissen* [1991] ECR I-745.
147. Note the very helpful article by Paul Davies, 'Posted Workers, Single Market in Protection of National Labour Law Systems', (1997) 31 CML Rev. p. 877.

Member States concerning the taking up and pursuit of activities as self-employed persons, while the latter provision (which takes effect by cross-referencing to the provisions on establishment) grants the Community power to enact harmonising provisions removing restrictions on the cross border provision of services.

The Directive endeavours to ensure that the host-state applies to the employment relationship with the posted worker (who may be a community or a third country national) certain basic standards of labour law, and it may also apply certain other basic standards.[148] Article 2(1) of the Directive defines a posted worker as one who, for a period of time carries on work in the territory of a state other than that in which he is established. It specifies three categories of such arrangements. There is some reason for doubt about the compatibility of certain of the provisions of the Posted Workers Directive with Articles 49 and 50 EC. The Directive would seem likely to be beneficial to posted workers, but it may not contain adequate machinery for ensuring that promises made to such workers are carried out.

According to paragraph 20 of the Preamble to the Posted Workers Directive, this instrument does not affect the laws of Member States concerning the access to their territory of third country providers of services, or national laws relating to the entry, residence or access to employment of third country workers. Two proposed directives exist on the provision of services by non-Community staff lawfully established in the EU (as in *Vander Elst*), and on the rights of such persons when self-employed.[149] The provisions of these directives are considered briefly at the end of the section on posted worker. They both purport to deal with the entry and sojourn of certain categories of third-country nationals.

2. Provisions of the Directive

According to Article 1(1) of the Directive, it only applies to posting, within the framework or the transnational provision of services. Thus, it is only applicable if there is an employment relationship between the posted worker and an undertaking established in the home state. There must be a provision of services to an undertaking in the host state, in accordance with an arrangement between the home state and host state undertakings. The former state must be in the Community.

Article 1(3) of the Directive sets out three types of arrangement. These take place: (a) where the host state and the home state undertaking have entered into a contract for the provision of the services in question; (b) where there is an administrative arrangement within a company or group of companies; (c) where a temporary employment undertaking or placement agency established in the

---

148. Posted Workers Directive, Article 3.
149. COM (1999) 3 final. For a useful brief account of these proposed directives, see Hailbronner, *Immigration and Asylum Law and Policy of the EU*, 'Kluwer International, 2000', pp. 206–210.

home state supplies labour to an undertaking established in the host state, In the latter case, there must be an employment relationship between the agency and the worker, if there is no such relationship, the situation is not covered by the Directive. According to Article 2(2) of the latter instrument, the law of the host state determines who is a worker.

The detailed and complex provisions of Article 3 set out standards which Member States must or may apply to posted workers. The basic standards which Member States are required to ensure apply to posted workers are set out in Article 3(1). This reference to basic standards is clearly to the basic standards of the host state's system of labour regulation. Jurisdiction to enforce claims by posted workers based upon the host state's legal provisions through the medium of the contracts of employment of individual posted workers, will sometimes fall upon the courts of the home state. This is because, as Davies explains,[150] Article 3(1) of the Brussels Convention of 1968 (as amended)[151] confers jurisdiction over contracts of employment primarily on the courts of the place where the employee habitually carries on his work. This will quite frequently be the home state. It should be clear that in such an event, the home state's courts will have to consider the basic standards of the host state's system of labour regulation.[152]

The basic standards which a Member State must ensure are applicable involve several items. These are working hours, holidays, minimum pay, the regulation of the conditions of supply of workers by agencies, health and safety, the protective rules for pregnant workers, working young mothers and children and young persons, and equal treatment of men and women and other provisions on non-discrimination. The relevant standards which a Member State must ensure are applicable may be contained in their laws, regulations or administrative provisions. In addition, they may be included in certain types of collective agreements or arbitration awards. However, Member States are only required by Article 3(1) to apply collectively agreed standards to posted workers in the building industry. Nevertheless, Article 3(10) of the Directive permits Member States to apply such standards to posted workers in other industries. This facility is subject to equality of treatment of national undertakings and undertakings posting workers, and to that of compliance with the Treaty. Furthermore, Article 3(1) permits (subject to the foregoing two requirements) the host state to apply to posted workers provisions of its laws, regulations and administrative provisions concerning matters additional to those set out in Article 3(1), with the proviso that such supplementary rules fall within the category of public policy provisions.

Article 3 of the Directive contains one detailed and narrowly drawn compulsory exemption and certain optional exceptions to certain of the provisions

---

150. *Op. cit.*, p. 378.
151. OJ 1978 L304/36.
152. It follows from Article 20 of the Rome Convention on the Law Applicable to Contractual Obligations, OJ 1980 L266/1 that Member States cannot evade the provisions of Directive

thereof. The compulsory exemption in Article 3(2) is inapplicable to the building industry. Such compulsory exemptions were mooted in the Commission's earlier drafts, but did not appear in the final text of the Directive.[153] The existing compulsory exemption applies where the cross-border provision of installation or assembly services is an integral part of a contract for the supply of goods; where the effective provision of the services depends on the deployment of skilled or specialist workers employed by the supplier of the goods; and where the period of posting does not exceed eight days. This exemption only applies to national rules relating to minimum pay and paid annual holidays.

The optional exemptions contained in Article 3(3)–(5) may not be used in relation to posted workers supplied by an agency. Article 3(3) allows Member States after having consulted the social partners, not to apply the rules governing minimum pay in respect of postings for less than one months' duration. Such a decision may, according to Article 3(4), be taken instead by collective agreement for particular sectors of activity. Furthermore, host states may allow collective agreements to withdraw, as far as a particular field of activity is concerned, a general exemption granted by the host state. Finally, Article 3(5) provides that host states may exempt, without consultation, posted workers from the minimum pay and paid holiday provisions, where the amount of work to be done by them is not significant. Article 4 of the Directive provides for an organised system for cooperation and exchanges of information between Member States.

3. Possible incompatibility of certain provisions of the Directive with EC Law

Although the above question is now largely of academic significance only, it remains one of considerable interest. It is now too late to bring an action for the annulment of provisions of the Directive, as the short time limit of two months from the publication of the Directive imposed by Article 230 EC for such annulment has now expired. It might however, still be possible to challenge particular measures taken by states under Article 3(1) thereof, which enables Member States to extend the Article 3(1) list of basic protections. As is pointed out by Davies, it can be cogently argued that Article 3(1) of Directive 96/71 and/or measures taken under Article 3(1) thereof by Member States may infringe Articles 49 and 50 EC, as these provisions have been interpreted in a number of decisions concerning the cross-frontier provision of services[154] which have

---

96/71 by invoking the provisions of Article 7(2) of that Convention. See Hailbronner *op. cit.*, pp. 210–211.

153. See Davies, *op. cit.*, pp. 583–4.

154. The need to comply with two different systems of law may well hinder or render less attractive the cross border provision of services: note for example Cases C-76/90, *Säger v. Dennemeyer & Co. Ltd.* [1991] ECR I-4221 at 4243, para. 12 and Case C-384/93, *Alpine Investments v. Minister van Financiën* [1995] ECR I-1141 at 1177–1178 (paras 35–38), which requires the abolition of non-discriminatory restrictions having the latter effect unless they are justified by imperative requirements in the public interest are suitable for

also been paralleled by corresponding decisions in the field of establishment.[155]

The compatibility of certain Belgian legislation governing posted workers with Articles 59 and 60 EC (now Articles 49 and 50 EC) was considered by the Court of Justice in *Arblad and Leloup*;[156] however the relevant events took place before the Posted Workers Directive came into force in 1999. The decision is considered briefly in the next chapter.

4. Recent Commission proposals

The Commission proposed that two EC Directives should be enacted in the field of the cross-border provision of services in February 1999.[157] The first of these proposals is for a Directive of the European Parliament and the Council on the posting of workers who are third-country nationals for the provision of cross-border services, whilst the second is a proposal for a Council Directive extending the freedom to provide cross-border services to third country nationals established within the Community.[158] Both these proposals are designed to eliminate the problems which have been encountered in the past by nationals of a non-member country who are legally present and allowed to take up employment or be self-employed in a Member State and who wish to move for the purpose of providing services in another Member State. Such provisions of services is now often impeded in practice by difficulties in obtaining visas, residence permits and work permits. The proposed introduction of the EC service provision card, which is common to both proposed Directives is intended to obviate such difficulties.

5. The 1999 proposal on the posting of third country national workers

The proposal for a Directive on the posting of workers who are third country nationals for the provision of cross-border services recommends the introduction of a new instrument, the EC service provision card, which, under Article 2(1) of the proposal, shall be issued by the Member State where the provider of the services is established if:

---

securing the objective which they pursue, and do not go beyond what is necessary to attain it.

155. See C-19/92, *Kraus v. Land Baden-Württemberg* [1993] ECR I-1663, para 32; Case C-55/94, *Gebhard v. Consiglio dell' Ordine degli Avvocati e Procuratori di Milano* [1995] ECR I-4165, para 37 and Case C-212/97, *Centros* [1999] 2 CMLR 551 at para 34.

156. Joined Cases C-369/96 and 376/96, [1999] ECR I-8453. Note also Case C-493/99, *Commission v. Germany*, n.y.r., in which the compatibility of certain German legislation on the hiring out of workers in the construction industry with Articles 43 and 49 EC is in question. Advocate General Ruiz-Jarabo Colomber took the view that this legislation is incompatible with the former provisions, in his opinion of 5 April 2001.

157. Commission Proposal of 12 February 1999, OJ 1999 C 76/12, COM(99) 3 final.

158. Commission Proposal of 12 February 1999, OJ 1999 C 67/17, COM(99) 3 final.

(a) the worker resides in that Member State in accordance with its legislation;
(b) he is affiliated to the social security scheme in the Member State responsible for sickness or industrial accident or is otherwise insured against the risk of sickness or industrial accident during his posting to one or more other Member States.

By virtue of Article 2(2) and 2(3) of the proposal, the EC service provision card may be issued for half a year or a year, depending on the period of employment before it is issued. It is renewable, if the conditions as to its issue are fulfilled once again.

Article 2(5) of the proposal provides that the Member State issuing the EC service provision card may not regard posting for the provision of services in another Member State as being an interruption of the posted worker's period of residence or paid activity. Thus, a secondment would not allow the Member State to refuse renewal of a residence or work permit, but must be regarded as equivalent to an authorized stay, and to work carried out in the relevant Member State.

Article 2(4) stipulates that the service provision card is issued to the service provider, which he or she places at the disposal of the posted employed worker described therein. According to Article 3(1) of the proposed Directive any Member State in which services are provided shall permit the entry and residence of a worker who is a third country national on its territory for the purpose of one or more provisions of services, if such person is in possession of the EC service provision card, and of an identity card or passport valid for the period during which the services are to be provided. Furthermore, Article 3(2) provides that Member States in which a service is provided may not require from the posted worker or the service provider in his capacity as employer: (a) an entry or exit visa; (b) a residence permit, other than one specified in paragraph 3; or (c) a work permit or permit for access to a job; or (d) impose any obligation equivalent to those in points (a), (b) and (c). Article 3(3) of the proposal stipulates that any Member State in which a service is provided may require the service provider to declare, before the worker enters the territory, the intended presence of that posted worker, the period of presence provided for, and the service provision or provisions for which he is to be posted. It also provides that Member States must grant residence permits to posted third-country national workers, if the total period required for the service provision or provisions in question exceeds six months out of a period of twelve months. Article 3(3) does not appear to make the grant of a residence permit contingent on the making of a declaration by the service provider.

According to Article 4(2) of the proposed Directive, Member States may not derogate from it except on grounds of public order, public security or public health, in which case Directive 64/221 shall apply *mutatis mutandis*. This provision appears to impose a limitation upon the competence of the immigration authorities of the host state in relation to a posted worker similar to that which is applicable to those categories of persons who benefit from freedom of movement. It may be that this protection is excessive, although as Hailbronner points out, it must be remembered that the provision only applies *mutatis mutandis* (other things being equal).[159] The provisions of the second sentence on Article 2(5) arguably impose restrictions on the issuing Member State which are capable of being burdensome. This sentence provides that the issuing Member State may not refuse, under national regulations, the readmission to its territory of the posted worker for any reason whatsoever. It makes no exception for public policy reasons for such a refusal.

It has been contended by Hailbronner[160] that insofar as the proposal governs the entry and sojourn of third country national posted workers, it cannot be properly based upon Articles 57(2) and 66 EC (now Article 47(2) and 55 EC) which the Commission submitted as its legal basis. It will be noted that the Posted Workers Directive, which had a similar basis, did not purport to affect national laws governing entry and residence. There seems to be considerable force in Hailbronner's argument that the proposed Directive should have a basis in Title IV EC insofar as it is intended to deal with the entry and residence of third country national workers. The existence of such a basis would require a unanimous vote in the Council, and would much diminish the role of the European Parliament.

It follows from Article 3(4) of the proposal that the Commission endeavours to secure equality of treatment with regard to particular social rights not covered by Directive 96/71/EC. Article 3(4) provides that:

> In order to facilitate the provision of services, any Member State in which a service is carried on shall ensure equality of treatment between third-country nationals and citizens of the Union posted as workers for the provision of services as regards the recognition of diplomas, certificates and other qualifications acquired within the Community with a view to performing the activity concerned, and issued by a competent authority of the Member State.

V. THE PROVISION OF SERVICES BY THIRD-COUNTRY NATIONALS ESTABLISHED WITHIN THE COMMUNITY

The proposal is based upon Article 59(2) EC (now Article 49(2) EC), which authorises the Council, acting by a qualified majority on a proposal from the Commission, to extend the provisions of the chapter on services in the EC Treaty (chapter 3) to nationals of a third country who provide services and are established within the Community. Such extension to third-country nationals would seem not only to involve the provisions of chapter 3, but the principles enshrined in all relevant secondary legislation applicable to nationals of Member States as providers of services, including the provisions of Council Directive 73/148/EEC

---

159. See, *Immigration and Asylum Law and Policy of the EU*, p. 208.
160. *Ibid.*, p. 209.

on the abolition of restrictions on movement and residence within the Community for nationals of Member States with regard to the provision of services. Thus it appears that the present proposal, unlike that considered immediately above, does not give rise to doubts concerning the infringement of the rights of Member States to control entry and residence, provided that the third country nationals act within the field of application of the freedom to provide services.[161]

The Commission's proposal suggests the extension of the freedom to provide services to third country nationals who are natural persons (and not also employees) established in a Member State for at least twelve months. However, the proposed Directive would not cover nationals of a third country who are recipients of cross-border services or a provider of such services in the transport section.[162] Third country national providers of services must be issued with an EC service provision card, which shall be valid for twelve months.[163] The service provision card will belong to the service provider, and contain details of him or her, together with the period for which it is valid, and particulars of the issuing authority and the issuing Member State. The provisions of Articles 2(4) second sentence, 3(1)–(3) and (4) of the proposed Directive extending the freedom to provide cross-border services to third country nationals established within the Community, which are concerned with the admission of such persons to the territory of the host state and their readmission to that of the home state, correspond exactly to those of Articles 2(5), second sentence, 3(1)–(3) and (4) of the proposed Directive on the posting of workers who are third country nationals for the provision of cross-border services.

---

161. *Ibid.* The writer also correctly says that third country providers of services established in a Member State may post third nationals under the same conditions as any EU citizens making use of the freedom to provide services.
162. See Article 1 of the Draft Directive.
163. Draft Directive, Articles 2(1) and 2(2).

4 Freedom of Establishment

I. INTRODUCTORY REMARKS: RELATIONSHIP BETWEEN FREEDOMS

Certain preliminary matters which relate equally to establishment and services, and which may sometimes have a wider ambit, are considered together in the earlier parts of this chapter for the sake of convenience. The later parts are primarily concerned with the right of establishment.

There are similarities between the three chapters of the EC Treaty dealing with the free movement of workers, freedom of establishment and freedom to provide services which have been recognised in many of the decided cases. Thus, for example, Article 43(2) EC permits freedom of establishment under the conditions laid down for its own nationals by the law of the country where such establishment is effected. Article 50(3) EC contains a similar provision. Both these two provisions appear capable of having a restrictive effect. One can find a number of other parallels between the rules on establishment and services. Thus, for example, both sets of rules are not only applicable to natural persons, but also to companies and other legal persons. In *Royer*[1] the Court held that all the three above-mentioned chapters were based on the same principles insofar as they concern the entry into and residence in the Member States of persons covered by Community law, and the prohibition of all discrimination against them. The prohibition of discrimination on the grounds of nationality, which is applicable both to freedom of establishment and to the cross-border provision of services is binding on all competent authorities as well as on legally recognised professional bodies.[2]

Non-discriminatory restrictions on the free movement of workers, freedom of establishment and freedom to provide services have also been held to infringe the directly applicable provisions of Articles 39, 43 and 49 EC in a number of recent cases. The Court first took this approach to non-discriminatory rules in the jurisprudence on the provision of services across frontiers. Non-discriminatory rules may have a market partitioning effect and require objective justification.[3] In some decisions, the Court has held that non-discriminatory professional

---

1. Case 48/75, [1976] ECR 497: see paragraph 12 of the judgment.
2. In Case 197/84, *Steinhauser v. Ville de Biarritz* [1985] ECR 1819, (Article 52 EC, now Article 43 EC, was held binding on a municipal council. In Case 36/74, *Walrave and Koch v. Association Union Cycliste Internationale and others* [1974] ECR 1405, Article 59 EC, now Article 49 EC, was held binding on a cyclists' association which was neither a state nor a public body.
3. This requirement was mentioned in Case 33/74, *Van Binsbergen v. Bestuur van de Bedrijfsvereniging voor de Metaalnijverheid* [1974] ECR 1299. However, the restriction in that case can be regarded as indirectly discriminatory. In Case C-76/90, *Säger v.*

rules always involve a restriction on free movement; which can only be justified if they satisfy the requirements set out in an identically framed "rule of reason". This "global" approach which, as pointed out in Chapter 1 was taken in the Court's recent decision in *Centros*,[4] a case concerning a Danish restriction on the establishment of a company, has been criticised by certain authors, including Daniele,[5] who thinks it might give rise to considerable difficulties. Whether or not this is the case, it is probable that such an approach will continue to be used by the Court. As is apparent from *Centros*, it has been extended beyond the area of professional activities.

Although the distinction may not always be of much significance, it will often prove difficult in practice to determine whether a particular activity involves the exercise of the right of establishment or the provisions of services across frontiers. The differentiation between these two activities was fully discussed by the Court of Justice in *Gebhard*,[6] which was mentioned in Chapter 2.

It appears to follow from this case that the essential feature of establishment is the carrying on of an economic or professional activity from a stable and continuous base in the host state. It will be remembered that the Court also held in *Gebhard* that the provider of services might to the extent necessary for the provision of these services, set up some form of infrastructure in the host state. As is pointed out by Hatzopoulous, this rule somewhat modifies that put forward in the *German Insurance*[7] case, in which it was held that any permanent presence in the host state automatically means that the rules on services are replaced by those on establishment. They would be so replaced, however, if a person or company established in a Member State provided services there for an indefinite period.[8]

In certain cases on services, the Court has extended the application of the relevant rules by treating the concept of services in an objective manner.[9] Thus, certain decisions such as *Kohll* have focused on the movement of the services and any hindrances thereto, rather than the particular situation of the parties. This approach is similar to that which is taken to the Treaty rules on goods, and places emphasis on the needs of a single market.[10]

Dennemeyer [1991] ECR I-4221, the Court adopted an approach to indistinctly applicable restrictions on the provision of services, which was similar to that which it had taken in relation to goods in the leading Case 8/74, *Procureur du Roi v. Dassonville* [1974] ECR 837.

4. Case C-212/97, *Centros Ltd v. Erhvervs og Selskabsstyrelsen* [1999] ECR I-1459.

5. See his article, 'Non-Discriminatory Restrictions on the Free Movement of Persons', [1997] 2 ELRev. 191.

6. See Case C-55/94, *Gebhard v. Consiglio dell' Ordine degli Avvocati e Procuratori di Milano* [1995] ECR I-4165. In this case, the Court also emphasised that the Treaty provisions on goods, services, workers and establishment should be similarly interpreted.

7. Case 205/84, *Commission v. Germany* [1986] ECR 3755.

8. Case C-70/95, *Sodemare v. Regione Lombardia* [1997] ECR I-3395 para 24.

9. Hatzopoulos, 'Recent Developments of the Case Law of the ECJ in the Field of Services', (2000) 37 CMLRev., p. 59; note for example Case C-158/96, *Kohll* [1998] ECR I-1931.

10. An analogy between the movement of goods and the cross-frontier supply of services where neither party moves was made by the Court of Justice in Opinion 1/94, in which

Whatever the (sometimes minuscule) difference between the provision of services and the exercise of the right of establishment, it is clear that the fundamental principle underlying the chapters on services and establishment has been thought of as the elimination of discrimination. Thus, many years ago the 1961 General Programme made it clear that directly and indirectly discriminatory restrictions on establishment were to be eliminated, and provided an indicative list of restrictions. It is apparent from such cases as *Bosman*,[11] *Terhoeve*,[12] and *Gebhard*,[13] that the emphasis on the need for discrimination has been modified both in relation to the free movement of workers, and in relation to freedom of establishment. It may indeed be the case that despite the criticisms of such authors as Daniele, the Court will move towards a single justificatory principle in respect of impediments to the exercise of all the four basic freedoms, i.e. freedom of movement of goods, persons, services and capital.[14]

Many would argue, however, that it still remains the case that it is easier to justify non-discriminatory national controls on establishment than it is to justify such controls on providers of services. This is the case because a person who establishes himself or who works in another Member State can be regarded as submitting himself to the legal order of that state to a greater extent than one who has a more transitory presence there, such as a service provider who may never, or only occasionally visit that state.[15]

Restrictions on freedom to provide services which discriminate directly on the basis of nationality can be justified under Article 55 EC, on grounds of public policy, security or health, which are fully considered in Chapter 7.[16] Other restrictions may be justified on a number of other public interest grounds, for example consumer protection or the protection of the recipient of the services.[17] It would appear that the principle stated in *Bond van Adverteerders* is applicable

---

it held certain aspects of GATS were within the Common Commercial Policy: see *Re Uruguay Round Treaties* [1994] ECR I-5267.

11. Case C-415/93, *Union Royale Belge des Sociétés de Football Association and others v. Bosman and others* [1991] ECR I-4921.

12. Case C-18/95, *Terhoeve* [1999] ECR I-345. In this case, the Netherlands rules on income tax and social security were considered under Article 39 EC. The Court found that rules which preclude or deter a national of a Member States from leaving his country of origin in order to exercise his freedom of movement constitutes an obstacle to that freedom; even if they are applied without regard to the nationality of the worker concerned.

13. *Ibid.* note 6.

14. See Case C-120/95, *Decker* [1998] ECR I-1831 at paragraph 44 of the judgment, and Joined Cases C-34 to C-36/95, *De Agostini and TV Shop* [1997] ECR I-3843 at paragraph 39 of the judgment. See also Hatzopoulos, *op. cit.*, pp. 71–2.

15. This consideration seems to have been implicit in the decision of the Court of Justice in Case 205/84, *Commission v. Germany* [1986] ECR 3755.

16. Case 352/85, *Bond van Adverteerders v. Netherlands* [1988] ECR 2085.

17. See the cases on freedom to provide services mentioned in Kapteyn and Verloren van Themaat, *Introduction to the Law of the EC*, (3rd edn, Gormley (ed.) 1998), pp. 758–760. Article 86(2) EC provides a further justification for restrictions on the provision of services.

as well to directly discriminatory restrictions on freedom of establishment. Non-discriminatory restrictions have been sometimes treated as being outside the scope of Article 43 EC (ex Article 52 EC),[18] but it is now clear from such cases as *Kraus*,[19] *Gebhard*[20] and *Centros*,[21] that such restrictions may require justification by overriding requirements in the general interest. Such justification was held to exist in *Pfeiffer Großhandel GmbH v. Löwa Warenhandel GmbH*[22] in which a restriction on the right of establishment brought about by an indistinctly applicable provision of national law whose aim was to protect trade names against the risk of confusion was held to be so justified.

II. RELEVANT SECONDARY LEGISLATION AND THE COURT'S APPROACH TO ITS LIMITATIONS

Council Directive 73/148 of 21 May 1973[23] on the abolition of restrictions on movement and residence within the Community for nationals of Member States with regard to establishment and the provision of services resembles Directive 68/360. The Directive applies to persons who are nationals of a Member State who are established or who wish to establish themselves in another Member State in order to pursue activities as self-employed persons, or who wish to provide services in that state. Furthermore, it applies to nationals of a Member State wishing to go to another Member State as recipients of services. It is also applicable to the families of such persons, defined in the same way as in Article 10 of Regulation 1612/68.[24]

Articles 2 and 3 of the Directive require Member States to grant the right to leave and enter a Member State to the categories of persons mentioned in Article 1 simply on the production of a valid identity card or passport. There is an exception for members of the family who do not have the nationality of a Member State, and who are thus required to produce an entry visa or equivalent document on entering a Member State. According to Article 4 of Directive 73/148, a right of permanent residence evidenced by a permit is granted to persons who establish themselves in a self-employed activity. A right of temporary residence is granted to persons who provide or receive services, which is of equal duration to the period for which the services are provided or received. When such a period exceeds three months, the Member State in which the services are performed must issue a right of abode. By Article 6 of the Directive, an applicant for a residence permit or a right of abode may only be required to produce an

---

18. Note for example Case 182/83, *Robert Fearon v. Irish Land Commission* [1984] ECR 3677 and Case 221/85, *Commission v. Belgium ("Clinical Biology Services")* [1987] ECR 719.
19. Case C-19/92, *Kraus v. Land Baden-Württemberg* [1993] ECR I-1663, paragraph 32.
20. Case C-55/94, *Gebhard* [1995] ECR I-4165, paragraph 37.
21. Case C-212/97, *Centros* [1999] ECR I-1459, paragraph 34.
22. Case C-255/97, [1999] ECR I-2835, paragraph 21.
23. OJ 1973 L172/14.
24. Directive, Article 1(1)(a)–(d) and (2).

identity card or passport, and proof that he or she is one of the persons within the ambit of the Directive.

Council Directive 75/34 of 17 December 1974[25] provides for the right of nationals of a Member State to remain in their territory of another Member State after having carried on an activity there as a self-employed person. This right is also enjoyed by the members of the family of such a person, as defined in Article 1 of Directive 73/148.[26] The conditions which have to be complied with by the relevant person in order to be entitled to such a right are very similar to those set out in Article 2(1)(a)–(c) of Regulation 1251/70, which is applicable to employed persons. It will be noted that persons providing or receiving services do not come within the scope of Directive 75/34.

Regulation 1612/68, which is concerned to a considerable extent with equal treatment in employment, is not paralleled by any corresponding instrument applicable to self-employed persons, established in a Member State other than their own, or providing services in such a state. Nevertheless, it seems that where such self-employed persons and their families are lawfully resident in a Member State other than their own, they may sometimes be able to invoke the principle of non-discrimination contained in Article 12 EC and thus claim equal treatment in relation to social and tax advantages, and also in relation to housing and education. Much would appear to depend on the length of their stay in the host state.

Thus, in *Commission v. Italy*[27] the Italian government contended that because Article 9 of Regulation 1612/68 was inapplicable, reduced rate mortgage loans and social housing did not have to be made available to self-employed nationals of other Member States on identical terms to those granted to Italian nationals. The Court disagreed with this standpoint, taking the view that the self-employed migrant needs housing, and that any restriction on access thereto, and of relevant facilities granted to nationals in order to lessen the financial burden on them must be regarded as an obstacle to the pursuit of the occupation itself. It seems from this decision that under Article 43 EC, there must be a link between the relevant benefit, and the ability to perform the self-employed activity. The Court also took the view that if the self-employed person is already established in his home state and provides services in the host state for a relatively brief period, there may be no need for housing. One may add the same proviso in relation to certain other social benefits for transitory migrants. However, the impact of *Maria Martinez Sala* in this area remains somewhat uncertain.

---

25. OJ 1975 L 14/10.
26. This definition is the same as that in Article 10 of Regulation 1612/68.
27. Case 63/86, [1988] ECR 29.

III. EC TREATY PROVISIONS AND EXCEPTIONS

1. The exception for the exercise of official authority

Article 45 EC stipulates that the provisions of the chapter relating to the right of establishment shall not apply, so far as any particular Member State is concerned, to activities which are connected, even occasionally, with the exercise of official authority. This provision is also applicable to the supply of services.[28] It is clearly rather similar to the derogation contained in article 39(4) EC.

The exception contained in what is now Article 45 EC (ex Article 55 EC) was invoked in *Reyners v. Belgium*.[29] In this case, Reyners, a Dutchman, was born, educated and resident in Belgium, and he had a doctorate in Belgian law. He was refused admission to the Belgian bar as he did not have Belgian nationality. He brought an action before the Belgian Conseil d'Etat claiming that this refusal was contrary to Article 52 EC (now Article 43 EC). The Belgian court made a reference to the European Court of Justice under Article 177 EC (now Article 230 EC). One of the Belgian government's arguments in support of the rule maintained by the Belgian bar that the profession of *avocat* was limited to Belgian nationals was that the whole of the profession was exempted from Article 52 EC because it was connected organically with the public service of the administration of justice. The European Court refused to accept this contention, which was also supported by the Luxembourg government. It held that (like what was then Article 48(4)), Article 55 EC (now Article 45 EC) had to be interpreted in a Community sense. It added that the most typical activities of the profession of *avocat*, in particular, such as consultation and legal assistance and also representation and the defence of parties in court, even where the intervention or assistance of the *avocat* is compulsory or is a legal monopoly, cannot be considered as connected with the exercise of official authority. Article 55 EC (now Article 45 EC) had, according to the Court, to be restricted to those activities which have a direct and specific connection with the exercise of official authority.

A similar narrow interpretation to Article 55 EC (now Article 45 EC) was given by the Court in the later case of *Thijssen v. Controledienst voor de Verzekeringen*.[30] In this case, the Court found that the position of commissioner of insurance companies and undertakings was not excluded from the provisions of the chapter on establishment or services. Despite the fact that this post involved checking upon companies and making reports on possible infringements of the penal code, the power possessed by the commissioner to prevent insurance companies from carrying out certain decisions was not a definitive one, and did not affect the ultimate power of approval or refusal possessed by the Office de Contrôle des Assurances.

---

28. Article 55 EC.
29. Case 2/74, *Reyners v. Belgium* [1974] ECR 631.
30. Case C-42/92, [1993] ECR I-4047.

2. The impact of Articles 295 and 86(2) EC

Article 295 EC provides that the EC Treaty shall in no way prejudice the rules in the Member States governing the system of property ownership. This provision allows the nationalisation of undertakings, provided no discrimination on the grounds of nationality contrary to Article 12 EC occurs and provided that the specific prohibitions of discrimination contained in Articles 44(2)(c) and 294 EC are respected.[31] The expropriation of land has been held by the Court to be permitted by Article 295 EC.[32] Provided the three conditions set out in Article 86(2) EC are fulfilled, Member States may make an exception to prohibition contained in Article 43 EC.[33] The Court is disinclined to interpret Article 90(2) EC widely.[34]

3. The direct effect of Article 43 EC and some consequences thereof

Article 52 EC (now Article 43 EC) was held to have a direct effect in *Reyners*, which has been mentioned above. This was despite the fact that Articles 54(2)(c) (now Article 44(1) EC) and Article 57(1) (now Article 47(1) EC) required that directives should be adopted. The Court held that Article 52 EC imposed an obligation to attain a precise result, the fulfilment of which had to be made easier by, but not dependent on the implementation of a programme of progressive measures. According to the Court, after the expiry of the transitional period, the directives provided for by the chapter on the right of establishment had become superfluous with regards to implementing the rule on nationality, since this was sanctioned by the Treaty itself with direct effect. Nevertheless, the Court emphasised that "these directives have not lost all interest, since they preserve an important scope in the field of measures intended to make easier the effective exercise of the right of freedom of establishment."

Despite the judgment in *Reyners*, it appeared to be the case that where

---

31. Article 294 EC provides that Member States shall accord nationals of the other Member States the same treatment as their own nationals as regards participation in the capital of companies or firms within the meaning of Article 48 EC, without prejudice to the other provisions of the Treaty.
32. Case 182/83, *Robert Fearon Ltd. v. Irish Land Commission* [1984] ECR 3677. See Kapteyn and Verloren van Themaat, *op. cit.*, pp. 738, 740.
33. Article 86(2) permits public service undertakings to avoid the application of Treaty rules where this is necessary for the performance of their tasks.
34. However it was held in Case C-266/96, *Corsica Ferries France* [1996] ECR I-3949 that an impediment to the free provision of services may not infringe Article 49 EC where the conditions for the application of Article 86(2) are satisfied. These are that the undertakings must have been entrusted with a sense of general economic interest, or having the character of a revenue producing monopoly; that the application in the Treaty rules would obstruct in law or in fact the particular tasks assigned to it; that in any case the development in trade must not be affected to such an extent as would be contrary to the interests of the Community.

educational, training, and professional ethics, and other requirements varied considerably between Member States, Article 52 EC could not be treated as having direct effects by itself, for the purposes of attacking a restriction on freedom of establishment. It appeared that Community legislation (in the form of directives) under Article 57(2) EC (now Article 47(2) EC)) was necessary in such cases for the purpose of coordinating the diverse requirements of the various Member States for the carrying on of a particular professional activity, and that impediments on freedom of establishment based upon such different requirements could not be impugned in the absence of such directives.[35]

However, perhaps somewhat surprisingly, this was not the approach taken by the Court. The first relevant case was *Thieffry*.[36] This case involved a Belgian national having a Belgian doctorate in law, who had practised as an advocate in Brussels. His doctorate was recognised by a French university (Paris I) as equivalent to the French licentiate's degree in law, and he subsequently obtained a French certificate of aptitude for the profession of *avocat*. The Court held that if Thieffry had already obtained an equivalent qualification and had satisfied the necessary practical training requirements, the state authorities could not refuse him admission to the French bar simply because he lacked French qualifications. The Court has ruled in the subsequent cases of *Heylens*[37] and *Vlassopoulou*.[38] that Article 52 EC (now Article 43 EC) prevents the national authorities from simply refusing, without an explanation, to allow nationals from another Member State to practise their profession or trade because their qualification is not equivalent to the corresponding national one. These cases made it clear that the person concerned must be given reasons for a refusal to recognise the equivalence of their qualifications, and must be granted a remedy of a judicial nature in the event of such refusal.

In the first of these cases, Heylens, a Belgian national who possessed a Belgian football trainer's licence was denied recognition of the equivalence of his diploma by the French Ministry of Sport, and he was not given reasons for such denial. He continued to practise as a trainer, and was prosecuted by UNECTEF, the French football trainer's union. The Tribunal de Grande Instance of Lille made a reference to the European Court of Justice. The Court held that because free movement of workers was one of the fundamental objectives of the Treaty, the requirement to secure free movement stemmed from Article 5 (now Article 10 EC). There was thus a duty on the French national authorities to assess the equivalence of the Belgian diploma with the French football trainers' diploma. Furthermore, the Court held that since free access to employment was a fundamental right which the Treaty confers individually on each worker in the

---

35. Note in this sense Craig and de Burca, *EU Law*, (2nd edn, Oxford University Press, 1998), p. 735.

36. Case 71/76, *Thieffry v. Conseil de l'ordre des avocats à la cour de Paris* [1977] ECR 765.

37. Case 222/86, *UNECTEF v. Heylens* [1987] ECR 4097.

38. Case 340/89, *Vlassopoulou v. Ministerium für Justiz, Bundes-und Europaangelegenheiten Baden-Württemberg* [1991] ECR 2357.

Community, the existence of a remedy of a judicial nature against any decision of a national authority refusing the benefit of such right was essential.

The Court also took the view that the imposition of a duty on the competent nationality authority to provide reasons for refusal, either in the decision itself or subsequently, was a necessary element in securing effective legal protection.

Vlassopoulou concerned a Greek national who possessed a Greek law degree and a doctorate in law from the University of Tübingen in Germany, and who practised German law in Germany for several years. The German authorities refused her application for admission to the Bar and authorisation to practise, because she had not passed the relevant German examinations (i.e. the First and Second State Examination), and was thus not qualified to practise. Her appeal against this decision was eventually heard by the German Supreme Court, which requested a preliminary ruling from the European Court of Justice. The Court held that even if applied (as is required by Article 43(2) EC) without any discrimination on the grounds of nationality, national requirements concerning qualifications might have the effect of hindering nationals of other Member States in the exercise of their right of establishment. This could be the case if the national rules in question took no account of the knowledge and qualifications already acquired by the person concerned. The Court added that a Member State which receives a request to admit a person to a profession under which access under national law, depends on the possession of a diploma or a professional qualification must take into account the diplomas, certificates and other evidence of qualifications which the person concerned has acquired in order to exercise the same profession in another Member State by making a comparison between the specialised knowledge and abilities certified by those diplomas, and the knowledge and qualifications required by the national authorities.

The Court added that if the necessary comparative examination by the national authorities of the relevant diplomas resulted in the conclusion that the knowledge and skills acquired were equivalent, the state must recognise the qualification. If, on the other hand, such a comparison revealed only partial correspondence, the host state was entitled to require the person concerned to show that he had acquired the knowledge and qualifications which were lacking. Furthermore, the Court also stipulates that any decision taken must be capable of being the subject of proceedings in which its legality under Community law could be reviewed, and the person concerned must be able to ascertain the reasons for the decision taken with respect to him.[39]

The interpretation of Article 52 EC (now Article 43 EC) in such cases as *Heylens* and *Vlassopoulou* leads to a situation comparable to that which exists under Directive 89/48 on the mutual recognition of higher education diplomas.

---

39. See paragraph 22 of the Court's decision in *Vlassopoulou*, which adopts a similar approach to that taken by the Court in paragraph 16 of *Heylens*. Note also the provision of Article 8(2) of Directive 89/48 on a general system for the recognition of higher education diplomas, OJ 1989 L19/16, which is in similar terms.

As is pointed out below, it may sometimes prove useful to invoke the principles established in these cases, where the two general directives of 1989 and 1992[40] are for some reason inapplicable, and there is no relevant sectoral directive.

IV. COORDINATING DIRECTIVES AND THE MUTUAL RECOGNITION OF QUALIFICATIONS

As is recognised in Article 2 of the two general system directives,[41] considered below, the mutual recognition of qualifications is of importance to its free movement of workers as to the self employed. However, it would appear that barriers to free movement arising from the non recognition of qualifications are of more significance in the context of freedom of establishment than in relation to the free movement of workers and freedom to provide services. For this reason, attempts to remove such barriers through coordinating or harmonising directives and through the mutual recognition of qualifications are discussed in the present chapter.[42]

Community legislation governing minimum standards of education and training for particular professions took place initially generally by means of complementary sets of directives for each sector regulated. An exception to this method of legislation came about, however, in the field of architecture, where the system of mutual recognition of diplomas only provides the requirements necessary for such recognition, and does not define any mandatory characteristics of the qualification allowing the pursuit of activities as an architect in each state.[43] The other six sectoral systems for the recognition of diplomas each comprised two different directives, one of which a coordinating directive set out the educational and training requirements necessary for the pursuit of a profession, whilst the other would set out the qualifications and diplomas awarded in the Member

---

40. Directive 92/51, OJ 1992 L209/29. This Directive has been subjected to minor amendments, more recently by Directive 97/38 (OJ 1997 L184/31). The two general system Directives have been amended recently and the Directives governing the professions of nurses responsible for general care, dentists, veterinary surgeons, midwife, architect, pharmacist and doctor have also undergone certain changes: see COM(2000) 527 final, 21-8-2000, which contains the Commission's Opinion on the EP's amendments to the Council's common position regarding such an amending proposal. The amending Directive was enacted on 14 May 2001: see OJ 2001 L 206/1, 13 July 2001.
41. Council Directive 89/48 on a general system for the recognition of higher education diplomas awarded on completion of professional education and training of at least three years duration, OJ 1989 L19/16 and Council Directive 92/51 on a general system for the recognition of professional education and training to supplement Directive 89/48, OJ 1992 L209/25.
42. This follows the precedents set by Kapteyn and Verloren van Themaat, *op. cit.*, p. 744 and Craig and de Burca, *op. cit.*, pp. 738–744.
43. Directive 85/384/EC, OJ 1985 L223/15.

States which would satisfy those requirements.[44] Special transitional directives and directives requiring restrictions to be removed applied to particular activities. It often transpired that protracted and difficult negotiations were necessary before agreement could be reached on the content of the directives, especially those relating to professional activities. It was suggested by the Commission in 1997[45] that a new directive should be enacted applying to the activities mentioned in the present paragraph a similar mechanism for the recognition of qualifications as is employed in the two general mutual recognition directives mentioned below.

1. The Lawyers' Directive of 1998

A directive on the provision of services by lawyers was enacted in 1977,[46] but although a Directive on the Establishment of Lawyers was under active consideration for many years, the Directive was not enacted until 1998.[47] This Directive is said to be based in particular on what are now Article 40 EC (ex Article 49 EC), Article 47(1) EC (ex Article 57(1) EC) and Article 5(2) EC (ex Article EC). It provides for the mutual recognition of certain professional legal qualifications obtained in the Member States and enables a person who is an EC national, and who holds such a qualification, to practise on a permanent basis in another Member State under his own professional title after having registered with the competent authority in that state.[48]

Such a registered lawyer is permitted to practice in partnership with host state lawyers where joint practice is permitted in the host state.[49] He is also permitted to advise on host state law, which includes European Community law,[50] and to undertake activities reserved for host state lawyers, subject to certain limitations.[51] Further, Article 11 of Directive 98/5 gives lawyers registered under it, after three years practice of host state law, the right for admission to the host state legal profession without having to pass an examination. Interestingly, insofar as these requirements reflect the case law mentioned above, decisions not to grant registration or to cancel registration must state the reasons on

---

44. The complementary pairs of directives related to doctors, nurses, midwives, dentists, veterinary surgeons and pharmacists.
45. COM (1997) 363, [1997] OJ C 264/5; and see the proposal for an EP and Council Directive supplementing the seven above-mentioned directives, and amending the two general Directives. The Council's common position may be found in OJ C 119/1, 24.2.2000. The European Parliament made eleven amendments to the Common Position, four of which proved acceptable to the Commission: see COM (2000)527 final. The relevant Directive has now been enacted by the Council: see OJ 2001 L 206/1, 13 July 2001.
46. Directive 77/249, OJ 1977 L78/17.
47. Directive 98/5, OJ 1998 L77/36.
48. Directive 98/5, Articles 1–3.
49. Directive 98/5, Article 11.
50. Directive 98/5, Article 5(1).
51. Directive 98/5, Articles 5(1)–5(3).

which they are based; in addition, a remedy must be available against such decisions in a court or tribunal in accordance with the provisions of domestic law.[52]

The Directive has been implemented in the United Kingdom.[53] The competent authorities for England and Wales are the Law Society and the Bar of England and Wales. Different authorities will be responsible for registration etc. in Scotland and Northern Ireland.

Luxembourg has brought an action for the annulment of the Directive against the Council and European Parliament (it was made under the co-decision procedure) on three grounds, i.e. that it violates Article 52(2) EC (now Article 43(2) EC), Article 57(2) EC (now Article 47(2) EC) and Article 190 EC (now Article 253 EC). Advocate General Jabaro Colomer has suggested all the arguments on behalf of the Luxembourg government should be dismissed in his Opinion of 24 February 2000. The Court also found that none of Luxembourg's pleas could be upheld.[54]

2. The two general systems for mutual recognition

(1)   Directive 89/48: the first general system Directive

Because of the slow progress which was made with the coordination or harmonisation of educational and training requirements for the various professions, the European Councils, meeting at Fontainebleau in 1984, decided to adopt a new approach, based not upon harmonisation but upon the mutual recognition of qualifications. This was not made applicable to individual professions, but instead to all fields of activity, where a higher education diploma is required. The first Directive to be based on these principles is Directive 89/48, enacted by the Council 18 December 1989.

As already indicated, this Directive and Directive 92/51, which supplements it, apply to workers[55] as well as to the self-employed. Both Directives are stated in the preambles thereto to be without prejudice to the application of Article 48(4) EC (now Article 39(4) EC) (exception for employment in the public service) and Article 55 EC (now Article 45 EC) (exception for the exercise of official authority). The Directive is only applicable to the pursuance of a regulated

---

52. Directive 92/51, Article 9.
53. The Law Society of England and Wales has made the European Lawyers' Registration Regulations 2000, with the concurrence of the Master of Rolls under Schedule 14 to the Courts and Legal Services Act 1990, as extended by the European Community (Lawyers Practice) Regulations 2000 in order to implement the Directive.
54. Case C-168/98, *Luxembourg v. Council and Parliament* [2000] ECR I-9131.
55. See Case C-234/97, *Bobadilla v. Museo del Prado and others* [1999] ECR I-4773 in which a Spanish art restorer working for the Prado in Madrid sought recognition of her degree of Newcastle Polytechnic, as it then was.

professional activity.[56] Such activities are not very clearly defined in Article 1(d) of Directive 89/48, or in Article 1(f) of Directive 92/51 (the supplementary Directive) which is in similar terms. In the earlier Directive, the first two modes of pursuit of a professional activity are said to be:

pursuit of an activity under a professional title, in so far as the use of the title is reserved to the holder of a diploma governed by laws, regulations, or administrative provisions

pursuit of a professional activity relating to health,

in so far as remuneration or reimbursement for such an activity is subject by virtue of national social security arrangements to the possession of a diploma.

It may be that Pertek[57] is correct is assuming that the second mode does not give rise to any difficulties of interpretation. It is also clear as he says, that health professionals sometimes enjoy a total or partial monopoly over the performance of certain activities, or of the use of a particular title. There seem to be more difficulties in understanding what is meant by the first mode, and in particular the meaning of the phrase "professional title". According to Pertek, it can be defined in a general way as the qualification or the denomination which is used in an activity for which remuneration is received, and which attests to a specific skill. He also says that the way in which it is granted is determined by a public authority. The qualification or denomination is protected by penal sanctions. These may simply consist of the fact that illegal pursuit of the profession is an offence.

Pertek's proposed definition encapsulates many of the features of a regulated professional activity. It is probably not correct to say that such an activity must always be pursued for the purposes of remuneration. It may also be that Pertek exaggerates the significance of sanctions. Furthermore, as is recognised by the third mode of definition outlined below, the way in which professional qualifications are granted is not always determined by public authorities.

This third mode of definition is set out in the second subparagraph of Article 1(d), which provides:

Where the first subparagraph does not apply, a professional activity shall be deemed to be a regulated professional activity if it is pursued by the members of an association or organisation the purpose of which is, in particular, to promote and maintain a high standard in the professional field concerned, and which, to achieve that purpose, is recognised in a special form in a Member State and:

---

56. It seems that a regulated professional activity need only be carried on in one Member States. Thus, Article 1(c) of Directive 89/48 provides that a regulated profession is the professional activity or range of professional activities which constitute the profession in a Member States.

57. Pertek, 'Free Movement of Professionals and Recognition of Higher Education Diplomas', [1992] 12 YBEL pp. 300–3.

awards a diploma to its members

ensures that its members respect the rules of professional conduct which it prescribes, and

confers on them the right to use a title or designatory letters, or to benefit from a status corresponding to that diploma.

It should be noted that a title or qualification of the above kind is not called a professional title but, if it exists, the relevant activity can be called a regulated professional activity. Pertek[58] takes what seems to be the correct view that such a title is not called a professional title because of the absence of public provisions governing the conditions for granting it. It appears that this extension was intended to cover the situation in the United Kingdom and Ireland, where chartered bodies sometimes grant persons the right to employ a title or qualification according to conditions which they lay down.[59]

According to the judgment of the Court in *Aranitis v. Land Berlin*,[60] the effect of Article 1(d) of Directive 89/48 and Article 1(f) of Directive 92/51 is that, where the conditions for taking up or pursuing a professional activity are directly or indirectly governed by legal provisions, whether laws, regulations or administrative provisions, that activity constitutes a regulated profession. It was also held in that case that the right to take up or pursue a profession must be regarded as directly governed by legal provisions where the laws, regulations or administrative provisions of the Member State concerned create a system under which that professional activity is expressly restricted to those who fulfil certain conditions and entry to it is denied to those who do not.

The recognition of a qualification earned by Ms Bobadilla, a Spanish art restorer who worked for the Prado in Madrid, and who had obtained her qualification at what was then Newcastle Polytechnic was considered by the Court of Justice.[61] The Spanish authorities had refused to recognise this qualification, saying that in order to obtain official recognition, Ms Bobadilla would have to sit a number of examinations in 24 subjects. This refusal was seemingly motivated by the fact that a collective agreement entered into in 1988 by the Prado and staff-representatives provides that the post of restorer is to be reserved to persons who possess the qualification awarded by the restoration department of the Faculty of Arts or the School of Fine Arts.

The question thus arose in the context of a reference for a preliminary ruling whether a profession governed by a collective agreement entered into by management and labour could be regarded as regulated within the meaning of Directive

---

58. *Op. cit.*, at page 304.

59. The Directive contains an Annex consisting of a non-exhaustive list of professional organisations or associations which have such a role. It principally consists of engineering and accountancy, bodies in the United Kingdom and Ireland.

60. Case C-164/94, [1996] ECR I-135. In this case, the Court extended its ruling in *Vlassopoulou*, which applied to a regulated profession, to an unregulated one.

61. Case C-234/97, *Bobadilla v. Museo Nacional del Prado and others* [1999] ECR I-4773.

89/48 or 92/51. The Court answered this question by saying that a profession could be regarded as being "regulated" where a collective agreement governed in a general way the right to take it up and pursue it, especially where that resulted from a single administrative policy laid down at national level, or even where the terms of a collective agreement entered into by a public body and its staff representatives were common to other collective agreements entered into on an individual basis by public bodies of the same kind. The latter rather extensive notion of a regulated profession evidently follows from the Court's desire to lend effectiveness to the Directives. The Court held that it was up to the referring court to determine whether the profession of an art restorer was a regulated profession, in the light of its ruling. The Court also held, following *Vlassopoulou*, with regard to non-regulated professions, that where a Member State did not have a general procedure for recognition of diplomas which was compatible with Community law, it was for the public body itself to investigate whether the diploma obtained in another Member State together, where appropriate with practical experience, is to be regarded as equivalent to the qualification required. This may give rise to considerable practical difficulties for public authorities and bodies in assessing the relevant knowledge and experience. Such recognition of equivalence is not required for regulated professions.

The 1989 Directive is not applicable to professions which are the subject of a separate Directive providing arrangements for the mutual recognition of diplomas by Member States. The principle of mutual recognition under Directive 89/48 may be applicable to higher education diplomas which have been awarded by a competent authority in a Member State after at least three years higher education (or an equivalent period part-time) and the completion of any necessary period of professional training in addition to the higher education course. According to Article 3 of Directive 89/48, where in a host state the taking up or pursuit of a regulated profession is subject to the possession of a diploma, the competent authority of the Member State may not, on the ground of inadequate qualifications, refuse to authorise a national of a Member State to take up or pursue that profession on the same conditions as are applicable to its own nationals, subject to certain provisos. These are that the applicant holds a diploma required in another Member State for the taking up or pursuit of the profession in question, or has pursued that profession for at least two out of the last ten years in a state which does not regulate that profession.[62]

Where the duration of the education and training of the applicant is at least one year shorter than that required in the host state, and where there is a

---

62. According to the Common Position adopted by the Council on 20 March 2000 (OJ 2000 C 119/1), which proposes the introduction of a new subparagraph into Article 3(b) of Directive 89/48, the two-year period referred to above would not be required where the applicant held a qualification awarded on completion of regulated education and training as defined in the proposed new Article 1(d)(a) of the Directive. The amending Directive was enacted on 31.7.2001: see OJ 2000 L 206/1. The draft provision remained unchanged in the Directive.

shortfall in the period of supervised practice required, the host state may require the provision of evidence of professional experience. The required period of professional experience may not exceed twice the shortfall in the duration of education and training required by the host state, or the shortfall in professional practice.

In any event, the required period of professional experience may not exceed four years.[63]

Article 4(1)(b) of Directive 89/48 provides that the host state may require the completion of an adaptation period of not more than three years in certain circumstances. These are:

(a) where the matters covered by the education and training received by the applicant differ substantially from those covered in the diploma required in the host state;[64] or

(b) where certain of the professional activities regulated in the host state are not regulated in the applicant's state of origin and that difference corresponds to specific education and training required in the host state and covers substantially different matters from those covered in the diploma possessed by the applicant; or

(c) where the profession regulated in the host state comprises professional activities which are not in the profession pursued by the applicant in the Member State from which he originates, and that difference corresponds to specific education and training required in the host state, and covers substantially different matters from those covered by the evidence of formal qualifications provided by the applicant.

The applicant may opt for an aptitude test rather than an adaptation period. Nevertheless, for professions whose practice requires precise knowledge of national law, and in respect of which the provision of advice and/or assistance concerning national law is an essential and constant part of the professional activity, the host Member State may stipulate either an adaptation period or an aptitude test. There has been a general tendency for Member States to require the latter kind of test as far as legal professions are concerned. The German requirements have been particularly strict. The above derogation for legal professions has been rather widely interpreted in France; it is doubtful whether the

---

63. Directive 89/48, Article 4(1)(a).

64. The Common Position of the Council in its proposed Directive amending the two general system and certain sectoral Directives, OJ 2000 C119/1, provides that the above subparagraph should be followed by one stipulating "If the host state intends to require the applicant to complete an adaptation period or take an aptitude test, it must first examine whether the knowledge acquired by the applicant in the course of his professional experience is such that it fully or partly covers the substantial difference referred to in the first paragraph". Where such a difference was covered, neither requirement could, it would seem, be imposed on the applicant. The provision remains unchanged in the amending Directive.

profession of commissaire-priseur, which benefited from it, can properly be regarded as a legal profession within the wording of the Directive. The Directive also contains a rather complex procedure according to which host states may introduce derogations for other professions.[65]

According to Article 4(2) of the Directive, a Member State cannot apply this requirement of periods of professional experience and adaptation cumulatively. This entails that the maximum "training" period is four years. According to Article 5, the host state may allow the applicant to perform that part of his training which consists of supervised professional practice in that state, on the basis of equivalence. Article 6(1) governs the provision of evidence of good character and of certain other matters to the competent authorities of the host state when such evidence is required by them. The latter state is required to accept as sufficient evidence in respect of nationals of other Member States wishing to take up a regulated profession in its territory, the production of documents issued by the competent authorities of the Member State of origin or the Member State from which the foreign national comes showing that these requirements have been met. Where such documents are not issued by the competent authorities of the relevant Member State, they may be replaced by a declaration on oath, or a solemn declaration, before a judicial or administrative authority by the person concerned. Article 6(2) governs the situation where the competent authority of the host Member State requires a national of that state wishing to take up or pursue a regulated profession to provide a certificate of physical or mental health.

In such an event, that authority is required to accept as sufficient evidence the production or the document required in the Member State of origin, or in the Member State from which the foreign national comes. Where these states do not impose any requirements of that nature on those wishing to take up or pursue the relevant profession, the host state is required to accept from such nationals a certificate issued by a competent authority in that state corresponding to the certificates issued in the host state.

The competent authorities of the host state are required by Article 7 to allow nationals of Member States who fulfil the conditions for the taking up and pursuit of a regulated profession in their territory to use the corresponding professional title in the host state and also their lawful academic title.

Article 8(1) is concerned with the provision of evidence of qualifications and experience. The host state is bound to accept as proof the certificates and documents issued by the competent authorities in the Member States, which the person concerned shall submit in support of his application to pursue the profession concerned. The designation of competent authorities by a Member State, empowered to receive the applications and take the decisions referred to in the Directive is provided for in Article 9(1). According to Article 9(2), each

65. Article 4(1)(b) and Article 10, *ibid.*

Member State is required to designate a person responsible for coordinating the activities of those competent authorities.

Member States were required by Article 12 to implement the Directive by 4 January 1991. Article 13 provided for a report from the Commission to the European Parliament and the Council on the state of application of the general system no more than 5 years after 4 January 1991. The Commission was required to present its conclusions as to any changes which might be made in the system. As already pointed out, the Commission has proposed amendments to both the two general system Directives,[66] certain of which have been enacted.

(2) Directive 92/51

This Directive supplements and follows a similar approach to that taken in the first general mutual recognition Directive, Directive 89/48. It is applicable to education and training other than the three year higher education countries covered by Directive 89/48, of at least one year's duration or of equivalent duration on a part-time basis, which qualify, the holder for a regulated profession. It also covers certificates awarded by a competent authority in a Member State after the conclusion of education and training course other than the abovementioned post-secondary courses of at least one year's duration, or after a professional or probationary practice period, which shows that the holder is qualified to take up a regulated profession.

(3) Some reflections on the general system Directives, and their Implementation

Both above Directives are intended to have a broad and general ambit, and to base recognition on the principle of mutual trust, without prior coordination of the relevant educational and training courses for particular professions. These Directives contain the basis principle that a host state may not refuse entry to a regulated profession to a national of a Member State who holds the necessary qualification for practice in another Member State. Both the two general system Directives enable the competent authorities of the host state, where they are able to show that there are substantial differences between its education and training which has been acquired and that required, to impose additional requirements on the applicant i.e. that he should have professional experience, sit an aptitude test, or complete a period of adaptation.

The general system has shown that it provides an appropriate manner of enabling people to pursue a regulated profession in another Member State. However, it seems certain Member States were slow to implement the Directives fully. There have been delays in Belgium and France in particular. Furthermore,

---

66. Note in particular the proposal submitted by the Commission to the Council on 3 December 1997, OJ C28/1, 26.1.1998. The Council adopted a common position on that proposal on 20 March 2000, see OJ C119/1, 27.4.2000.

as is pointed out in the Report of the High Level Panel,[67] it is clearly the case that the behaviour of certain competent authorities show a lack of willingness to apply the mutual trust on which the system is based. It may be that in some cases, perhaps in response to pressure from professional groupings, the presumption in favour of recognition has become secondary to that in favour of a need to impose secondary requirements. The competent authorities often engage in a detailed subject by subject comparison of the course followed by the applicant and that in the host state.

There is also a marked reluctance on the part of such authorities to take account of post diploma professional experience of the applicant, and to accept that such experience may relieve or do away with the additional requirements contemplated. Furthermore, a considerable number of applicants complain of the delays which they experience in getting a decision from the competent authorities. According to Article 8(2) of Directive 89/48, such a decision should be given in a reasoned manner not more than four months after the presentation of all the documents relating to the persons concerned. Such persons are frequently asked to provide additional documents or supplementary information long after the initial application was submitted, and the prescribed time period is rarely respected. However, according to Article 8(2) of Directive 89/48, they should have an appeal to a national court or tribunal in the absence of a reasoned decision as well against the decision itself.

As already pointed out, there seems to be inadequate progress in the free movement of persons in the public sector. According to the Report of the High Level Panel,[68] some Member States consider that the two general systems for the recognition of diplomas do not apply to this sector. In view of the jurisprudence of the European Court of Justice, this approach is clearly wrong, except insofar as a limited range of posts involving, as far as Article 39(4) EC is concerned, participation in the exercise of powers conferred by public law and entailing duties designated to safeguard the general interests of the state.[69]

The provisions of the two general system Directives which are sufficiently clear, precise and unconditional may be invoked against public bodies in the Member States, insofar as they are subject to the authority or control of the state.[70] Many professional bodies come within the latter category.

(4)   Qualifications obtained in non-Member States

The directives in the field of recognition of qualifications do not cover non-Community nationals. However, Annex VII to the EEA Agreement applies

---

67. See p. 29, thereof.
68. Page 37, *ibid.*
69. See Case 149/79, *Commission v. Belgium* [1980] ECR 3881. The Court has also taken a narrow view of the exception based on the exercise of official authority contained in Article 45 EC: see Case 2/74, *Reyners v. Belgium* [1974] ECR 631.
70. See Case C-188/89, *Foster v. British Gas plc* [1990] ECR I-3313 at paragraph 18, where the principle expressed is wider than that in paragraph 20 of the judgment.

certain of them, to nationals of the EEA states, including Directive 89/48 on the general system, as well as the directives establishing sectoral systems for the recognition of diplomas, and Directive 77/249 to facilitate the effective exercise by lawyers of freedom to provide services, in so far as it relates to higher education. Furthermore, the directives do not apply to qualifications obtained outside the Community. Nevertheless, when Directive 89/48 was adopted, a Council recommendation was made[71] that the governments of the Member States should allow nationals of Member States who had obtained a diploma certificate or other evidence of formal qualifications in a non-Member State to receive recognition of it within the Community.

It was held by the Court in *Tawil-Albertini v. Ministre des Affaires Sociales*[72] that a French national who had obtained a dental qualification in Lebanon which was subsequently recognised by the Belgian authorities as being equivalent to a Belgian qualification and which allowed him to practise in Belgium was not entitled to have this qualification recognised in France. This was so even though he was also authorised to practise in two other Member States. The Court found that the qualification could not be treated as within the Community directive on dentistry[73] simply because of the recognition of the equivalence of the qualification in certain Member States. This principle would appear applicable to any of the sectoral directives and to the two mutual recognition directives.[74]

It was held, however, in *Haim v. Kassenzahnärztliche Vereinigung Nordrhein*[75] that if a Member State (in this case Germany) chooses to recognise a qualification obtained in a non-Member State by a Community national, it must take account of training periods or professional experience acquired in another Member State in order to discover whether the national training period has been completed. Non-Community nationals are unable to take advantage of Community directives, whether general or sectoral, for the purpose of claiming recognition of any professional qualification they may have obtained in a Member State.

V. AMBIT OF ARTICLE 43 EC

As already indicated, certain of the early cases gave support to the idea that Article 52 EC (now Article 43 EC) had no application to non-discriminatory restrictions. Thus, in *Commission v. Belgium (Clinical Biology Services)*[76] the Court rejected the Commission's action which maintained the incompatibility

---

71. Recommendation 89/49, OJ 1989, L19/24.
72. Case C-154/93, [1994] ECR I-451.
73. Council Directive 78/687.
74. Craig and de Burca, *op. cit.*, p. 743.
75. Case C-319/92, [1994] ECR I-425. See also the Opinion of Jacobs AG in *Hocsman v. Ministre de l'emploi et de la Solidarité*, Case C-238/98, [2000] ECR I-6623.
76. Case 221/85, [1987] ECR 719.

with Article 52 EC of a national regulation preventing social security reimbursement for clinical biology services provided by private laboratories, whose members, partners and directors were not all persons authorised to perform medical analysis. The effect of these rules seemed to have been that persons engaged in clinical biology tests would have to maintain a primary establishment in Belgium, although they did not refer to the nationality or seat of the person or company providing the service.

The Commission argued that restrictions on freedom of establishment were not confined to discriminatory measures, but also included measures which were indistinctly applicable to nationals and foreigners, when they constituted an unjustified restriction for the latter. Advocate General Lenz asked the Court not to follow the approach of the Commission which had relied on *Klopp*[77] and which he distinguished.

He said that the Court's decision in that case in favour of a German lawyer, who had been refused admission to the Paris Bar simply because he had an office in Düsseldorf was based upon the idea that a Member State might not require a lawyer to have only one establishment throughout the Community.[78] The single practice rule of the Paris Bar, which was indistinctly applicable to nationals and non-nationals provided that a lawyer could have only one office, which must be in the district of the Tribunal de Grande Instance where he was admitted. However, the Advocate General took the view that non-discriminatory rules governing the exercise of a profession could not be tested by reference to the principle of proportionality.

The Court took a similar view to the Advocate General; finding that Article 52 EC (now Article 43 EC) only required the equal treatment of nationals and non-nationals. It attempted to explain *Klopp* on the basis that the national treatment should equally benefit those who set up a secondary establishment. Marenco suggests that this statement appears to mean that the secondary establishment in another Member State must be treated on the same basis as the main establishment of nationals.[79] The Court concluded that the rule in *Clinical Biology Services* (*Commission v. Belgium*) was indistinctly applicable, and its provisions and objectives did not lead to the conclusion that it was adopted for discriminatory purposes or that it produced discriminatory effects. With

---

77. Case 107/83, *Ordre des Avocats v. Klopp* [1984] ECR 2971.
78. Such refusal would seem to contravene the right of secondary establishment contained in the Treaty. According to Marenco, it was objectionable on other grounds: see his article 'The Notion of Restrictions on the Freedom of Establishment and Provision of Services in the Case Law of the Court', (1992) 11 YBEL 110, 121. He says that the effect of the rule was to prevent all establishment in France by foreigners established elsewhere whilst for French nationals, it only prevented the acquisition of a secondary establishment. In practice it seems this rule bore more heavily on foreign lawyers than on French lawyers, and could not be justified according to the Court, on the basis of the need of advocates to maintain contact with their clients and judges, and to respect professional rules.
79. *Op. cit.*, p. 124.

respect to the Court, it is difficult to accept the absence of such effects upon clinical laboratories whose primary establishment was in another Member State.

The same seems to be true of the Court's decision in *Fearon*,[80] in which it found that certain Irish legislation relating to the compulsory acquisition of land applied equally to Irish nationals and non nationals, and did not infringe Article 52 EC. The requirement that a company could only benefit from an exemption from the compulsory purchase of land if its shareholders and members tended on the land clearly had a more restrictive effect on persons established elsewhere. It may be that the restrictions in *Clinical Biology Services* can be justified on public health grounds,[81] but this seems somewhat doubtful. The restrictions in *Fearon* may perhaps be justified on the ground that the national agricultural policy contained in the Land Acts was compatible with general Community policies. However, the Court did not mention the question of justification in either case. The Court seems to have departed decisively from its approach in these cases in recent years.

In addition to *Klopp*, the Court made a number of other decisions in which it condemned the single practice rule. Thus, in *Commission v. France*[82] the Court of Justice found a French rule applicable to nationals and to non-nationals prohibiting doctors and dentists established in another Member State for practising in France was too restrictive, and was not justified by the need to ensure continuity of medical treatment or the application of French rules of medical ethics in France. Furthermore, the four *INASTI* cases[83] (INASTI is a Belgian social security agency for independent workers) apply similar principles to those in which the single practice rule was condemned. According to the applicable Belgian law, a self-employed person who already contributed to a Belgian social security scheme as a salaried worker did not have to contributed again in respect of his independent activity. Self-employed persons who did not contribute to a Belgian scheme were required to pay social security contributions in Belgium, even where they were salaried workers in another Member State and were compulsory affiliated to a social security scheme in that state.

The Court found that the above rules applied without direct or indirect discrimination on the grounds of nationality. However, the Court cited *Klopp* and observed that freedom of establishment was not limited to setting up one establishment within the Community, but comprised the power to set up more

---

80. Case 182/83, *Robert Fearon & Co. v. Irish Land Commission* [1984] ECR 3677.
81. See Craig and de Burca, *op. cit.*, p. 747.
82. Case 96/85, [1986] ECR 1475. See also Case C-106/91, *Ramrath v. Ministre de la Justice* [1992] ECR I-3351, in which the Court held that a Luxembourg rule providing that a person was prohibited from establishing himself in Luxembourg and practising as a company auditor there on the ground that he was established and so authorised in another Member States violated the provisions of the EC Treaty governing the right of establishment.
83. Cases 154–155/87, *RSVZ v. Wolf* [1988] ECR 3897; Case 143/87, *Stanton v. INASTI* [1968] ECR 3877; and Case C-53/95, *INASTI v. Kemmler* [1996] ECR I-703.

than one place of work therein. The totality of the Treaty provisions governing the free movement of persons was, according to the Court, designed to facilitate the pursuit by Community nationals of occupational activities of all kinds within the Community. Thus, any national regulation tending to place these nationals at a disadvantage when they wish to extend their activities beyond the territory of a single Member State, and which was not justified by any added social security protection granted to such Community citizens, was incompatible with Article 48 EC (now Article 39 EC) and Article 52 EC (now Article 43 EC).[84] As Marenco points out, it is difficult to believe that the rules in the four *INASTI* cases in fact had no indirectly discriminatory effect.[85]

It is clear that non-discriminatory rules which do not restrict the right of secondary establishment may breach Article 43 EC. This was made fairly clear in *Gullung*[86] in which the non-discriminatory rule requiring an advocate to be registered with the Bar in France was held to be justified, because it pursued an objective worthy of protection, namely the observance of moral and ethical principles and the disciplinary control of the activity of lawyers. In *Kraus v. Land Baden-Württemberg*,[87] the Court took a similar approach holding that Articles 48 and 52 EC (now Articles 39 and 43 EC) precluded the invocation of a national rule governing the use of an academic title, which applied equally to nationals and non-nationals, but which was "liable to hamper or render less attractive the exercise by Community nationals, including those of the Member State, which enacted the measures of fundamental freedoms guaranteed by the Treaty."[88]

The fourfold test employed in *Gebhard*[89] and *Centros*[90] has already been mentioned above. It will be remembered that in these cases, the Court held that national measures liable to hinder or render less attractive the exercise of fundamental freedoms guaranteed by the Treaty must be applied in a non-discriminatory way; must be justified by imperative requirements in the general interest;[91] must be suitable for obtaining the objective which they pursue and

---

84. See Case 143/87, *Stanton* [1988] ECR I-3877, paragraph 13.

85. Marenco, *op. cit.*, p. 122.

86. Case 292/86, *Gullung v. Conseil de l'Ordre des Avocats* [1988] ECR 111.

87. Case C-19/92, [1993] ECR I-1663.

88. See page 1697 of the judgment. In Case C-190/98, *Volker Graf*, 9 March 1999, (2000) 1 CMLR 741 the Court reiterated that non-discriminatory rules which impeded the free movement of workers would infringe Article 48 EC (now Article 39 EC), but that the rules governing entitlement to compensation on termination of employment in question made such compensation dependent on a future and hypothetical event, and could not be regarded as hindering freedom of movement.

89. Case C-55/94, [1995] ECR I-4165.

90. Case C-212/97, 9 March 1999, [1999] ECR I-1459.

91. Thus, for example, in Case C-222/95, *Société civile immobilière Parodi v. Banque H. Albert de Bary et Cie* [1997] ECR I-3899, the Court held that before the entry into force of the Second Banking Directive of 1989 OJ 1989 L386/11 there were imperative reasons capable of justifying the imposition by a Member State which was the state of destination of a

must not go beyond what is necessary to attain it. The Court also held in *Gebhard* that Member States must take account of the possible equivalence of diplomas, and where necessary proceed to a comparison of the knowledge and qualifications of the person involved, and those required by the national rules.

Although such cases as *Gebhard* and *Kraus* contain propositions concerning non-discriminatory restrictions, it seems that the restrictions in these cases were indirectly discriminatory. Thus, in *Gebhard*, the rules of the Milan Bar Council that a person wishing to pursue an activity as an advocate and use the title *avvocato* must be admitted to the Milan Bar, were more likely to hinder non-nationals than Italians. In the same way, the German rule that the holder of a foreign academic qualification needed
special permission to use it was more likely to have an adverse effect on a non-national rather than on a national, although the plaintiff in the action was, in fact, a German national, and could not therefore complain about discrimination on grounds of nationality.

1. Can a national invoke Article 43 against his own state?

Problems have arisen in certain of the cases concerning the situation of nationals of a Member State who wish to establish themselves or provide services in their own state. Similar problems have been encountered by workers, who have been held unable to rely on Article 48 EC (now Article 39 EC) or Regulation 1612/68 against their own Member State on behalf of themselves, nor have members of the family of workers in a Member State been held entitled to join them in that state in certain cases.[92] It seems that it is now clear that where there are rules of Community law governing the recognition of qualifications, whether these are contained in a sectoral directive or one of the two general recognition directives, they may be invoked by nationals of the host state, as well as by nationals of other states, against the public authorities of the former state.[93]

---

mortgage loan of conditions which went further than the minimum conditions required by the First Banking Directive (OJ L1977 L33/30), as far as access to the activity of credit institutions and their supervision were concerned. The minimum conditions had already been implemented in the Member States from which the loan originated: see Usher, *The Law of Money and Financial Services in the EC*, (2nd edn, Oxford EC Law Library, 1999), p. 90.

92. See Case 175/78, *R v. Saunders* [1979] ECR 1129 (woman held unable to invoke Article 48 EC impugn an order restricting her to a certain part of the national territory); Joined Cases 35 and 36/82, *Morson and Jhanjan v. Netherlands* [1992] ECR 3723 (Dutch nationals held unable to bring parents into the Netherlands from Surinam); and Case C-370/90, *R v. Immigration Appeal Tribunal and Singh ex parte Home Secretary* [1992] ECR I-4265 in which the Court held because a British spouse of an Indian national had been working in Germany, she was entitled under Community law to bring him into the United Kingdom.

93. Thus in Case-234/97, *Bobadilla v. Museo Nacional del Prado and Others* [1999] ECR I-4773, the Court of Justice held that if the profession of art restorer was regulated in

It appears, however, that in the absence of a rule of Community law providing for the recognition of a qualification, nationals will only be allowed to challenge a restriction on their establishment in their own Member State if they are able to rely upon some Community element, for example the fact that (as in *Kraus*), they have moved and obtained a qualification in another Member State. It may be possible to explain the controversial case of *Bouchoucha*,[94] in which a French national who had obtained a diploma in osteopathy in the UK, and who was prosecuted for practising as an osteopath in France (where he would have been required to have been a doctor by French law to carry on such a practice), was held not entitled under Community law to have his qualifications compared with someone qualified under national law, on the basis that there was a suspicion of the abuse of a lesser qualification by the European Court, or simply on the alternative one that the case was wrongly decided. There was then no Community directive on osteopaths, but one would have thought the comparison already mentioned was made necessary by *Heylens* and *Vlassopoulou*. There was clearly a Community element in the case, since Bouchacha had gone to the United Kingdom to receive his vocational training, and then returned to France.

The Court's decision in *Werner v. Finanzamt Aachen-Innenstadt*[95] is easier to understand. In that case the Court held that Article 52 EC (now Article 43 EC) did not prevent the imposition of a heavier tax burden on a German citizen subject to German tax law and practising in Germany if he were non-resident in Germany than if he were resident there. The Court obviously thought the rules governing establishment were inapplicable. However, the Court adopted a different approach in *Asscher*[96] which was discussed in the previous chapter. Asscher was a Netherlands national, resident in Belgium, who earned income as a director of two companies, one in the Netherlands and another in Belgium. He paid national insurance contributions in Belgium alone. Because he was not resident in the Netherlands and because he earned more than ten per cent of his income elsewhere, he was subjected for higher rate of taxation in the Netherlands and was held entitled to invoke what is now Article 43 EC (ex Article 52 EC) against his own state. This was because he had exercised his free movement rights, and was being penalised for maintaining two different establishments in two different countries. The Dutch differential rates of taxation were held to be unjustified, there being no objective basis for them.

Spain, a young woman who held a degree in fines arts restoration from Newcastle Polytechnic was entitled to seek its recognition in Spain (where she worked) under Directive 89/48 or Directive 92/31. See also Case 246/80, *C. Broekmeulen v. Huisarts Registratie Commissie* [1981] ECR 2311, in which a Dutch medical doctor who had qualified in Belgium invoked an EC directive on the recognition of medical qualifications in order to work as a general practitioner in the Netherlands, although he had not received the training for general practice needed in that state.

94. Case C-61/89, *Bouchoucha* [1990] ECR I-3551.
95. Case C-112/91, [1993] ECR I-429.
96. Case C-107/94, *Asscher v. Staatsecretaris van Financiën* [1996] ECR I-3089.

VI. ESTABLISHMENT AND COMPANIES

1. Beneficiaries

According to Article 48 EC:

> Companies or firms formed in accordance with the law of a Member State and having their registered office, central administration, or principal place of business within the Community shall, for the purposes of this chapter (on establishment) be treated in the same way as natural persons who are nationals of Member States. "Companies and firms" means companies and firms constituted under civil or commercial law including cooperation sometimes, and other legal persons constituted under civil or commercial law, including cooperative societies, and other legal persons governed by public or private law, save for those which are not profit making.

Thus, Article 48 EC require Member States to recognise companies as legal subjects enjoying the right of establishment if they are incorporated in accordance with the law of a Member State, and have their registered office, central administration or principal place of business within the Community. States which take the view that the law applicable to a company is the place of the company's headquarters argue that two of the preconditions have to be linked, and that a company's actual seat (i.e. its central administration or principal place of business) as well as its registered office must be situated within their territory. Companies established under a foreign law may thus be denied recognition in such countries. Such problems do not arise in countries in which the law applicable to a company is treated as that of its state of incorporation."

Complex conflict of laws problems arise insofar as a company or other legal person wishes to transfer its head office or primary establishment to another Member State without registering as a company or firm under the law of the host state. These problems arise from the differing governing law and recognition theories[97] that the Member States apply to companies, and from those relating to the manner in which these states deal with the prospect of the transfer of the head office of the company, or the relocation of the place were it is incorporated.[98] Many attempts have been made to provide a satisfactory selection to the problems which arise when a company incorporated in one jurisdiction wishes to relocate its activities into another.

---

97. Two German judgments have refused to recognise companies incorporated abroad, but actually running their businesses from their real seats in Germany, and treated them simply as private companies in the process of formation: *OLG Düsseldorf* [1994] WM, p. 808; *L.G. Marburg* [1994] RIW 63. According to German law, the law which governs a company is that system of law where the real seat of the company is situated, which system also governs its recognition.

98. For a very helpful discussion of these matters see Drury, 'Migrating Companies', (1999) 24 ELRev. 354.

Thus, Article 293 EC (ex Article 220 EC) envisages the need for conventions between Member States on the mutual recognition of companies and firms and on the retention of their legal personality when they wish to transfer their seat from one Member State to another. A Convention on the Mutual Recognition of Companies was actually concluded, but it failed to come into effect because the Dutch government did not ratify it.

Nevertheless, in the judgment of the Second Chamber in *Segers*, it was held to be immaterial that a company was formed in the first Member State (the United Kingdom) only for the purpose of establishing itself in another Member State by means of a branch there (in the Netherlands) where its entire business was to be conducted. The Court also held that such a company had to be given equal treatment to companies of the host state so far as social security matters were concerned. Thus, a Member State could not exclude the company's director from a national sickness benefit scheme. Such discrimination against an employee was held to indirectly restrict the freedom of the company to establish itself through the medium of an agency, branch or subsidiary, and not to be justified by the need to prevent fraud. The decision in *Segers* has been criticised on the ground that the Court of Justice should have treated the case as one of primary establishment.

The *Daily Mail* case, which received much critical comment, gives rise to the conclusion that a company has no right under Community law to change its primary establishment from one state to another. The case involved an attempt by a company registered in England to move its central management and control to the Netherlands, whilst maintaining its status as a United Kingdom company for reasons of taxation. Such a migration was permissible under English and Dutch company law, but the United Kingdom Treasury wished to place certain restrictions on the transfer, which the Daily Mail contended restricted its freedom of establishment in a manner contrary to Article 52 EC (now Article 43 EC).

The Court took the view that in the case of a company, the right of establishment is generally exercised by the setting up of agencies (as in *Centros* which is discussed immediately below), branches or subsidiaries, and may also be exercised by means of the formation of a company in another Member State. However, the Court pointed out that companies are creatures of the law, and in the present state of Community law, creatures of national law. The Court also indicated that the legislation of the Member States varies widely in regard both to the factor providing for a connection to the national territory required for the incorporation of a company, and the question whether a company incorporated under the legislation of a Member State may subsequently modify that connecting factor.[99] It also mentioned that the legislation of other states

---

99. As the Court mentioned, certain states require that not only the registered office but also the real head office or central administration or the company should be situated in their territory. These include France, Germany, Italy, Luxembourg and Portugal. The removal of the central administration from that territory may presuppose the winding up of the company. This is not true of all countries which accept the real seat or *siège réel* doctrine.

permits companies to transfer their central administration to a foreign country, but certain of them, such as the United Kingdom, make that right subject to certain restrictions, and the legal consequences of a transfer, particularly with regard to taxation, vary from one Member State to another.[100]

The Court thus found that the question whether and how the registered or real head office of a company incorporated under national law may be transferred from one Member State to another were problems not resolved by the rules governing the right of establishment. Furthermore, it said that Articles 52 and 58 EC (now Articles 43 and 49 EC) could not be interpreted as conferring on companies incorporated under the law of a Member State a right to transfer their central management and control, and their central administration to another Member State, while retaining their status as companies incorporated under the legislation of another Member State.

The dispute in *Centros* was concerned with the Danish authority's refusal to register a branch of a United Kingdom company which had never conducted business in the United Kingdom, in Denmark. The Court held that the companies could set up a branch (which, in the particular circumstances was equivalent to a primary establishment) in another Member State although it had never conducted business in the state of registration, and it was formed in the particular Member State in order to avoid the host state's rules regarding the minimum capital contribution, which would have applied had a local Danish private company been formed. Some would argue that the decision of the Court in *Centros*[101] is incompatible with the Court's decision in the *Daily Mail* case, but that does not seem necessarily to be the case. Nothing was said about the "real seat" doctrine in the decision: both the state in which the company was formed (the United Kingdom) and that in which the branch was set up, (Denmark) like Switzerland, the Netherlands, and Liechtenstein, adhere to the incorporation theory, according to which the law governing a company and its recognition is that of the place where it was incorporated. Although the Court's decision in *Centros* covered a number of matters, such as fraud or abuse, the effect of Article 56 EC (now Article 46 EC), and possible justifications for restrictions on the freedom of establishment of companies, the Court said absolutely nothing about the *Daily Mail* case. However, there may be certain *dicta* in *Centros* which are capable of being interpreted as throwing doubt on the siege reel, or real seat doctrine.[102] One can only await with interest future developments in the jurisprudence of the Court of Justice concerning this and related matters.

---

100. The United Kingdom requirement of Treasury consent to a departure was abolished by the Finance Act 1990. Section 105 of that Act, which has been consolidated into s. 185 of the Capital Gains Act 1998, treats a cessation of UK residence as a deemed disposal of the departing company's capital assets. A company which ceases to reside in the UK must settle its outstanding tax liabilities before such departure.

101. Case C-212/97, *Centros Ltd. v. Erhvervs-og Selskabsstyrelsen* [1999] ECR I-1459.

102. Note in particular paragraphs 21 and 22 of the judgment. A lively academic debate, based on their two contrasting papers, took place between Professors Behrens and Wolf Henning

It is clear from the Court's judgment that whilst fraud or abuse of rights may preclude reliance upon freedom of establishment, evidence of such fraud will necessitate more than the mere intent to avoid national legislation which itself has a restrictive effect on such freedom, and more than the simple fact that the company carriers on no business in the place of incorporation. The Court's approach to fraud or abuse of rights in *Centros* somewhat elaborates that which it has taken in a number of earlier cases, particularly concerning services, such as in *Van Binsbergen*.[103] The Court emphasised that subject to the above reservation, the host state might take any appropriate measure for combating or penalising fraud, either in relation to the company itself or in relation to its numbers, where it has been established that they are in fact attempting, by means of the formation of the company, to evade their responsibilities towards private or public creditors established in the host state.

The Court found that minimum capital requirements could not be a matter of public policy and thus within Article 56 EC (now Article 46 EC). Furthermore, when using the fourfold test familiar from *Alpine Investment* and *Gebhard*, the Court found that the practice indulged in by the Danish authorities of refusing to register the branch of a company incorporated in another Member State where it did no business was not such as to attain the alleged objective of protecting creditors, because if the company in question had conducted business in the United Kingdom, its branch would have been registered in Denmark even though Danish creditors would have been equally opposed to risk.

The Court also emphasised the importance of the disclosure requirements of the Fourth Council Directive on the annual accounts of certain types of companies[104] and of the Eleventh Council Directive concerning disclosure requirements in respect of branches opened in a Member State by certain types of company governed by the law of another state,[105] as means of creditor protection.

It also held that it was possible, contrary to the arguments of the Danish authorities, to adopt measures which were less restrictive or which interfered less with fundamental freedoms by, for example, making it possible in law for public creditors to obtain the necessary guarantees.

In view of what has been discussed above, it is interesting to note that there are special formulations in the recitals to two important directives obliging

---

Roth. Both papers were given at a symposium on this case held at King's College London on 28–29 April 2000. Professor Behrens argued that it followed from *Centros* that it was beyond the competence of Member States to request any specific link between a company in another Member State and the state of incorporation. Professor Wolf Henning Roth adopted the more conservative view that *Centros* had no effect on the rules of private international law, and that there were advantages in the real seat doctrine, which has been readopted in the German Introductory Law to the Civil Code of 1999.

103. Case 33/74, [1974] ECR 1299.
104. Council Directive 78/660, OJ 1978 L 222/11.
105. Council Directive 89/666, OJ 1989 L 395/36.

Member States to ensure that the head office[106] of a credit institution or an investment firm is situated in the same Member State as the registered office, and also providing that authorisation shall be refused where it is clear that the credit institution has opted for the legal system of one Member State in order to avoid the stricter standards in force in another Member State in which it intends to carry on business.[107]

2. Discriminatory and other rules imposing restrictions and disadvantages on companies having their registered or principal office in another Member State

There is a considerable case law governing such rules, in addition to *Segers* and *Centros*, which have been discussed in some detail above. These cases began with *Commission v. France*,[108] and they help to show how the principle of freedom of establishment applies to companies. It was made clear in *Commission v. France* that a Member State could not treat companies on a different basis for tax purposes, depending on what kind of establishment was present in their jurisdiction. The Court found that France could not treat branches of foreign companies whose principal establishments were in other Member States differently from French based insurance companies (including French subsidiaries of foreign companies). The Court did not however rule out the possibility that, in tax law, a distinction based upon the residence of a company might sometimes be justified.

The important decision of the Court in *Commission v. France* was reaffirmed in the recent cases of *Royal Bank of Scotland*[109] and *St Gobain*.[110] The first of these cases was principally concerned with differential tax treatment for national companies and companies incorporated in another Member State. The second was concerned with the refusal to grant to local branches of companies established in another Member State the tax advantages accorded to local companies. The differential treatment was condemned in both cases. In the first of these, no justification were put forward: in the second, the justifications advanced were rejected.

The earlier decision in *R. v. IRC ex parte Commerzbank AG*[111] is also of importance in the context of branches. In that case the Court held that tax disadvantages imposed on a German company (which traded in the UK through the medium of a branch established here) on the basis on the company's fiscal

---

106. This term probably has the same connotation as central administration, real seat or *siège réel*.
107. See the recitals to Council Directive 89/646 (Second Banking Directive) OJ1989 L386/11 and Council Directive 93/22 (Investment Services Directive) OJ 1993 L141/27.
108. Case 270/83, [1986] ECR 273.
109. Case C-311/97, *Royal Bank of Scotland v. Elliniko Dimosio (Greek State)* [1999] ECR I-2651.
110. Case C-307/97, *Compagnie de Saint Gobain, Zweigniederlassung Deutschland v. Finanzamt Aachen-Innenstadt* [1999] ECR I-6161.
111. Case C-330/91, *R. v. IRC ex parte Commerzbank AG* [1993] ECR I-4017.

residence rather than its seat were indirectly discriminatory, because most companies are fiscally resident in the place where they have their seat. A similar approach was taken by the Court of Justice in *ICI v. Colmer (HMIT)*[112] in which fiscally resident companies were denied certain advantages because the majority of their subsidiaries were not so resident.

In *Halliburton Services v. Staatsecretaris van Financiën*[113] the Court held that a Member State's refusal of tax relief to a transaction within a group of companies because a company involved in the transaction was incorporated in another Member State constituted a breach of the EC Treaty if such tax relief would have been granted had the company been incorporated in the first state.

X AB and Y AB[114] is another rather interesting case concerning Swedish legislation which denied Swedish companies which had exercised their right of free establishment to form subsidiaries in other Member States the right to be granted tax concessions on certain inter-group transfers. The Court mentioned that, even though the rules on freedom of establishment are primarily designed to make sure that foreign nationals and companies are treated in the host state in the same way as nationals of that state, they also prevent the Member State of origin from hindering the establishment in another Member State of one of its nationals or a company incorporated under its legislation which comes within Article 58 EC (now Article 49 EC). The national legislation in question thus violated Community law. No attempt was made to justify it on any grounds.

A point of interest in *X and Y AB* is that the Court referred expressly to the *Daily Mail* case. It is unlikely that it would have done so if, as some of the many commentators on the case think,[115] it had been overruled by *Centros*.[116]

The imposition of conditions concerning the keeping of accounts and the situation where the losses were incurred on a non resident company which had a branch but not a principal establishment in the relevant state, for the purpose of determining allowable losses and liability to tax was held to be permissible in *Futura Participations*.[117] However, the specific restrictions imposed by

---

112. Case C-264/96, [1998] ECR I-4695. In this case, a reference to the European Court of Justice was made by the House of Lords.

113. Case C-1/93, [1994] ECR I-1137.

114. Case C-200/98, *X AB and Y AB v. Rikskatteverket* [1999] ECR I-8261. This and certain other recent cases on tax discrimination were helpfully analysed by V Edwards in her paper, "*Centros* as a milestone on the road to freedom of establishment", presented to the symposium on *Centros* held at King's College on April 28–29, 2000.

115. Because both countries adhere to the *siège réel* (real seat) doctrine, there was a great deal of comment on *Centros* in German and Austrian legal journals.

116. The status of the real seat doctrine may be determined by the European Court in the near future: the Amtsgericht of Heidelberg referred a relevant case, *Wohnbau*, to the Court of Justice in March 2000. The Austrian Supreme Court has recently held that the real seat theory should be set aside if it conflicts with freedom of establishment, see *S. V. Companies Registrar Graz*, [2001] 1 CMLR 38.

117. Case C-250/95, *Futura Participations SA Singer v. Administration des Contributions* [1997] ECR I-2471.

Luxembourg were examined carefully by the Court from the viewpoint of proportionality, and the accounting requirement was found to be excessive.

In *Futura Participations*, the Court emphasised that effectiveness of fiscal supervision was an overruling requirement of general interest capable of justifying a restriction on the exercise of fundamental freedoms guaranteed by the Treaty. It reiterated this statement in its judgment in *Société Baxter and others v. Premier Ministre and others*.[118] However, the public authorities were unsuccessful in their claims in both cases. *Baxter* concerned the deductibility of research expenditure from a special levy imposed on pharmaceutical undertakings in France. It was contended that limiting the right of deduction to expenditure required on research carried out in France disadvantaged the secondary establishment of pharmaceutical undertakings established in other Member States as compared with those established in France, because research is generally carried out in the Member State where the principal establishment is situated. The Court accepted this argument. It said that "national legislation which absolutely prevents the taxpayer from submitting evidence that research expenditure carried out in other Member States has actually been carried out cannot be justified in the name of effectiveness of fiscal supervision."

In *Baars v. Inspecteur der Belastingen Particulieren*[119] the Court found that provisions of Netherlands law which granted an exemption from wealth tax where assets were invested in shares of a company established in the Netherlands and such shareholding conferred on the shareholder a definite influence over the company's decisions but granted no such exemption where the company was established elsewhere was contrary to Article 43 EC, and could not be justified on the ground of the need to safeguard tax cohesion.

Most of the decisions on the taxation of companies have involved (or have been said to involve) direct or indirect discrimination. The Court has shown itself unwilling for rather obvious policy reasons to apply Article 43 EC to non-discriminatory obstacles in the field of taxation. It will be noted that it did make use of the fourfold classification used in *Gebhard* and *Kraus* in *Centros*, but *Centros* was not concerned with taxation, but with the Danish authorities refusal to register a branch.

---

118. Case C-254/97, *Société Baxter, B. Braun Médical SA, Société Fresenius France and Laboratoires Bristol-Myers-Squibb SA v. Premier Ministre, Ministère du Travail et des Affaires sociales, Ministère de l'Economie et des Finances and Ministère de l'Agriculture, de la Pêche et de l'Alimentation* [1999] ECR I-4809, at paragraph 18; see also judgment in *Futura Participations* at paragraph 31.
119. Case C-251/98, *C. Baars v. Inspecteur der Belastingen Particulieren/Ondernemingen Gorinchem* [2000] ECR I-2787.

5 Freedom to Provide and Receive Services

I. INTRODUCTION

Article 49 EC (ex Article 59 EC) provides as follows:

> Within the framework of the provisions set out below, restrictions on freedom to provide services within the Community shall be prohibited in respect of nationals of Member States who are established in a state of the Community other than that of the person for whom the services are intended.

The Council may, acting by a qualified majority on a proposal from the Commission extend the provisions of the chapter to nationals of a third country who provide services and who are established within the Community.[1]

Article 50(3) EC provides that:

> Without prejudice to the provisions of the Chapter relating to the right of establishment, the person providing the service may, in order to do so, temporarily pursue his activity in the state where the service is provided under the same conditions as are imposed by that state on its own nationals.

Although Article 50 does not mention the situation, it is now clear that the relevant articles of the EC Treaty on services are applicable where a person moves temporarily to another Member State to receive services.[2]

As already indicated, the cross-border provision of services may take place without either party moving. The reservation concerning the conditions on which the services are provided contained in Article 50(3) EC (like the similar reservation contained in Article 43(2) EC) has been somewhat restrictively construed by the Court of Justice, which has taken the view that national regulation

---

1. See the Commission proposal of 27 January 1999 COM (1999) 3 final for a Council Directive extending the freedom to provide cross-border services to third country nationals established as self-employed persons within the EU. The proposal is based upon Article 49(2)EC. This document also contains another proposal (based on Articles 47(2) and 55 EC)) for a Directive of the EP and Council on the posting of workers who are third country nationals for the provision of services. It is intended, like the former proposal, to prevent problems from arising in relation to visas, residence permits and work permits. Both proposals provide for the issuing of an EC service provision card.
2. Joined Cases 286/82 and 26/83, *Luisi and Carbone* [1984] ECR 377 and Case 186/87, *Cowan* [1989] ECR 195. However, in Case C-70/95, *Sodemare* [1997] ECR I-3395, the Court expressly excluded the situation where a person goes to another Member State and establishes his principal residence there in order to receive services from the scope of Article 49 EC.

applicable to permanently established natural persons and firms may not necessarily be applied to the temporary activities of such persons and firms established in other Member States. Service providers in a host state benefit from a wide principle of equivalence and mutual recognition so far as their qualifications obtained in the home state are concerned.

It is clear from Article 55 EC, which makes reference to Article 45 EC, that companies formed in accordance with the law of a Member State and having their registered office, central administration or principal place of business within the Community are treated in the same way as natural persons who are nationals of the Member States so far as the cross-border provision of services is concerned. However, as is also the case with the right of establishment, where the central administration or principal place of business is outside the Community, the company's activities must have an effective and continuous link with the economy of a Member State. Such a link may not depend on nationality, particularly the nationality of the parties or of the member of the managerial or supervisory bodies or of persons holding the capital.[3]

Services are defined in Article 50(1) EC as those normally provided for remuneration, in so far as they are not governed by the provisions relating to freedom of movement for goods, capital and persons. Thus services which are funded by the state in the educational, social or cultural field do not come within Article 49 EC.[4] Although the wording of Article 50 EC would seems to lead to the conclusion that the chapter on services is subordinate to those on the basic freedoms, and the European Court has repeatedly confirmed this view in its judgments, it has given a broad and comprehensive interpretation to the concept of services, and has in fact, materially extended the ambit of the rules[5] in a number of decisions.[6] Article 50(3) EC contains a non-exhaustive list of kinds

---

3. General Programme for the abolition of restrictions on freedom to provide services, JO 1962 32.

4. Case 263/86, *Belgium v. Humbel* [1988] ECR 5365.

5. Note in this sense that Hatzopoulos, 'Recent Developments in the Case Law in the Field of Services', (2000) 37 CMLR, p. 43 at 45. However, in Case C-158/96, *Kohll* [1998] ECR I-1931 and Case C-120/95, *Decker* [1998] ECR I-1831, the Court held that the Luxembourg social security rules concerning medical treatment constituted a barrier to the freedom to provide services and could not be objectively justified, insofar as they made it hard for a person to reclaim the cost of medical treatment outside Luxembourg. The difference between these cases and those on education is that the former services were provided for remuneration, the cost eventually being refunded by the insurance company. See also Case C-157/99, *BSM Geraets-Smits v. Stichting Ziekenfonds VGZ*, n.y.r. In this case the Court held that hospital services provided in the context of a sickness insurance scheme providing benefits in kind could be classified as services within the meaning of the Treaty.

6. Thus for example the apparently residual character of the chapter on services was ignored in Case C-484/93, *Svensson and Gustavsson v. Ministre du Logement* [1995] ECR I-3955, in which it was held that bank loans in another Member State to buy a house fell within the scope of the 1988 Directive on capital movements (OJ 1989) L178/5, but that such

of services, making it clear that these include industrial, commercial, professional and craft activities. Services in the field of transport are covered by the special provisions of Part II, Title IV of the EC Treaty relating to transport. According to Article 51(2) EC, the liberalisation of banking and insurance services connected with movements of capital shall be effected in step with the liberalisation of movements of capital.

Since the liberalisation of capital movements has now been achieved, Article 51(2) EC may now be of little relevance except perhaps where the current provisions on monetary movements allow restrictions to be imposed, as may be the case with Article 58(1)(a) EC.[7]

The official authority exception and the public policy, public security and health derogations provided for in Articles 45 and 46 EC relating to establishment are made applicable by Article 55 EC to services. The relevant derogations, as is the situation with workers and establishment, are subject to the provisions of Council Directive 64/221.

II. SCOPE OF THE SERVICES PROVISIONS

1. The direct effect of Article 49 EC

Van Binsbergen[8] concerned a Dutch national who changed his residence whilst acting as legal adviser to *Van Binsbergen* before a Dutch social security court. The Dutch national was told that he could no longer continue to represent his client because, under Dutch law, only persons established in the Netherlands could act as legal advisers. A reference was made to the European Court of Justice under what was then Article 177 EC (now Article 234 EC) to determine whether the Dutch rule infringed it. The Court found that directives implementing the General Programme for the abolition of restrictions on freedom to provide services had two functions, one being to abolish restrictions, and another to facilitate the effective exercise of the freedom to provide services.

The Court held that, as far as the first function was concerned where the restriction was one based upon the ground of nationality or establishment, no directive was required. Once the transitional period had expired, Article 59 had become directly effective and the lawyer could rely on it.[9]

---

transactions also constituted services within the meaning of Article 59 EC (now Article 49 EC). See also Case C-118/96, *Safir v. Skattemyndighten i Dalarnas Län* [1998] ECR I-1897.

7. Note the valuable discussion of this provision in Usher, *The Law of Money and Financial Services in the EC*, (2nd edn, Oxford EC Law Library 1999), pp. 32–3, 56–7 and 235–8. It is suggested by Usher that it may now be the view of the Court that a situation covered by another Treaty freedom does not fall within Article 58(1)(a), which permits distinctions to be made between taxpayers on the basis of their residence.

8. Case 37/74, [1974] ECR 1229.

9. *Van Binsbergen* also established the important principle that a Member State is entitled to take measures to prevent a provider of services whose activity is wholly or principally

2. Distinction from other fundamental freedoms

The relationship between services and establishment was considered in some detail in the preceding chapter. It appears that the Court has not always been ready to recognise the subordinate nature of the rules on services in relation to those on the free movement of capital. In fact, it has frequently adopted the view that when these two sets of rules are in conflict, those on services prevail.[10] Thus, for example in *Safir*,[11] which was concerned with the Swedish method of taxation of life assurance premiums, the Court was asked to interpret the Treaty provisions on services and capital. It indicated that the provision of insurance was a service within the meaning of Article 50 EC (formerly Article 60 EC), and limited its analysis accordingly.

The distinction between a worker and a service provider is normally apparent, because the latter, unlike a worker, is *ex hypothesi*, a self-employed person. However, as Hatzopoulos[12] indicates, there are certain marginal cases in which the freedom to provide services and the freedom of movement of workers come close. This happens when a provider of services moves to another Member State together with his workforce, who may or may not, according to the relevant circumstances, be able to claim rights from the freedom of movement of workers. In either of the latter contingencies, the situation is treated as governed by the rules concerning the freedom to provide services. This is subject to the right of the host state to extend its legislation or collective agreements to any person who is employed, even temporarily within the territory, irrespective of the country in which the employer is established.[13]

In *Rush Portuguesa*, a Portuguese company engaged Portuguese workers to build a railway in France shortly after Portugal had acceded to the European Community. At the relevant time, the rules relating to freedom to provide services were binding on Portugal, but not those governing the free movement of workers, which were not yet in force. According to French law, only the French *Office d'Immigration* could recruit foreign workers. The Court of Justice held that the right to move freely to provide services also included the right for

---

directed towards another territory from exercising the freedom to provide services in order to avoid the legislation applicable in the state of destination. The principle has been confirmed in subsequent cases. The Court also recognised in *Van Binsbergen* that national regulatory rules could be objectively satisfied by the general good.

10. This approach was taken by Advocate General Elmer in his Opinion in Case C-484/93, *Svensson and Gustavsson* [1995] ECR I-2955, but the Court of Justice took the view that the contested provisions, contained in a Luxembourg housing scheme, which favoured loans being contributed by banks established in Luxembourg, were contrary both to the rules on freedom to provide services and those on capital: see Hatzopoulous, *op. cit.*, p. 43 at pp. 47–49.

11. Case C-118/96, *Jessica Safir* [1998] ECR I-1897.

12. *Op. cit.*, p. 49.

13. Case C-113/89, *Rush Portuguesa* [1990] ECR I-1417, at paragraph 18.

the company to use its own Portuguese workers. A rather similar conclusion was reached in *Vander Elst*[14] in which the relevant workers, who had Belgian but not French work permits, and who came from Morocco, with which the Community has an association agreement, were employed in French territory by a Belgian Company. The Court found that the situation involved the supply of services and not the exercise of the right of establishment, and the French legislation requiring a work permit infringed Articles 59 and 60 EC (now Articles 49 and 50 EC).

In *Arblade and Leloup*[15] the Court had to consider the limits imposed by Community law on the freedom of Member States to regulate the social protection of persons working on their territory. The relevant persons, who were employees of two service providers established in France, were deputed to work for these undertakings in Belgium, on two construction projects for comparatively short periods of time. When the matters in the main proceedings took place, Directive 96/71 on posted workers, which was considered in the chapter on the free movement of workers, was not in force. The enactment of this Directive was, of course, influenced by the jurisprudence of the Court.[16]

The Court found that the fact that the Belgian rules, which were applicable to all persons present in national territory, were categorised as public order rules, did not exempt these rules from compliance with the EC Treaty, because otherwise the primary and uniform application of community law would be undermined. It proceeded to consider whether the indistinctly applicable restrictions imposed by the Belgian legislation on the freedom to provide services could be justified by overriding reasons relating to the public interest,[17] insofar as that interest was not already safeguarded by the rules to which the provider of the service was already subject in the state of establishment, and also whether the same result could have been obtained by less restrictive rules. The Court took the view that provisions of a collective labour agreement guaranteeing a minimum wage were justified, but that in order for their infringement to justify the criminal prosecution of an employer established in another Member State, those provisions must be sufficiently precise and accessible, such that they do not render it impossible or excessively difficult in practice for such an employer to determine the obligations with which he is required to comply.

A similar approach was adopted by the Court in *Arblade and Leloup* to that

---

14. Case C-43/93, *Vander Elst v. OMI* [1994] ECR I-3803.

15. Joined Cases C-369/96 and C-376/96, [1999] ECR I-8453.

16. Note especially *Vander Elst*, paragraph 21, in which the criteria distinguishing the provision of services from the free movement of workers are set out, and Case C-272/94, *Guiot* [1996] ECR I-1905 in which it was made clear that the social protection of workers could be an overriding requirement justifying restrictions on the provision of services.

17. The social protection of workers has been treated as an overruling reason relating to the public interest in Case 279/80, *Webb* [1981] ECR 3305 at paragraph 19; the same approach was taken to the social protection of workers in the construction industry in Case C-272/94, *Guiot* [1996] ECR I-1905.

which it had taken in *Guiot*[18] to the provisions of the Belgian Collective Labour Agreement of 1988 requiring the employer to make contributions towards the bad weather stamps (*timbres-intempéries*) and the loyalty stamps (*timbres-fidélités*) schemes. It found that this obligation could be justified only if the contributions payable resulted in a social advantage for the workers and furthermore, if these workers did not enjoy in the state of establishment, by virtue of the contributions already paid by the employer in that state, protection which was essentially similar to that afforded by the rules of the Member State in which the services were provided.

As far as obligations to draw up certain documents and keep them in certain places for a certain time were concerned, the Court found that their compatibility with the Treaty essentially depended on whether they were needed in order to enable the monitoring of compliance with the relevant Belgian legislation, and on whether comparative obligations existed in the state where the undertaking was established. In *Arblade and Leloup*, as also in *Rush Portuguesa* and *Guiot*, the Court showed its preference for applying the rules on services rather than those on establishment.

The Court took the view in *HM Customs and Excise v. Schindler*[19] that where the provision of services has an ancillary effect on the distribution of goods (in this case lottery tickets), the situation should be treated as governed by Article 59 (now Article 49) EC and not by Article 30 (now Article 28) EC. This principle has been applied in other comparable cases.[20]

3. Extension of the scope of the rules governing services

The scope of the rules on services appears to have been considerably extended in the recent jurisprudence of the Court of Justice,[21] which concerned whether expenses incurred by Mr Vestergaard, a Danish national, established in Denmark, in respect of professional training courses conducted in Crete by periods established in Denmark, could be deducted as operating costs from the

---

18. Case C-272/94, *Guiot* [1996] ECR I-1905.
19. Case C-257/92, [1994] ECR I-1039.
20. See Case C-55/93, *Van Schaik* [1994] ECR I-4837 and Case C-266/96, *Corsica Ferries France* [1998] ECR I-3949. Note also Hatzopoulos *op. cit.*, p. 43 at pp. 51–5. The writer points out that where more than one fundamental freedom is involved, the Court of Justice has sometimes opted for the cumulative application of different Treaty provisions: note in particular Case C-348/96, *Donatella Calfa* [1999] 2 CMLR 1138, in which the Court made reference to Articles 48, 52 and 59 (now Articles 39, 43 and 49) EC in the final paragraph of its judgment. In Case C-124/97 *Läärä*, [1999] ECR I-6067 the Court held that it was impossible for it to decide on the impact on the rules governing the free movement of people of the relevant legislation, because it had inadequate information about its impact on the importation of slot machines. The Court thus only dealt with the impact of the legislation on the provision of services.
21. A full account of this tendency is given by Hatzopoulos, *op. cit.*, p. 43 at 59–62.

income of a company of which Mr Vestergaard was a sole shareholder. The Court answered this question in the affirmative. It mentioned the extensive ambit of Article 59 EC (now Article 49 EC) and mentioned five cases in which this broad scope had been recognised in the judgment.

Thus, the Court emphasised that Article 59 EC (now Article 49 EC) applies not only where the person providing a service and the recipients thereof are established in different Member States,[22] but also wherever a provider of services offers these services in a Member State other than that in which he is established, wherever the recipient of the services may be established.[23] In *Commission v. France*,[24] which was cited in the latter case, the Court also seems to have placed considerably less emphasis on the flow of services between Member States than on the objective situation of the parties. As Hatzopoulos points out, this objective application of the rules on services is similar to that of those governing goods.[25] Thus, in *Kohll*,[26] the Court emphasised at paragraph 46 of the judgement that the freedom to provide services was underpinned by the fundamental principle of freedom of movement.

In its decision in *Debauve*,[27] the Court held that the provisions of the Treaty on freedom to provide services could not be applied to acts whose relevant elements were confined to one Member State. However, in recent years the Court has applied the provisions of services to situations which are internal to one Member State, but which may have some limited effect on inter state trade. This seems to have been the case in *SETTG*, which was cited in *Bent Vestergaard* as authority for a different proposition. In this case, the Court condemned the Greek requirement that tourist guides in possession of the requisite national licence should be bound by an employment relationship with the agencies for which they worked which only had an effect on Greek tourist guides, because in a previous judgment,[28] the Court had held that tourist guides from other Member States could provide services in Greece without possessing the Greek national licence. The Court justified its approach on the ground that in some circumstances the measure could have some effect on intra-state trade.

However in *RI SAN Srl*,[29] a case involving questions concerning the procedure for choosing the entity entrusted with running an Italian waste collection service,

---

22. See Case C-381/93, *Commission v. France* [1994] ECR I-5145.
23. See Case C-398/95, *SETTG v. Ypourgos Ergasias* [1997] ECR I-3113.
24. See Case C-381/93, [1994] ECR I-5145.
25. Hatzopoulos, *op. cit.*, p. 43 at p. 60.
26. Case C-158/96, [1998] ECR I-1931.
27. Case 52/79, *Procureur du Roi v. Debauve* [1980] ECR 833. Mancini AG argued in Case C-352/85, *Bond van Adverteerders v. Netherlands* [1988] ECR 2085 that because television services were capable of transcending frontiers, the provision of such services came within Article 59 EC (now Article 49 EC). The Court did not find it necessary to consider his suggestion.
28. Case C-198/89, *Commission v. Greece* [1991] ECR I-727.
29. Case C-108/98, [1999] ECR I-5219, paragraph 24.

the Court found that Article 55 EC (now Article 45 EC) did not apply to a situation in which all the facts were confined to within a single Member State and which did not therefore have any connecting link with one of the situations envisaged by Community law in the area of the freedom of movement for persons and freedom to provide services. The difference between this case and *SETTG* seems to be the absence in the former case of any possible connecting link with Community law.

4. Circumvention of the law and fraud

The Court has considered the above matters in its case law concerning freedom to supply services, freedom of establishment, the free movement of goods, social security, the free movement of workers, the common agricultural policy and company law.[30] The cases have involved attempts by nationals of a Member State, under cover of the rights created by the Treaty, improperly to circumvent their national legislation, or to improperly or fraudulently take advantage of provisions of Community law. The Court has held that Member States may take measures designed to prevent such activities.

The first decision of this nature in the field of services was *Van Binsbergen*[31] in which the Court held that a state must be able to stop persons whose activities were entirely or mainly directed towards its territory from trying to avoid the rules which would apply to them if they were established there. The Court held that such persons could be denied the benefit of the provisions relating to services and be treated under the provisions of establishment. It reiterated the approach which it took towards the use of the law as a cloak for fraud in *Van Binsbergen* in a number of subsequent cases.[32]

However, the recent jurisprudence of the Court on this matter as far as it relates to the free movement of services, has shown an alteration in its position. Thus, for example in *TV 10 SA*,[33] the Dutch authorities took the view that a television broadcaster established in Luxembourg which broadcast the great bulk of its programmes to the Netherlands, was to be treated as a domestically established undertaking. The Court of Justice, which departed from its previous case law, adopted the view that "the circumstance that *TV10* established itself in the Grand Duchy of Luxembourg in order to escape the Netherlands legislation does not preclude its broadcasts from being regarded as services within the meaning of the Treaty." It made it clear that the latter position was distinct

---

30. The relevant cases are referred to in paragraph 24 of the Court's judgment in Case C-212/97, *Centros* [1999] ECR I-1459.
31. Case 33/74, [1974] ECR 1299, paragraph 13.
32. See Case 39/75, *Coenen v. Social-Economische Raad* [1975] ECR 1547 and the insurance cases, i.e. Case 220/83, *Commission v. France* [1986] ECR 3663; Case 252/83, *Commission v. Denmark* [1986] ECR 3713; Case 205/84, *Commission v. Germany* [1986] ECR 3755 and Case 206/84, *Commission v. Ireland* [1986] ECR 3817.
33. Case C-23/93, *TV 10 SA* [1994] ECR I-4795.

from the measures that a Member State might take to prevent a provider of services established in another Member State from evading its legislation.

Furthermore, in *VT4*,[34] in which the facts resembled those of *TV10*, the Court took the view that the Treaty did not prohibit an undertaking from exercising the freedom to provide services even though it did not do so in the Member State of establishment. It has been suggested (it is submitted correctly) by Roth[35] that where a service provider is totally inactive in the state of his establishment, that service provider can no longer argue that because he satisfies the relevant rules in his home state, he is not required to comply fully with those of the host state.

As pointed out in the chapter on freedom of establishment, the Court further considered the problem of abuse of EC law in *Centros*. It will be remembered that in this case which, as is pointed out by Hatzopoulos,[36] transferred the *TV10* solution to the field of the establishment of companies, the Court held that the intention of the parties to circumvent EC law did not preclude the application of the relevant Treaty rules, but allowed Member States to adopt measures to prevent attempts by its nationals to abuse such rules. The Court held (in paragraph 25, of its judgment) that national courts might, on a case by case basis, take account on the basis of objective evidence of abuse or fraudulent conduct on the part of the persons concerned so as to deny them, where appropriate, the benefit of the relevant provisions of Community law on which they seem to rely, they must nevertheless assess such conduct on the basis of objective criteria.[37] According to paragraph 28 and 29 of the judgment in *Centros*, neither the choice of the most favourable place of formation, nor the fact that the companies did not carry on any business there, is sufficient to prove the existence of abuse or fraudulent conduct.

No doubt future case law will indicate what is sufficient for the latter purposes. It is also noteworthy that the Court held that although combating fraud cannot justify a practice of refusing to register a branch of a company which has its registered office in another Member State, this does not prevent the host state from adopting any appropriate measure for preventing or penalising fraud either in relation to the company itself, if need be in cooperation with the Member State in which it was registered, or in relation to its members, where it has been established that they are attempting, by means of the formation of the company, to evade their obligations towards private or public creditors established on the territory of the Member State concerned.

---

34. Case C-56/96, *VT4* [1997] ECR I-3143.
35. Roth, 'Wettbewerb der Mitgliedstaaten oder Wettbewerb der Hersteller, Plädoyer für eine Neubestimmung des Art. 34 EGV', (1995) 159 ZHR 1, p. 78.
36. *Op. cit.*, p. 64.
37. Note in the same sense Case C-206/94, *Brennet v. Paletta* [1996] ECR I-2357, "*Paletta II*", paragraph 24.

5. Freedom to receive services

The above freedom is not mentioned in the EC Treaty but it is referred to in the General Programme on the abolition of restrictions on the provision of services, as well as in Article 1(1) of Directive 64/221 and in Article 1(1)(b) of Directive 73/148. The former provision refers to freedom of movement for employed or self-employed persons or the recipient of services, whilst the latter one places an obligation on Member States to abolish restrictions on the movement and residence of nationals of Member States wishing to go to another Member State as recipients of services. In *Luisi and Carbone*,[38] the Court made it clear that the relevant provisions of the EC Treaty applied to recipients as well as providers of services. The plaintiffs in the main action were fined for exceeding the maximum permitted amount of foreign currency which could be exported from Italy for use abroad. They argued that since they had exported the currency paid by them for services as tourists and a consideration for medical treatment in another Member State, the currency restrictions were in breach of Community law. The Court of Justice was asked whether the circumstances fell within the Treaty provisions on capital, or whether they were covered by the rules concerning the liberalisation of payments connected with services contained in the Treaty.

The Court found that the rules on services were applicable. It held that it was clear from the General Programme which required the abolition of impediments for payments for services, especially where the provision of such services is limited on by restrictions in respect of the payments therefore, which requirement was implemented by Council Directive 63/340/EEC,[39] that the freedom to provide services included the freedom for recipients of service to go to another Member State in order to receive a service there without being obstructed by restrictions, even as to payments. The Court also held that persons receiving medical treatment and persons travelling for the purpose of education or business are to be regarded as recipients of services. It seems to follow from *Sodemare*[40] however, that persons who establish their principal residence in another Member State in order to receive services there for an indefinite period of time are not covered by the rules governing services, but those governing establishment.

According to Articles 2 and 3 of Directive 73/148, a person who is a national of a Member State and who wishes to go from one Member State to another to provide or receive services there must be granted to leave the relevant Member State and enter the host state simply on the production of a valid identity card or passport. These rights are also enjoyed by the members of the family of such

---

38. Joined Cases 286/82 and 26/83, *Luisi and Carbone v. Ministero del Tesoro* [1984] ECR 377.
39. JO 1963; p. 1609.
40. Case C-70/95, *Sodemare* [1997] ECR I-3395. Services performed for tourists were also in question in Case C-348/96, *Calfa* [1999] ECR I-11; 2 CMLR 1138, in which a life ban from its territory imposed by Greece on an Italian tourist found in possession of drugs was found disproportionate and the very negation of the freedom to provide services.

a person. It is not clear whether there are any grounds on which a state may refuse to allow a person within its jurisdiction to leave it for the purpose of receiving services in another Member State. In *SPUC v. Grogan,*[41] Advocate General van Gerven appeared to take the view that it would be a disproportionate restriction on the freedom to travel to another Member State where their provision was lawful. The services in question were those of abortion clinics. It was not necessary for the Court to consider this question in its judgment, but a similar one came up before the Irish Supreme Court, in proceedings initiated by the Irish Attorney General intended to restrain a young woman from leaving Ireland for the purpose of terminating her pregnancy. It was submitted that she had a right to travel under Community law. However the matter was resolved in favour of the young woman purely as a matter of domestic constitutional law.

In another case[42] which was dealt with by domestic courts in the United Kingdom, an indirect restriction upon the freedom of a woman to travel to another Member State in order to receive medical services taking the form of artificial insemination was under consideration. She had been refused permission under the Human Fertilisation and Embryology Act to use a quantity of her husband's sperm, taken from him when he was unconscious before his death, and unable to give consent. She wished to take the sample to another Member State where its use would have been legal, but the Health Authority refused to release it, on the ground that this would be illegal under the relevant legislation. Her action in the High Court failed, but she succeeded in the Court of Appeal on the ground that such a refusal would constitute an unjustifiable interference with her right under EC law to travel for the purpose of receiving services. Recipients and providers of services may obtain a right of abode or residence permit provided that they show the national authorities of the host state the identity card or passport with which they entered the territory, and proof that they are a recipient or provider of services.[43] The right of residence for persons providing or receiving services is of the same duration as that for which the services are provided.

It is of interest to determine what rights are available to recipients of services other than those mentioned above of entry and residence. It would seem that they are in a rather similar position to those who provide services in a host state, and that, to some extent, they may be able to claim equal treatment to nationals of the host state, in accordance with the provisions of Articles 12 and 49 EC.[44] However, it would seem that there are certain social benefits which

---

41. Case C-159/90, *SPUC v. Grogan* [1991] ECR I-4685.
42. *R. v. Human Fertilisation and Embryology Authority ex parte DB* [1997] 2 CMLR 591.
43. Directive 73/148, Article 6.
44. This is the position of persons established in such a state: note for example Case 197/84, *Steinhauser v. City of Biarritz* [1985] ECR 1819; Case 63/86, *Commission v. Italy* [1988] ECR 29; and Case 305/87, *Commission v. Greece* [1989] ECR 1461.

may be unavailable to the temporary migrant.[45] However, the availability of such benefits cannot be entirely excluded.

In *Cowan*[46] the Court held that the failure to compensate under the French criminal compensation scheme a British tourist who was receiving services in France, and who was mugged in Paris, constituted discriminatory treatment within the meaning of Article 49 EC (ex Article 59 EC). This case shows a more positive approach to the granting of equal access to social benefits to temporary migrants than that taken in *Commission v. Italy* (social housing).

In *Commission v. Spain*[47] the Court of Justice found that a system by which Spanish nationals and residents were entitled to free admission into museums whilst other Member State nationals over the age of 21 had to pay an entrance fee infringed Articles 6 and 59 EC (now Articles 12 and 49 EC). This (and possibly *Cowan*) appears to conflict with *Humbel*,[48] in which the Court held that Article 59 EC (now Article 49 EC) did not apply to the receipt of services funded by the state in the educational, social and cultural field. It seems that the Court took the view in *Cowan* that the service being received was not the compensation, and that in *Commission v. Spain* was not the entry fee. These services were instead those of establishments patronised by the tourists in each case, for which they paid remuneration, thus bringing them within the scope of the Treaty. Thus, the refusal to grant the relevant benefits had at least some tangible connection with the receipt of services as a tourist.[49]

The exact scope of the principle of non-discrimination as applied to recipients of services is unclear, but it may be that the use of the concept of European citizenship by the Court in the future will reinforce the present increasing tendency to prohibit discrimination against such persons. Thus, in paragraph 14 of its judgment in *Bickel and Franz*,[50] the Court stated that "the exercise of the right to move and reside freely in another Member State is enhanced if the citizens of the Union are able to use a given language to communicate with the administrative and judicial authorities of a state on the same footing as its nationals." However, the Court's reservations in *Humbel* according to which

---

45. This seems to follow from Case 63/86, *Commission v. Italy* [1988] ECR 29 in which case the Court held that providers of services would in most cases not satisfy the conditions, of a non-discriminatory nature, for access to social housing.

46. Case 186/87, *Cowan v. Le Trésor Public* [1989] ECR 195.

47. Case C-45/93, *Commission v. Spain* [1994] ECR I-911.

48. Case 263/86, *Belgium v. Humbel* [1988] ECR 5365. It is clear from Article 50 EC that the services must be economic in nature, i.e. they must be provided for remuneration. In Case C-157/99, *Geraets-Smits*, the Court held, (contrary to the opinion of the AG) that the hospital services in question were provided for remuneration which was furnished by the sickness funds.

49. See in this sense Craig and de Burca, *EU Law: Text, Cases and Materials,* (2nd edn, OUP, 1998), pp. 769 and 774.

50. Case C-274/96, [1998] ECR I-7637.

Article 49 EC is only applicable to services provided for remuneration is likely, for obvious economic reasons, to remain of some significance.

III. JUSTIFICATIONS FOR RESTRICTIONS

1. Treaty rules

Justifications for restrictions may result from specific provisions of the EC Treaty such as Articles 45, 46 and 86(2) EC, or from the now familiar concept of overriding (or imperative) reasons of public interest.[51] Article 46 EC was implemented by Council Directive 64/221, which allows special measures to be taken in relation to the entry and residence of foreign nationals on the grounds of public policy, public security and public health. The compatibility of the expulsion for life of a tourist who was convicted of a drugs offence was in question in the Court's preliminary ruling in *Donatella Calfa*.[52] The Court applied well established principles concerning the exercise of powers of exclusion and deportation on public policy grounds which it had formulated in the contest of its jurisprudence on restrictions on the free movement of workers in this case. The limitations on the free movement of persons on grounds of public policy, public security and public health are fully considered in a later chapter.

In *Corsica Ferries France*,[53] the Court held that an obstacle to the free movement of services may not infringe Article 49 EC (ex Article 59 EC) when the conditions for the application of Article 86(2) EC (ex Article 90(2) EC) were present. Article 86(2) provides that undertakings charged with the provision of services of general economic interest may, under certain conditions, escape the application of the Treaty rules where this is necessary fore the accomplishment of the special tasks assigned to them. *Corsica Ferries France* concerned Italian legislation which made it obligatory for large vessels entering certain Italian ports to make use of mooring services provided by a state monopoly, which was alleged to charge both excessive prices and differential prices in different ports.

The Court concluded that there were reasons of public security which would justify the grant of exclusive rights in relation to mooring services. It adopted the view that the mooring services were of general economic interest within the meaning of Article 86(2) EC (ex Article 90(2) EC). A universal service had to be provided at anytime and to any user in order to ensure safety in the waters of the ports. The Court adopted the view that, in order to sustain this universal service, the price charged for mooring services might include a supplement to cover the financial burden of providing the universal mooring service, and that differential tariffs would not infringe Article 49 EC. Thus, where a service activity

---

51. Both Articles 45 and 46 EC and the public interest exception were considered by the Court of Justice in Case C-67/98, *Questore di Verona v. Zenatti* [1999] ECR I-7289; [1999] 1 CMLR 201, which concerned the Italian legislation relating to the taking of bets.
52. Case C-348/96, [1999] ECR I-11; 2 CMLR 1138.
53. Case C-266/96, [1998] ECR I-3949.

has the features of a universal service, Article 86(2) EC will justify the imposition of restrictions on the free provision of services. However, it does not seem that Member States may establish such universal services without having some objective justification for doing so.

2. Other grounds for justifications developed by the Court

The Court has often found that rules imposing restrictions on the provision of services were justified by imperative or overriding reasons of public interest. Such justification is now thought not to be available except where the relevant restrictions apply without any discrimination in law or in fact. It may be that this concept of overriding reasons has sometimes also been applied to discriminatory measures.

The first time that the Court adumbrated such an approach to restrictions in the field of the provision of services was in its decision in *Van Binsbergen*.[54] In that case, the Court held that specific requirements imposed on a person providing services would not be incompatible with the Treaty when they have as their purpose the application of professional rules justified by the general good in particular rules relating to organisation, qualifications, professional ethics, supervision and liability which are binding on any person established in the state where the service is provided. It also held that even the imposition of a requirement of establishment on persons concerned with the administration of justice was permissible where it was objectively justified in order to ensure the observance of professional rules of conduct.

Thus, according to the Court's judgment in *Van Binsbergen*, a restriction may be justified if it adopted in pursuance of a public interest which is not incompatible with Community aims; and the rules are indistinctly applicable both to persons established within the state and those established outside it, and the rules are objectively justified. Such objective justification involves the determination of whether there is a genuine need for the rule, whether it is appropriate in achieving its purpose, and whether the interest furthered by the rule is incapable of being met by less restrictive means. The Court held that the residence requirement could not be justified in *Van Binsbergen*, because the public interest in the administration of justice could be complied with by imposing a requirement that the non-resident lawyer providing services in the Netherlands should maintain an address for service there.

The Court has adopted the view that an economic aim cannot relate to the general interest, but it has been accused[55] of using this principle, recently stated in *SETTG v. Ypourgos Ergasias*[56] in an inconsistent way. In the latter case, the Court held that maintaining industrial peace was an economic aim, and could

---

54. Case 33/74, [1974] ECR 1299.
55. Hatzopoulos, *op. cit.*, at pp. 78–9.
56. Case C-398/95, [1997] ECR I-3113.

not constitute a reason of general interest, justifying restrictions on the provision of services. However, it has been suggested by Hatzopoulos that objectives of an economic nature have sometimes been admitted as justifying such restrictions. Thus, in two judgments of the Court concerning the compatibility of the Luxembourg social security system[57] with Article 28 (ex Article 30) EC and 49 (ex Article 59) EC, the Court stipulated that aims of a purely economic nature could not justify a barrier to a fundamental freedom recognised by the Treaty. Nevertheless, it went on to state that "the risk of seriously undermining the financial balance of the social security system may constitute an overriding reason in the general interest capable of justifying a barrier of that kind."[58] Although the cases are difficult to reconcile, it may be that the Court is willing to recognise economic aims of a structural character as overriding reasons, but is not willing to extend this recognition to economic aims of other kinds.

The principles according to which restrictions on the provisions of services could be justified set out in *Van Binsbergen* were also applied by the Court in *Webb*,[59] a case involving manpower services. In this case, the Court also made it clear that, when deciding whether a restriction on the provision of services was proportionate and necessary, the Court must consider whether the provider was subject to similar restrictions or requirements in the Member State in which he or she was established. It would seem that a restriction is unlikely to be upheld by the Court if it is incompatible with fundamental rights which form part of Community law. This may follow from *ERT*,[60] in which the Court held that it could review whether when a Member State relied on the derogation permitted by Article 56 EC (now Article 46 EC) to justify rules which are likely to obstruct the exercise of the freedom to provide services, the Court could review whether this justification was compatible with the fundamental rights the observance of which is ensured by the Court. A similar principle would seem to apply to one of the imperative reasons resulting from the public interest recognised by the Court.

The principles set out by the Court in *Van Binsbergen* and *Webb* were applied and to some extent refined in the four insurance cases decided by the European Court in 1986.[61] These cases were direct actions under Article 169 EC (now Article 226 EC), in which the Court applied the threefold test set out above directly to the restrictions in question.[62] Thus, in *Commission v. Germany*, the

---

57. Case C-120/95, *Decker* [1998] ECR I-1831 Case C-158/96, *Kohll* [1998] ECR I-1931.

58. *Decker*, paragraph 39; *Kohll*, paragraph 41.

59. Case 279/80, [1981] ECR 3305.

60. Case C-260/89, *Elliniki Radiophonia Tileorassiae v. Dimotiki/Etaria Pliroforissis and Sotirios Kouvelas* [1991] ECR I-2925.

61. See Case 205/84, *Commission v. Germany* [1986] ECR 3755; Case 206/84, *Commission v. Ireland* [1986] ECR 3817; Case 220/83, *Commission v. France* [1986] ECR 3663; and Case 252/83, *Commission v. Denmark* [1986] ECR 3713.

62. Note in this sense Craig and de Burca, *op. cit.* p. 778. On the insurance cases, note in particular D Edward, 'Establishment and Services; The Analysis of the Insurance Cases', (1989) 12 EL Rev. 231.

Court considered an authorisation and residence requirement imposed under German legislation on companies established in other Member States which were providing particular types of insurance services in Germany. The authorisation and establishment requirements applied to all EC undertakings, wherever established, which were providing services in Germany.

The Court placed emphasis on the burdensome nature of the authorisation requirement in respect of insurance activities carried on by non-established insurers. It found that this requirement (like that of establishment) constituted a restriction on the freedom to provide services, as it increased the cost of the insurance services in the state in which they were provided, in particular where the insurer conducted business in that state only occasionally.[63] It found that such requirements were lawful only if justified by imperative reasons relating to the public interest, and that the interest was not already protected by the rules of the state of establishment, and that the same result could not be reached by less restrictive rules.[64] The Court accepted that the insurance section was a sensitive area from the viewpoint of the protection of the consumer both as a policy holder and an insured person. It also said that the co-ordinating directives already enacted in the field of insurance had not dealt with all important matters relating to the assets and reserves of insurance companies. Thus, the Court found that an important public interest was in question.

After applying the above-mentioned criteria, the Court found that one category of requirements was lawful and the other unlawful. As far as direct insurance was concerned, the Court found that a Member State was entitled to ensure the observance of its own rules on technical reserves and on the conditions of insurance relating to services provided on its territory, provided that these rules did not go further than necessary to protect policy holders and persons assured, and that there was no duplication of control. However, as far as coinsurance was concerned, the Court held that the requirement that the lead insurer should be authorised was unnecessary. Because the clients were large undertakings, the arguments drawn from consumer protection could not be sustained, a fact which was confirmed by the absence of any authorisation for the other consumers.

The Court rejected the German requirement of establishment, as it had the corresponding Dutch requirement in *Van Binsbergen*. It said that such a requirement could completely frustrate the aims of Article 59 EC, and that it would be necessary to demonstrate that it was "indispensable for achieving the objective pursued."[65]

The reasoning in the three *Tourist Guide*[66] decisions is rather similar to that in the insurance cases. In these cases, France, Italy and Greece were found to

---

63. *Commission v. Germany*, paragraph 28.
64. *Ibid*, paragraph 29.
65. *Ibid*, paragraph 52.
66. These cases are Case C-154/89, *Commission v. France* [1991] ECR I-659; Case C-180/89, *Commission v. Italy* [1991] ECR I-709; and Case C-198/89, *Commission v. Greece* [1991] ECR I-727.

have infringed Community law. This infringement consisted of national provision requiring a tourist guide to possess a licence obtained after an examination even when accompanying groups of tourists from another Member States and the service was performed at places other than museums or historic monuments. The national provisions in question were indistinctly applicable to nationals and foreigners, and did not necessarily duplicate conditions already fulfilled. The Court accepted that the relevant provisions pursued interests which could constitute overriding reasons such as the appreciation of artistic, historic and archaeological treasures, the spread of knowledge of the cultural and artistic heritage, the conservation of that heritage and consumer protection. Nevertheless, the Court held that all the relevant requirements as to the passing of an examination and the obtaining of a licence could not be imposed on a tourist guide established in another Member State, without preventing the provisions of the freedom to provide services having any useful effect.[67]

The Court of Justice found that less stringent rules could have been used to achieve the desired result. The use of local guides, which would have been encouraged by the relevant measures, would have resulted in difficulties, especially of a linguistic character for the tourists. The measures were thus held to be disproportionate to the aims pursued.

3. The treatment of indistinctly applicable rules

In its subsequent case law, the Court made it quite clear that restrictions which were neither discriminatory in law of in fact might come within the ambit of Article 59 EC (now Article 49 EC) and thus need to be justified on the grounds already explained. It has also made it clear that the Court's jurisprudence on objective justification set out in such decisions as *Van Binsbergen* and the four insurance cases is applicable outside the field of professional activities.

Before the Courts decision in *Säger v. Dennemeyer*[68] which confirmed such an assumption there were reasons to think that a restriction which was non-discriminatory in law and fact still came within the ambit of Article 59 EC (now Article 49 EC) and required objective justification. This conclusion followed from the fact that one of the grounds for the justification of a restriction was that it was indistinctly applicable; however indistinctly applicable rules are capable of imposing a dual burden on providers of services and this was the case in certain of the decisions mentioned above. It also appeared from the *Lawyers' Services Case*,[69] and especially from the opinion of Advocate General de Cruz Vilarca in that case, that genuinely non-discriminatory rules might come within Article 59 EC (now Article 49 EC) and require objective justification in accordance with the criteria mentioned above. The *Lawyers' Services Case* was

---

67. Case C-154/89, *Commission v. France* [1991] ECR I-659, paragraph 12.
68. Case C-76/90, [1991] ECR I-421.
69. Case 427/85, *Commission v. Germany* [1988] ECR 1123.

concerned in part with the rule which used to be contained in Paragraph 52(2) of the German *Bundesrechtsanwaltsordnung* according to which an advocate (*Rechtsanwalt*) who wished to practise before one of the German superior courts had to be admitted to do so by that judicial body. This rule was indistinctly applicable to lawyers established in Germany and those established in another Member State.

The Court found that lawyers established in Germany had the right to practise before one and sometimes two German judicial authorities, but that a lawyer providing services who was established in another Member State was not in a position to be admitted to practise before a German court. It thus held that the rule of territorial exclusivity could not be applied to activities of a temporary nature pursued by lawyers in other Member States, because the conditions at law and fact applicable to such lawyers were not comparable to those applicable to lawyers established on German territory.[70]

It is in fact difficult to see how the territoriality rule burdened a lawyer established in another Member State more than the one established in Germany. As the Advocate General indicated, it would have had the same impact on a German lawyer established and admitted to practice in a region (land) different from that in which he or she wished to provide a legal service as it would on a lawyer established in another Member State. De Cruz Vilaca AG took the view that the territoriality rule did not infringe Article 59 EC (now Article 49 EC). The view is taken in Craig and de Burca's textbook that the case supports the view that even genuinely non-discriminatory restrictions will infringe Article 59 EC (now Article 49 EC) unless objectively justified.[71]

The idea that indistinctly applicable rules may breach the rules contained in Article 30 EC (now Article 28 EC) governing the free movement of goods unless they are necessary to satisfy certain mandatory requirements was accepted by the Court in *Cassis de Dijon*.[72] Since its decision in *Säger v. Dennemeyer*[73] it has taken an approach to services similar to that applied in *Cassis de Dijon*, to goods. However, as is shown below, there remain some differences between the Court's approach to the freedom to provide services and the free movement of goods. Dennemeyer was a United Kingdom provider of computerised patent renewal services, who provided such services in Germany. In that country, this activity was reserved to patent attorneys by law, and the latter needed authorisation which was granted only on the basis of a professional qualification. *Säger*, a German patent agent, challenged Dennemeyer's right to provide such services in Germany. Dennemeyer argued that the German rules were an obstacle to the free movement of services, and infringed Articles 59 and 60(3) EC (now Articles 49 and 50(3) EC).

---

70. See paragraphs 41 and 42, of the Court's judgment.
71. *EC Law: Text, Cases and Materials*, (2nd edn, OUP, 1999), p. 712.
72. Case 120/78, *Rewe-Zentral AG v. Bundesmonopolverwaltung für Branntwein* [1979] ECR 649.
73. Case C-76/90, [1991] ECR I-421.

Advocate General Jacobs said that it was not easy to see why a person established in one Member State who provides services in other Member States should be required to comply with the detailed requirements in force in each state. Such a requirement would make a single market unattainable in the field of services. He added that services should be treated in the same way as goods, and that non-discriminatory restrictions on the provision of services should be treated in the same way as non-discriminatory restrictions on the provision of goods under the *Cassis de Dijon* line of case law. He said that this appeared particularly appropriate where the nature of the service was not such as to involve the provider moving physically between Member States, but is instead provided by post or telecommunications. The Advocate General took the view that "if an undertaking complies with the legislation of the Member State in which it is established, it should be able to provide services in another Member State, even though the provision of such services would not normally be permissible under the laws of the second Member State."

The Court basically agreed with the Opinion of the Advocate General. It held that Article 59 (now Article 49) EC applied to indistinctly applicable measures which might prohibit or impede the activities of a service provider established in another Member State where he lawfully provides services.[74] It set out four criteria with which restrictive rules were required to comply which are very similar to those which it subsequently adopted in *Gebhard*.[75] First, rules limiting the freedom to provide services must be justified by imperative reasons relating to the public interest. These rules must apply to all persons and undertakings pursuing an activity in the state of destination insofar as that relevant interest is not protected by the rules to which the service provider is subject in the state of establishment. The requirements must be objectively necessary to ensure compliance with professional rules and must not exceed what is necessary to attain these objectives. Given the fairly simple character of the services provided, the restriction on trade was found disproportionate in *Säger*. The four criteria set out by the court relating to justification are similar to the two principles set out in *Cassis de Dijon*[76] but it is noteworthy that, whilst the latter case provides examples of mandatory requirements, which have been added to by the Court of Justice in its subsequent jurisprudence, and which may permit the justification of indistinctly applicable measures, *Säger* provides no examples of what must be treated as "imperative reasons of public interest". Abundant examples have, however, been provided by the Court in its considerable volume of relevant case law. Both *Säger* and *Cassis de Dijon* make use of the principles of proportionality and the recognition of the rule to which the service provider, or the person

---

74. See paragraph 12 of the Court's judgment.
75. Case C-55/94, [1995] ECR I-4165.
76. Case 33/76, *Rewe-Zentrale AG v. Direktor der Landeswirtschaftskammer Rheinland* [1976] ECR 1229 ("*Cassis de Dijon*").

marketing the goods in the host state, is subject to, in the host state or the state of importation.[77]

4. Justification in cases unconnected with professional rules

Säger and the other cases so far mentioned in this section on reasons justifying restrictions and the free movement of services were all concerned with professional rules. However, similar criteria for justification to those set out in *Säger* have been accepted in cases unconnected with such rules. Thus, a similar approach to that taken in *Säger* was employed by Van Gerven AG in *Society for the Protection of the Unborn Child v. Grogan.*[78] In this case, the applicant society obtained an injunction from the Irish Supreme Court preventing the distribution in Ireland by Irish student bodies of information about the availability of abortion services in the United Kingdom. It was undisputed that the student associations had no connections with abortion clinics in other Member States.

In 1983, after heated debate, a constitutional amendment approved by referendum added Article 40.3.3 to the Irish Constitution, which acknowledged the right to life of the unborn. The provision of such information was found by the Supreme Court to be contrary to the 1983 amendment. It did not however overturn the High Court's decision to refer questions to the European Court of Justice for a preliminary ruling. The defendant in the action begun in the Irish High Court had argued that the restriction imposed by Irish law on freedom to provide abortion services contravened Article 59 EC (now Article 49 EC).

The Advocate General found that although the restriction was indistinctly applicable, it constituted an impairment to the free provision of abortion services. However, it was justifiable for imperative reasons of public interest, the protection of the life of unborn children, and was not disproportionate.

The Court took a different approach from the Advocate General finding that the medical termination of pregnancy for remuneration was a service within Article 60 (now Article 50) EC. It found that the arguments put forward by SPUC concerning the morality of abortion could not influence its decision on the former matter. It held that it was not its task to substitute its assessment for that of the Member States where abortion was practised legally. Nevertheless, it held that the link between the activities of the students' associations and the medical termination of pregnancies carried on in clinics in another Member State was too tenuous for the prohibition on the dissemination of information to be regarded as a restriction within Article 59 (now Article 49) EC.

The approach taken by the Court in *Säger* was clearly adopted again by the Court in *HM Customs and Excise v. Schindler*[79] a case which had nothing to do

---

77. See Weatherill and Beaumont, *op. cit.*, pp. 686–7 and Steiner and Woods, *Textbook on EC Law*, (7th edn, Blackstone Press, 2000), pp. 331, 338–9 in this sense.
78. Case C-159/90, *SPUC v. Grogan* [1991] ECR I-4685.
79. Case C-275/92, [1994] ECR I-1039.

with professional qualifications and rules. The Schindlers, who were acting agents for a German lottery promoter sent advertisements and application forms from the Netherlands to the United Kingdom, inviting participation in a German lottery. These items were seized by the Commissioners acting in accordance with a British policy of controlling large scale lotteries, no matter what the nationality of the promoter or which Member State from which they originated. A request for a preliminary ruling was made to the European Court of Justice, which found that the measures in question constituted a restriction on cross-border lottery services, which was likely to prohibit or otherwise impede them. However, it was found that the measures were justified by overriding reasons of public interest. The laws contributed to the prevention of crime, prevented the encouragement of habitual gambling, and had other positive features. The Court also found that the measures were not disproportionate because of the considerable rule of thumb.

It is of interest to note that the Court of Justice held that similar justifications existed for the Finnish legislation which grants to a single public body exclusive rights to operate slot machines in *Läärä*.[80] The Court employed a fourfold test for justification similar to that which it had used in *Säger* in paragraph 31 of its judgment.[81] It also mentioned Articles 55 and 56 EC (now Articles 45 and 46 EC) as possible grounds of justification for the relevant restrictions. It should be remembered that these articles permit restrictions which are justified by virtue of a connection, even on an occasional basis, with official authority, or on grounds of public policy, public security or public health.

5. Alpine Investments and certain rules on the free movement of goods

The decision of the Court of Justice in *Alpine Investment*[82] is not only of interest insofar as it confirmed that generally non-discriminatory rules are within the Treaty provision on freedom to provide services, but also because in this case, the Court failed to extend the *Keck*[83] case law or *Groenveld*[84] to services. In the former case the Court found that certain selling arrangements did not fall within Article 30 EC (now article 28 EC) unless they were discriminatory in law or in fact. The decision in *Keck* seems to have been influenced by the principles of subsidiarity.[85] In *Groenveld* the Court held that measures which are indistinctly applicable will not infringe Article 34 EC (now Article 29 EC) even if they are

---

80. Case C-124/97, *Läärä* [1999] ECR I-6067.
81. The same fourfold test may be seen in paragraph 34 of the Court's judgment in Joined Cases C-369/96 and C-374/96, *Arblade and Leloup* [1999] ECR I-8453.
82. Case C-384/93, [1995] ECR I-1141.
83. Case C-267/91, *Keck and Mithouard* [1993] ECR I-6097.
84. Case 15/79, *Groenveld v. Produktschap voor Vee en Vlees* [1979] ECR 3409.
85. See Snell and Andenas, 'Exploring the Outer Limits – Restrictions on the Free Movement of Goods and Services' (1999) 11 EBL Rev. p. 252 at pp. 262-3 for some other possible background influences on the judgment in *Keck*.

capable of hindering directly or indirectly, actually or potentially, trade within the Community.

Alpine Investments concerned the Dutch prohibition on cold calling potential consumers of financial services. This prohibition applied to all service providers established in the Netherlands, and affected calls made by them to prospective customers in that country and in other Member States. The Court, which followed the approach taken by Advocate General Jacobs, held that non-discriminatory restrictions of this kind came within Article 59 EC (now Article 49 EC). In paragraph 28 of its judgment, the Court found that the restriction deprived the operators concerned of a rapid and direct technique for marketing and contacting potential clients in other Member States. It could, however, be justified by the need to protect the reputation of Dutch firms in the financial services sector and was proportionate to this aim. Thus, the Court took the view that a rule which was genuinely non-discriminatory, but which impeded the access to the market in services in another Member State would require justification under Community law, in accordance with the fourfold test explained above. It has been argued, however, that the practical use of the concept of market access may give rise to considerable difficulties for the Court of Justice and national courts, and that it has been made little use of in cases concerning services by it since its decision in *Alpine Investments*.[86]

The decision in the latter case has thus given rise to a good deal of criticism, but it was followed by the Court insofar as refusal to apply the principles set out in *Keck* in the field of services was concerned in *De Agostini and TV Shop*.[87] Following that decision, which applied different rules to goods and services, it is less easy to conclude that *Keck* may be applicable in a suitable case concerning services. The Court distinguished *Keck* in paragraph 28 of its judgment in *Alpine Investments*, stating that the rules in question in the latter case directly affected access to the market in other Member States. In *Keck*, in which a French rule forbidding sales at a loss was in question, this rule only affected access to the market in one Member State. It did not therefore seem such a serious impediment to the functioning of the common market as that in *Alpine Investments*.[88] Several different explanations are offered of the different approach taken by the Court in the two cases. The best seem to be those put forward by Weatherill[89] and Hatzopoulos.[90]

---

86. Note in particular, Craig and de Burca, *EU Law*, pp. 604–7; Daniele, 'Non discriminatory Restrictions to the Free Movement of Persons' (1997) 22 EBL Rev. 191, and Torgersen, 'The Limitations to the Free Movement of Goods and the Free Movement of Services – in Search of a Common Approach' (1999) 11 EBL Rev. 371.
87. Joined Cases C-34 to C-36/95, [1997] ECR I-3843.
88. Note the explanation of the difference between *Keck* and *Alpine Investments* given by Snell and Andenas, *op. cit.*, p. 252 at p. 264.
89. Weatherill, 'After Keck: Some thoughts on how to clarify the clarification' (1996) 33 CMLRev. 885.
90. *Op. cit.*, at pp. 67–8.

The first writer thinks that the difference in approach can be regarded as a "fine tuning" of *Keck*, which limits its scope of application by including elements of the direct market access and integrated cross-border market strategy theories.[91] The latter writer adopts the view that, because of the nature of services, a distinction between selling arrangements and other measures parallel to that which was introduced in the field of goods by *Keck*, is inappropriate to services. No such distinction is applicable in relation to the free movement of workers: it was rejected in *Bosman*.[92]

In *De Agostini and TV Shop*,[93] the Court had to determine whether certain Swedish legislation on TV advertising was compatible with Articles 30 and 59 EC (now Articles 28 and 49 EC). The Court found that the legislation, which prohibited forms of TV advertising aimed at children under 12, and which it held to be concerned with selling arrangements, was not contrary to Article 30 EC (now Article 28 EC) unless it was not genuinely indistinctly applicable. It thus applied the rules in *Keck*. Nevertheless, it held that the same legislation could be treated as a restriction contrary to Article 59 EC (now Article 49 EC) unless justified by some overriding requirements or by Article 46 EC. It is now more difficult to contend that *Keck* would be applicable to the provision of services in a suitable case. However, the "centralising" effect of *Alpine Investments* has been subjected to some criticism.

A second important distinction between the rules relating to services and goods is that, since *Alpine Investments*, the Court of Justice has failed to apply the principle stated in *Groenveld*,[94] and followed in subsequent cases, concerning the impact of Article 34 (now Article 29) EC on the exportation of goods, to services. Article 34 has only been applied to restrictions which have a clearly discriminatory effect on exports in the relevant case laws.[95] Although the view has been taken by Daniele that the Court should have applied the *Groenveld* case law in *Alpine Investments*,[96] it clearly did not do so. The restriction on cold calling in the latter case was obviously not discriminatory, but the Court treated it as requiring justification in so far as the supply of services to other Member States was concerned. The Court adhered to the same approach in *Commission v. France*.[97] This case concerned French legislation which imposed heavier

---

91. Restrictions which prohibit the implementation of such marketing strategies are thought of by some commentators as particularly harmful to the functioning of the common market. See the opinion of Jacobs AG in Case C-412/93, *Leclerc-Siplec v. TFI Publicité SA and MG Publicité* [1995] ECR I-179.
92. Case C-415/93, [1995] ECR I-4921.
93. Cases C-34–36/95, [1997] ECR I-3843.
94. Case 15/79, *Groenveld* [1979] ECR 3409.
95. Article 29 provides that quantitative restrictions on the export of goods and all measures having equivalent effects shall be prohibited between Member States. There is some doubt whether this provision is applicable to marketing rules.
96. Daniele, *op. cit.*, 192, 199.
97. Case C-381/93, [1994] ECR I-5145.

charges on boats engaged in intra-Community transport than upon boats engaged in internal maritime sabotage only. The legislation in question applied without distinction as to the nationality of the boat or the company operating it, but it had a restrictive effect on the movement of transport services towards other Member States.

The Court decided that such a restrictive measure "which has the effect of making the provision of services between Member States more difficult than the provision of services purely within one Member State" infringes Article 49 EC.

6. General comments

The very considerable recent jurisprudence of the Court of Justice in the field of services would seem to reflect the increasing importance of trade in services. The Court has attempted to distinguish between the services and establishment in two important recent cases, *Gebhard* and *Reisebüro Broede.*[98] It is interesting to note that when particular cases have involved both services and capitals the Court has not always taken account of the subordinate nature of the freedom to provide services. The ambit of the rules concerning services has been extended in recent years. In certain decisions, the Court has applied these rules to situations which appear to be internal to one Member State, and to have only an insignificant effect on trade within the Community. Some would apply a *de minimis* rule to such situation, treating them as within the relevant Community rules only if they involve restrictions having a substantial effect on market access. Owing to the difficulty of determining and defining such an effect, the better view may be that such an approach in justified only where the relevant restrictions have some direct causal effect on trade between Member States.

As pointed out in the previous chapter, there has been an increasing tendency in the recent jurisprudence of the Court to equate the justification rules relating to restrictions of the free movement of persons to those relating to goods, services and capital. This tendency was recently manifested in *Centros.*[99] It has already been suggested above that despite this tendency, there still appear to be some differences between the treatment of service providers and other persons exercising their right of freedom of movement.[100]

---

98. Case C-3/95, [1995] ECR I-6511. In this case the Court upheld the rules formulated by it in *Gebhard*. It found that the German rule prohibiting undertakings established in other Member States from obtaining judicial recovery of debts owed to others was justified on the ground of the protection of creditors and the sound administration of justice.
99. Case C-212/97, [1999] ECR I-1458.
100. See Hatzopoulos, *op. cit.*, p. 43 at pp. 73–4. The writer suggests that for Article 49 EC to be infringed by a national measure, this measure need only be liable to dissuade some categories of intra Community service providers or recipients, and that it is enough that within these categories, only certain providers of recipients are adversely affected whilst some benefit. The case law of the Court of free movement of workers and freedom of establishment is, according to him, not so far reaching.

It seems apparent from *Alpine Investments*[101] and *De Agostini and TV Shop*[102] that the principles enshrined in the *Keck*[103] case law are inapplicable to services. The rules contained in *Groenveld*[104] concerning the impact of Article 29 EC on export restrictions were held to be inapplicable to services in *Alpine Investments*[105] and *Commission v. France*.[106] This failure to apply *Groenveld* has been examined and criticised by a number of writers.[107] However, the view is now taken by some authorities that there is now some room for a unitary approach to export and import restrictions in the field of goods.

The categories of overriding (or imperative) reasons of public interest which are capable of justifying restrictions on the free provision of services have expanded considerably in recent years. They now include such reasons as environmental protection,[108] the effectiveness of fiscal supervision,[109] the social protection of workers in the construction industry,[110] and the requirements of road safety.[111] As indicated above, the Court of Justice exercises control over restrictive measures by examining their suitability (or necessity), and their proportionality to the objective pursued. It has also been shown that the Court has stipulated that an economic aim cannot constitute a reasons relating to the public interest, but the approach to economic objectives in the relevant case law may be somewhat inconsistent.[112] Thus, in *Decker*[113] and *Kohll*[114] the Court held that the risk of seriously undermining the financial balance of the social security system might constitute an overriding reason in the general interest capable of

---

101. Case C-384/93, [1995] ECR I-1141.
102. Cases C-34–36/95, [1997] ECR I-3843.
103. Case C-267/91, *Keck and Mithouard* [1993] ECR I-6097.
104. Case 15/79, [1979] ECR 3409.
105. Case C-381/93, [1995] ECR I-1141.
106. Case C-381/93, [1994] ECR I-5145.
107. Note for example Bernard, 'Discrimination and Free Movement in EC Law' (1996) 45 ICLQ 82; Weatherill, 'After Keck: Some thoughts on how to clarify the clarification', 33 CMLRev. (1996) 885; Daniele, 'Non-discriminatory Restrictions on the Free Movement of Persons', (1997) 22 EL Rev. 21; and R. Greaves, 'Advertising Restrictions and the Free Movement of Goods and Services', (1998) 23 ELRev. 303.
108. Case C-18/93, *Corsica Ferries Italia* [1994] ECR I-1783 at 1823.
109. Note, for example, Case C-204/90, *Bachmann v. Belgium* [1992] ECR I-249.
110. Case C-272/94, *Guiot* [1996] ECR I-1905; Joined Cases C-369/96 and 376/96, *Arblade and Leloup* [1996] ECR I-8453.
111. Case C-55/93, *Van Schaik* [1994] ECR I-4837 at 4858.
112. Hatzopoulos, *op. cit.*, p. 43, at pp. 79–80. See also Case C-398/95, *SETTG v. Ypourgos Ergasias* [1997] ECR I-3113.
113. Case C-120/95, *Decker* [1998] ECR I-1831.
114. Case C-158/96, *Kohll* [1998] ECR I-1931. See also Case C-157/99, *Geraets-Smits v. Stichting Ziekenfonds VGZ*, judgment of 12 July 2001, n.y.r.

justifying a barrier to the free movement of goods and services. In *Bachmann*,[115] the coherence of a tax system was held as justifying a barrier. These objectives would appear to be of a fundamental economic nature.

---

115. Case C-204/90, *Bachmann v. Belgium* [1992] ECR I-249. This decision has been distinguished in later cases, but never formally overruled.

6 Remaining Categories of Persons Enjoying the Right of Residence

I. INTRODUCTION

In addition to the categories of persons mentioned above, i.e. migrant workers,[1] persons in search of employment,[2] self-employed persons,[3] service providers and recipients of services, retired workers[4] and self-employed persons[5] and students,[6] certain other categories of persons enjoy the right of residence. These are employed and self-employed persons who have ceased their occupational activity, who are covered by Council Directive 90/365,[7] and the residual class of persons covered by Council Directive 90/364[8] who do not enjoy the right of residence under other provisions of Community law. Persons of independent means in this residual class, like retired persons who have ceased their occupational activity have to comply with a means test. In the discussion which follows below, these two directives will be compared with one another, and with that applicable to students, which was considered in chapter 3.

The two Directives on retired persons and the residual class of persons were both based upon Article 235 EC (now Article 308 EC). They may be contrasted in this respect with the Directive on students, which was based upon Article 6(2) EC (now Article 12(2) EC).

II. BENEFICIARIES AND DURATION OF THE RIGHT OF RESIDENCE

As far as retired persons are concerned, Article 1(1) of the Directive provides for the right of residence to be granted to nationals of Member States who have pursued an activity as an employee or self-employed person, and to members of their families as defined in Article 1(2). These cover, irrespective of their nationality, the spouse and the dependent relatives of the holder of the right of residence and his or her spouse in the ascending or descending line. Article 1(1) of Directive 90/364 provides for the grant of the right of residence to nationals of Member States who do not enjoy the right under other provisions of Community law,

---

1. See Article 39(3)(c) and Council Directive 68/360, OJ 1968 L257/13.
2. See Case C-292/89, *Antonissen* [1991] ECR I-745.
3. See Council Directive 73/148, CJ 1973 L172/14.
4. See Council Regulation 1251/70, OJ Spec Ed 1970, L142/24, p. 402.
5. See Council Directive 75/34, OJ 1975 L14/10.
6. See Council Directive 93/96, OJ 1993 L317/59.
7. OJ 1990 L180/30.
8. OJ 1990 L180/26.

and to members of their families as defined in Article 1(2). This definition is the same as that of family members under Article 1(2) of Directive 90/365, and is also applicable irrespective of nationality.

The right of residence enjoyed by retired persons and persons belonging to the residual category of persons of independent means is of unlimited duration, subject to the fulfilment of certain conditions described below. It differs in this respect from that of students, whose right is linked to the duration of their course.

III. REQUIREMENTS GOVERNING THE RIGHT OF RESIDENCE

According to Article 1(1) of Council Directive 90/365, a retired person who is a national of a Member State must be the recipient of an invalidity or early retirement pension or old age benefits, or a person in respect of an industrial accident or disease of an amount sufficient to avoid him and his family members becoming a burden on the social security system of the host state. These persons must also be covered by sickness insurance in respect of all risks in the host state. The resources of the applicant will be deemed sufficient when they are higher than the level of resources below which the host state may grant social assistance to its national, account being taken of the circumstances of family members. Where this test cannot be applied in a Member State, the resources of the applicant will be deemed sufficient if they are higher than the level of the minimum social security pension paid by the host Member State. It follows from Article 3 of Council Directive 90/365 that the right of residence will continue for so long as the beneficiaries comply with the above requirements.

The rules governing the right of residence of the residual class of persons of independent means contained in Article 1(1) of Council Directive 90/364 are very similar to those described above. The Member State national and members of his family must be covered by sickness insurance in respect of all risks in the host Member State, and have sufficient resources to avoid becoming a burden on the social assistance system in the host state during their period of residence. These resources will be deemed sufficient where they are higher than the level of resources below which the Member State may grant social assistance to its nationals, taking into account the personal circumstances of the applicant and where appropriate those of family members who are admitted. If this test cannot be applied, the resources of the applicant will be deemed sufficient if they are higher than the level of the minimum social security pension paid by the host Member State. By virtue of Article 3, the right of residence remains for so long as the beneficiaries of the right fulfil the conditions already mentioned.

In 1993, the Commission's Green Paper suggested that consideration might be given to giving the right of residence to less affluent people.[9] Such a step may well be politically impossible at present.

---

9. See Handoll, *Free Movement of Persons in the EU*, (Wiley 1995), p. 119.

IV. RESIDENCE PERMITS

According to Article 2(1) of the two above mentioned Directives (the same rule is contained in Article 2(1) of Council Directive 93/96, which is applicable to students), the exercise of the right of residence must be evidenced by the issue of a residence permit where a member of the family does not hold the nationality of a Member State, he or she is to be issued with a residence document of the same validity as that issued to the national on whom he or she depends.[10] When issuing the residence permit, the Member State may only require that the applicant presents a valid identity card or passport and provides proof that the conditions set out in Article 1 have been met.

In addition to the above provisions, Article 4(1) of Council Directive 90/364 and Directive 90/365 both stipulate that the validity of the residence permit may be limited to five years on a renewable basis. However, where they deem it necessary, Member States may require revalidation of the permit at the end of the first two years of residence.[11] Furthermore, Article 2(2) of each Directive stipulates that Article 6(1)(a)[12] of Directive 68/360,[13] which provides that the residence permit must be valid throughout the territory of the issuing Member State, shall apply *mutatis mutandis* to the beneficiaries of the Directive.

V. RIGHTS OTHER THAN RESIDENCE

Article 2(2) of Directives 90/364 and 90/365 also provide that Articles 2 and 3 of Directive 68/360 which provide for the right to leave and enter a Member State are applicable *mutatis mutandis* to the beneficiaries of the Directive.[14] Article 2(2) of each Directive also provides that the spouse and dependent children (but not other dependants) of a national of a Member State entitled to the right of residence shall be entitled to take up any employed or self-employed activity anywhere within the territory of the host Member State, even if they are not nationals of a Member State.[15]

VI. PERMISSIBLE DEROGATIONS

Finally Article 2(2) of each Directive provides that Member State shall not derogate from the provisions thereof except on grounds of public policy, public health and public security, in that event Directive 64/221 shall apply. A similar rule is applicable to students.

---

10. This rule is also applicable to students.
11. For the different rules applicable to students, see Article 2(1) of Council Directive 93/96.
12. The provision has now been replaced by Article 6(1)(b) of the Directive, as amended.
13. OJ Spec Edition 1968 L257/13.
14. Article 2(2) of Council Directive 93/96 is in similar terms.
15. The same rule is applicable to students: see Article 2(2) of Council Directive 93/96.

7 Derogations on Grounds of Public Policy, Security and Health: Impact of Council Directive 64/221

I. INTRODUCTORY REMARKS

It has been noted above that the Treaty provides for derogations from the requirements of the chapters on the free movement of workers, freedom of establishment and freedom to provide services. Thus Article 39(3) EC, which sets out the rights attaching to the free movement of workers, states that these rights are subject to limitations justified on the grounds of public policy, public security and public health. Article 46(1) EC, which is contained in the chapter on establishment, stipulates that the provisions of this chapter and measures taken in pursuance thereof shall not prejudice the applicability of provisions laid down by law, regulation or administrative action providing for the special treatment of foreign nationals on grounds of public policy, public security or public health. It is clear from Article 55 EC that the provisions of Article 46 EC are applicable to the provision of services.[1]

The above derogations, like the concepts of "public service", and "exercise of official authority", have been given a fairly narrow scope in the jurisprudence of the European Court of Justice. However, their scope has been further defined in secondary legislation, i.e. in Directive 64/221.[2] The rights contained in this Directive have been the subject matter of a recent communication by the Commission clarifying and amplifying the Court's case law.[3]

The 1964 Directive is applicable to the measures relating to entry and deportation from their territory and the issue or replacement of residence permits which Member States may adopt on grounds of public policy, security and health in relation to the employed, the self-employed and the recipients of services. It is also applicable to those coming within the residual Directive on persons of independent means (Directive 90/364), the Directive on retired persons (Directive 90/365) and the Directive on students (Directive 93/96). Furthermore it applies

---

1. It was so applied in Case C-158/96, *Kohll* [1998] ECR I-1931; Case C-266/96, *Corsica Ferries France* [1998] ECR I-3949 (in which Article 46 was applied together with Article 86(2) EC); Case C-348/96, *Calfa* [1999] ECR I-11; and in Case C-324/97, *Commission v. Italian Republic* [1998] ECR I-6099. Only in the second of these cases was the derogation held to be sufficient.
2. [1963–4] OJ Spec EC 117.
3. COM (1999) 372. According to the Commission, such amplification was necessary in view of the passage of time since the enactment of the Directive, the importance of the rights contained in it, and the new context within which it will operate after the introduction of European citizenship.

to the families of the three aforementioned categories of persons as defined in the relevant Directives. Article 8(1) of the proposed Directive on family reunification provides that a Member State may refuse to allow the entry and residence of a family member on grounds of public policy, domestic security or public health; however it makes no reference to Council Directive 64/221/EC.

As already indicated, the latter Directive is inapplicable to companies and thus the derogations applicable to such bodies under the establishment and services chapters of the EC Treaty are governed solely by Article 46 EC, and by the general principles of Community law, in particular those of non-discrimination, proportionality, and the protection of fundamental rights.[4]

The above general principles also apply in cases where Council Directive 64/221 is also applicable. This follows *inter alia* from the opinion of Advocate General La Pergola in *Calfa*, a case which concerned the life expulsion of an Italian national from Greece as the automatic result of her conviction for possessing a small quantity of drugs for personal use when on holiday in Crete. The Greek court, which heard her appeal against expulsion on the ground that this was not compatible with her right to receive services under Article 46 EC, referred two questions to the European Court. The Advocate General placed considerable emphasis on the principle of non-discrimination and proportionality in his submission, and unsurprisingly found the sanction of life exclusion to be disproportionate. The Court found it necessary to consider both Article 46 EC and Council Directive 64/221 in the judgment, and referred to certain of the Court's decisions on the expulsion of EC nationals from other Member States. It upheld the Opinion of the Advocate General, but focussed instead on the narrower ground of the failure of the Greek court which ordered expulsion to appraise (in accordance with what was required by the jurisprudence of the European Court) the seriousness of the threat posed by Ms. Calfa.

It follows from the Court's judgment in *Bond van Adverteerders*,[5] a case concerning prohibitions on advertising and subtitling having the non-economic objective of preserving the pluralistic and non-commercial character of the Dutch broadcasting system (as well as from the opinion of Advocate General Mancini in that case), that the Court will tend to interpret Article 46 EC by reference to cases decided under Directive 64/221.

II. OUTLINE OF THE PROVISIONS OF COUNCIL DIRECTIVE 64/221

Article 2(2) of the above Directive makes it clear that the grounds of public policy, public security or health may not be invoked to serve purely economic

---

4. Note, in the latter connection, Case 260/89, *ERT v. DEP* [1991] ECR I-4925 in which the Court held that when Articles 56 and 66 (now Articles 46 and 55) EC are used to justify rules which are likely to justify the exercise of the freedom to provide services, such justification must be interpreted in accordance with the general principles of law and, in particular, of fundamental human rights.

5. Case 352/85, [1988] ECR 2085.

ends. It has already been shown that the same is true of the general interest exceptions for non-discriminatory national measures which place limitations on the free movement of persons.[6] Articles 3(1) and (2) of the Directive contain important provisions which will require further consideration below. The former provision provides that measures taken on grounds of public policy or public security shall be based exclusively on the personal conduct of the individual concerned. Article 3(2) provides that previous criminal convictions shall not in themselves constitute grounds for the taking of such measures.

The public health exception is the subject matter of Article 4 of the Directive. This provision makes reference to the diseases listed in the Annex to the Directive, and also provides that diseases or disabilities occurring after a first residence permit shall not justify refusal to renew the residence permit or expulsion from the territory. The first of the two categories of diseases mentioned in the Annex are diseases which might endanger public health. These are diseases subject to quarantine listed by the World Health Organisation: active tuberculosis; syphilis; and infectious or contagious parasitic diseases which are the subject of provisions for the protection of nationals. The second category involves diseases and disabilities which might threaten public policy or public security, and includes drug addiction, profound mental disturbance, manifest conditions of psychotic disturbance with agitation, delirium, hallucinations or confusion.[7]

Articles 5–9 make provision for procedural protections for persons against whom one of the grounds mentioned in the Directive is being pleaded. These procedural grounds are more fully considered in a later section of this chapter.

Many of the provisions of Directive 64/221 are directly effective and may be invoked by individuals before national courts. The cases heard by the European Court have tended to involve the concept of public policy rather than public security or public health. The Court considered the protection of public health as a ground for justifying a restriction on the provision of services in *Kohll*.[8] In that case the Court accepted that a restriction upon the reimbursement of medical treatment provided in other Member States imposed by a Luxembourg measure could be justified under Article 46 EC, in so far as the maintenance of a treatment facility or medical service on national territory is essential for the public health and even the survival of the population. It did not find that such a justification was present in the instant case, because no evidence had been submitted suggesting that the rules are indispensable for that purposes.

III. THE DISCRETION GRANTED TO THE MEMBER STATES

The Court has considered the discretion given to the Member States by Article 39(3), 46(1) and 55 EC to derogate from the provisions of the Treaty relating

---

6. See Case C-398/95, *SETTG v. Ypourgos Ergasias* [1997] ECR I-3091. It is unfortunately not entirely clear from the case law what the Court envisages by economic objectives.

7. In its Communication on the Directive (COM (1999) 372) the Commission states that all the Community instruments stipulated that the free movement of persons with HIV/AIDS must be safeguarded.

8. Case C-158/96, *Kohll* [1998] ECR I-1931.

to the free movement of persons on grounds of public policy, public security and public health, as well as the relevant provisions of Council Directive 64/221 concerning the exercise of this discretion in a number of decisions. The first of these, which set out principles which have subsequently undergone development and alteration, was *Van Duyn v. Home Office.*[9]

IV. THE COURT'S DECISION IN *VAN DUYN*

In *Van Duyn*, the Court of Justice had to consider a challenge to a decision not to allow a Dutch woman who had obtained a post in the Church of Scientology entry into the United Kingdom. A reference had been made to the European Court of Justice under Article 177 EC (now Article 234 EC) by the English High Court. As already indicated, Article 3(1) of Council Directive 64/221 provides that action must be based exclusively on personal conduct. The European Court found that Article 3(1) was directly effective, and could be pleaded in national courts. The Court defined conduct rather widely, finding (in paragraph 17 of its judgment) that although past association cannot in general justify a decision refusing a person the right to move freely within the Community, 'present association which reflects participation in the activities of the body or the organisation as well as identification with its aims and designs' may amount to personal conduct.

The question thus arose whether the conduct in question could be regarded as sufficiently threatening to one of the interests recognised in Article 39(3) EC (ex Article 48(3) EC). The United Kingdom treated Scientology as being contrary to the public good, but had not imposed a ban on it. Thus, a British national would not have suffered any penalty by reason of taking up employment with the organisation. The Court conceded that the concept of public policy had to be interpreted narrowly, and that its scope could not be determined unilaterally by each Member State. However, it admitted that the particular circumstances justifying recourse to the concept of public policy may vary from one state to another, and from one period to another. Thus, the competent national authorities must be granted an area of discretion within the limits imposed by the Treaty.

The Court thus decided that when the state regards an activity as socially harmful and has taken administrative measures against it, that state cannot be required before it may rely upon the concept of public policy to make such activities unlawful. The decision in *Van Duyn* has been widely criticised on the ground that the activity in question was not known to have been dangerous, and that the Court's judgment permitted the taking of steps against non-nationals where no comparable steps would be taken against nationals. The Court's statement that a state cannot deny entry and residence to its own nationals does not provide a satisfactory explanation of the latter approach. No steps whatsoever were taken against British citizens who were members of the Church of

---

9. Case 41/74, [1974] ECR 1337.

Scientology, and thus the treatment of nationals of other Member States who belonged to this organisation appears to have involved arbitrary discrimination, although the Court's decision may have been politically expedient at the relevant time because of the impending referendum on the United Kingdom's continued membership of the EC.

V. THE NEED THAT THE PERCEIVED THREAT BE COMBATED EFFECTIVELY

The question whether deportation would constitute arbitrary discrimination on the ground of nationality was considered by the Court in *Adoui and Cornuaille v. Belgium*,[10] in which two French prostitutes who wished to carry on their trade in Belgium appealed against a decision by the Belgian authorities refusing them residence permits. The Liège Court, which heard their appeal, referred a number of questions to the Court of Justice. In answering these questions the Court found that Member States could not deny residence to non-nationals by reason of conduct which when perpetrated by nationals did not result in any repressive measures or other genuine and effective measures designed to combat it. Unfortunately, the Court did not particularise what sort of repressive measures a state might take.

The need to minimise discrimination against non-nationals was also emphasised in *Rutili v. Minister for the Interior*.[11] In that case, an Italian, resident in France and married to a French woman, had worked as a trade union official in that country for several years. An order was made by the French Minister for the Interior prohibiting him from residing in certain *départements*, and the residence permit for an EC national which was given to him contained a prohibition on residence in these districts. He challenged the territorial limitation on the validity of his residence permit in the French courts, and a reference was made to the European Court of Justice. The Court held that the term "measures" used in Council Directive 64/221 could include individual decisions. It somewhat controversially also held that a derogation on the basis of public policy, public security or public health can only apply to a total ban on residence in a Member State; a partial restriction on the residence of nationals of another state may not be imposed unless such restriction can be imposed upon nationals. Thus, whilst a Member State can deport a person who is thought to be a threat to the requirements of public policy, it cannot normally impose a partial ban on the access of such a person to a particular part of the national territory.

The need for a Member State to demonstrate that the sanctions imposed on non-nationals, although perhaps not identical to those imposed on nationals, are effectively designed to combat conduct regarded as contrary to public policy, and justify expulsion in the case of a national of another Member State, was

---

10. Cases 115 and 116/81, [1982] ECR 1665.
11. Case 36/75, [1975] ECR 1219.

emphasised by Advocate General La Pergola in *Calfa*.[12] It is not clear what criteria should be used for the purpose of determining whether restrictions are approximately equal.

VI. THE MEANING OF "PERSONAL CONDUCT"

Council Directive 64/221 does not give much indication as to what might constitute personal conduct serious enough to make it possible to invoke the public policy or security exceptions. The meaning of such "personal conduct" was considered by the Court in *Van Duyn*, in which the Court held that participation in the activities of an organisation could constitute personal conduct within the meaning of Article 3(1). Article 3(2) does make it clear that previous criminal convictions do not in themselves constitute reasons for taking measures on grounds of public policy or public security. Both these provisions have been considered in a number of cases heard by the Court.

Thus in *Bonsignore*,[13] the Court had to consider the situation of a young man of Italian citizenship who had fatally wounded his brother in a shooting accident. He was found guilty of causing death by negligence, but no penalty was imposed on him. However, a deportation order was made against Bonsignore, and on appeal the German court made a reference to the European Court of Justice, asking whether a deportation order could be made for reasons of a general preventive nature, or whether the reasons had to be specific to the individual. The Court found that it followed from Article 3(1) of the Directive that only the "personal conduct" of those affected by the measures was to be regarded as determinative. This concept of "personal conduct" was held to express the requirement that a deportation order could only be made for breaches of the peace and security which might be committed by the individual affected.

However, Member States are allowed to take general preventive measures in some circumstances, especially in relation to gatherings of people originating from different Member States, for example sports events, rock concerts and political demonstrations. Member States have been led to take measures to facilitate safety and public order at football matches. Certain such measures have been adopted under the Third (Justice and Home Affairs) Pillar.[14]

The Court also emphasised in *Rutili* that Article 3 of Council Directive 64/221 requires that Member States should base their decision on the individual circumstances of any person under the protection of Community law, and not on general considerations. The Court also held that the personal conduct involved must constitute a genuine and sufficiently serious threat to public policy in order

---

12. See paragraph 7 of his Opinion. See also the case note on *Calfa* by Cathryn Costello, (2000) 37 CML Rev., pp. 817–827.
13. Case 67/74, *Bonsignore v. Oberstadtdirektor der Stadt Köln* [1975] ECR 297.
14. Note, for example, Joint Action with regard to Cooperation on Law and Order and Security [1997] OJ L147/1, 5 June 1997. See also Steiner and Woods, *Textbook on EC Law*, (7th edn, Blackstone Press, 2000), p. 361.

that the derogation on this ground might be invoked. It found that the limitation placed by Directive 64/221 in respect of the control of aliens was a manifestation of a more general principle, enshrined in the European Convention on Human Rights, that no restrictions should be placed on the rights secured other than such as were "necessary for the protection of those interests of a democratic society".

The relevance of criminal convictions had to be considered in *Bouchereau*.[15] The latter was a French national residing in England who had two convictions for the possession of drugs. After the second conviction, the Marlborough Street Magistrates wished to make a recommendation for deportation against him, and made a reference to the European Court asking whether such a recommendation would be a measure within Council Directive 64/221, and whether past conduct which resulted in criminal convictions could be taken into account despite the wording of Article 3(2).

The Court of Justice held that a deportation order was a "measure" within the meaning of the Directive. It also held that the existence of previous criminal convictions could only be taken into account in so far as they constituted evidence of personal conduct that was a present threat to public policy, or showing a propensity to act in the same way in the future. However, the Court also held that it was possible that past conduct alone might constitute such a threat to the requirements of public policy. It is difficult to understand how the latter can be the case in the absence of any propensity to commit future offences. The Court found that Bouchereau's conduct was not of a sufficiently serious character to justify his deportation. It held that deportation on the public policy ground was only permissible in the presence of a genuine threat to public policy, affecting one of the fundamental interests of society.

As indicated above, the Court once again considered the concept of "personal conduct" in *Calfa*. In that case, the Court held that Calfa could only be expelled on the basis of personal conduct besides the commission of the drugs offence. It did not make it clear how an appraisal of such personal conduct was to take place. It has already been mentioned in the chapter on services that the Court did not consider the possible impact of the provisions of the EC Treaty in *Calfa*. Furthermore, neither the Court nor the Advocate General found it necessary to consider the impact of the European Convention on Human Rights in this case. Such consideration would have been more appropriate had Ms Calfa been a long term resident in Greece.[16]

---

15. Case 30/77, [1977] ECR 1999.

16. Note in this present connection, Costello, 'Casenote on Calfa', (2000) 37 CML Rev., p. 814, at pp. 826–7. See also *R. v. Secretary of State for the Home Department*, [2000] 2 All ER 1086 in which the Court of Appeal held that the deportation of an Italian national would be a disproportionate measure, even though he had committed serious criminal offences, because he had lived in the United Kingdom since childhood. The Court of Appeal made reference to Article 6 TEU which requires the Union to respect fundamental rights, and to Article 8 of the ECHR which provides that everyone has a right to respect for his private and family life.

VII. PROCEDURAL SAFEGUARDS

Persons seeking to enforce their rights to enter and reside in other Member States enjoy a number of procedural safeguards. The relevant provisions are expressed in clear and mandatory language and appear to have direct effect.

VIII. PROVISIONS CONCERNING RESIDENCE

According to Article 3(3) of Council Directive 64/221, when a person's identity card or passport has expired, this shall not justify his or her expulsion from the host country. The Court held in *Procureur du Roi v. Royer*[17] that the right of residence does not depend on a residence permit, which is of evidential value only of a right based on the Treaty itself. The same principle is applicable to identity cards and passports.[18] Furthermore, according to Article 3(4), the state which issued the identity card or passport must allow the holder of such document to enter its territory without any formality, even if the document is no longer valid (e.g. through expiry) or the nationality of the holder is in dispute.

A person who is awaiting a decision by a Member State to grant him or her a residence permit must be allowed to remain temporarily in that state pending such decision. The latter must, according to Article 5(1), be made as soon as possible and not more than six months from the date of application for the permit.

By virtue of Article 7, the person concerned must be officially notified of any decision to refuse the issue or renewal of a residence permit, or to expel him from the territory. The period allowed for leaving the territory must be stipulated in the notification. Except in cases of urgency, it must not be less than fifteen days if the person has not yet been granted a residence permit, and not less than six months in all other cases.

IX. REQUIREMENT OF INFORMATION OF GROUNDS FOR DECISION

By Article 6, the individual concerned must be informed of the grounds on which the decision taken in his case is based, unless this is contrary to the requirements of state security. The latter reservation does not seem to have been considered by the Court of Justice. The applicant is required to be given a precise and comprehensive statement of grounds, enabling him to take effective steps to prepare his or her defence.[19] Furthermore, he or she must be able to comprehend the content and effect of this statement.[20] It appears from the Commission

---

17. Case 48/75, [1976] ECR 497.
18. Failure to comply with administrative formalities may result in a fine, but is never a ground for deportation: see Case C-378/97, *Wijsenbeek* [1999] ECR I-6207.
19. See Case 36/75, *Rutili* [1975] ECR 1210, para. 39, and Joined Cases 115 and 116/81, *Adoui and Cornuaille* [1982] ECR 1665, para. 13.
20. See note 17 above and Handoll, *Free Movement of Persons in the EU*, (Wiley, 1995), p. 232.

Communication already mentioned that the duty to give reasons applies also to decisions regarding the application for visas by family members who are third country nationals.

X. LEGAL REMEDIES AVAILABLE

Article 8 provides that the person concerned is to have the same legal remedies in respect of any decision on entry,[21] or refusing the issue or renewal of a residence permit, or ordering expulsion from the territory, are available to nationals of the state concerned in respect of acts of the administration.

The Court held in *Pecastaing*[22] that Article 8 required that persons protected under Community law should be granted rights of appeal no less favourable than those granted to the nationals of the Member State concerned. The scope of this duty was considered by the European Court of Justice in *R. v. Shingara and Radiom*.[23] The ECJ had to consider a situation in which two EC nationals who were refused entry to the United Kingdom on grounds of public policy were not entitled under English law either to appeal against the decisions or have them referred to a competent authority, but only to judicial review, whilst a United Kingdom national whose immigration status was uncertain and who was refused entry, would have a right of appeal. The applicants argued that they were not being granted the same legal remedies as United Kingdom nationals, as was required by Article 8. The Court of Justice did not accept this argument, finding that the position of a national of another Member State who was refused entry on public policy grounds was in no way comparable to that of a national whose immigration status was in doubt. It mentioned its reasoning in *Van Duyn* and *Adoui and Cornuaille*, where the Court mentioned that a Member State was not permitted to refuse entry and residence to its own nationals under public international law, whilst it could do so in the case of non-nationals, so that the distinction was justified. The Court's approach in this case does not seem entirely convincing in view of the wording of Article 8.

In *Royer*,[24] the Court of Justice held that in the case of the legal remedies referred to in Article 8 of Directive 64/221, the party concerned must at least have the opportunity of lodging an appeal and obtaining a stay of execution

---

21. Advocate General Léger in his Opinion of 30.3.2000 in Case C-357/98, *R. v. Secretary of State for Home Affairs ex parte Yiadom* held that a decision of the Home Secretary refusing a Netherlands national of Ghanaian origin leave to enter the UK given several months after she had been given temporary admission should be construed as a decision concerning expulsion, such that the remedies mentioned in Article 8 were open to her. The Court of Justice adopted the same approach in paragraph 38 of its judgment of 6 November 2000, [2000] ECR I-9265.
22. Case 98/79, *Pecastaing* [1980] ECR 691, para. 22.
23. Cases C-65/95 and C-111/95, *R. v. Secretary of State for the Home Department ex parte Shingara and ex parte Radiom* [1997] ECR I-3343.
24. Case 48/75, *Royer* [1976] ECR 497.

before the expulsion order is carried out. Thus, where a legal remedy referred to in Article 8 is available, the decision ordering expulsion may not be executed before the party concerned is able to avail himself of the remedy. In *Pecastaing*,[25] the Court held that Article 8 did not require Member States to allow the non-national to remain in the country for the duration of appeal procedures, provided that he or she was able to have a fair hearing, and present an adequate defence.

Article 9 was held to be directly effective in *Santillo*.[26] The Court indicated in *Pecastaing* that Article 9 was intended to supplement the deficiencies of Article 8. Its rather complex provisions are set out below:

1. Where there is no right of appeal to a court of law, or where such appeal may be only in respect of the legal validity of the decision, or where the appeal cannot have suspensory effect, a decision refusing renewal of a residence permit or ordering the expulsion of the holder of a residence permit from the territory shall not be taken by an administrative authority, save in cases of urgency, until an opinion has been obtained from a competent authority of the host state before which the person concerned enjoys such rights of defence and of assistance or representation as the domestic law of that country provides for. The authority shall not be the same as that empowered to take the decision refusing renewal of the residence permit or ordering expulsion.
2. Any decision refusing the issue of a fresh residence permit or ordering expulsion of the person concerned before the issue of the permit shall, where that person so requests, be referred for consideration to the authority whose prior opinion is required under paragraph 1. The person concerned shall then be entitled to submit his defence in person, except where this would be contrary to the interests of national security.

Article 9(1) applies where a residence permit has already been granted, while Article 9(2) applies where no such permit has been issued. The relationship between these provisions was considered by the Court of Justice in *R. v. Shingara and Radiom*, in which the Court held that the restriction on the rights granted by Article 9(1) to situations in which the person concerned has "no right of appeal to a court of law, or where such an appeal may be only in respect of the legal validity of the decision or where the appeal cannot have suspensory effect". Article 9(1) also applies to the rights given by Article 9(2).

In *Royer*, which has already been mentioned above, the Court also found that where no legal remedy under Article 8 was available, or where such a remedy was available but could not have any suspensory effect, the decision of expulsion could not be taken, save in cases of urgency, while the party concerned has had the opportunity to appeal to a competent authority under Article 9, and until that authority has reached a decision. However, in *Gallagher*,[27] the Court found

---

25. Case 98/79, *Pecastaing v. Belgium* [1980] ECR 691.
26. Case 131/79, *Santillo* [1980] ECR 1585, para. 13.
27. Case C-175/94, [1995] ECR I-4253.

that in that situation within Article 9(1) decision of the relevant competent authority must be obtained before the decision on expulsion is taken, whilst under Article 9(2) the opinion is obtained after the decision is taken.

The Court found in paragraph 18 of its judgment in *Pecastaing* that it followed from Article 9 that as soon as the opinion in question has been notified to the addressee an expulsion order may be executed immediately, subject always to the right of that person to stay on for the necessary time to avail himself of the remedies provided under Article 8. The Court of Justice came to a somewhat dubious conclusion about urgency in this decision. In such cases it is clear from Article 9(1) that neither suspension of the decision to deport nor obtaining the opinion of a competent authority is necessary. However, it is difficult to agree with the Court's conclusion that whether a matter is urgent may be determined by the administrative authorities, as opposed to the judicial ones.[28]

It follows from the relevant case law that a Member State has some measure of discretion as to the nature of the competent authority. Thus, in *Santillo*,[29] a recommendation for deportation made by a court was held by the ECJ to satisfy the requirement of an opinion of such an authority. The Court took into account the fact that the criminal court in question was independent from the Home Secretary who was responsible for making the deportation order. The Court held that Article 9(1) could only provide a satisfactory safeguard if (i) all the factors to be taken into consideration by the administration were put before the competent authority; (ii) the opinion of the competent authority is sufficiently proximate in time to the expulsion to ensure that there are no new factors to be taken into consideration; (iii) both the administration and the person concerned are in a position to take cognisance of the reasons which led the competent authority to give its opinion subject to the state security reservation in Article 6 of the Directive.

Despite the fact that the Home Secretary's deportation order was made nearly five years after Santillo had received his eight year sentence for serious sexual offences, coupled with a recommendation for deportation, the trial judge's opinion was found by Donaldson LJ[30] to be still valid, since there was no evidence of any change in the position since the recommendation. There is some reason for doubt whether the ruling of the ECJ was correctly applied.[31]

The requirement of the independence of the competent authorities referred to in Article 9 was once again emphasised in *Dzodzi*.[32] In that case the Court mentioned that Directive 64/221 does not stipulate how the competent authority

---

28. Note in this sense, O'Keefe, 'Practical Difficulties of the Application of Article 48 of the Treaty', (1982) 19 CML Rev. 35, 36–9.
29. Case 131/79, *R. v. Secretary of State for Home Affairs, ex parte Santillo* (1980) ECR 1585.
30. [1980] 1 CMLR 1; [1981] 2 All ER 867 (Court of Appeal); note the different outcome of *Proll v. Entry Clearance Officer Düsseldorf* [1988] 2 CMLR 387.
31. Note in this connection, Gormley, 'The Application of Community Law in the United Kingdom 1976–1985' (1986) 23 CML Rev. 287, 302–3.
32. Joined Cases C-297/88, 197/89, *Dzodzi v. Belgian State* (1990) ECR I-3763.

is to be appointed, and does not require it to be a court or composed of members of the judiciary. However, the Court said it was an essential requirement that it should be clearly established that the authority is to perform its duties in absolute independence, and is not to be directly or indirectly subject in the exercise of its duties to any control by the authority empowered to take the measures provided for in the Directive.

A similar approach to the independence of the competent authority was taken by the ECJ in *Gallagher*. Gallagher, who had been convicted of the possession of rifles for unlawful persons in Ireland, came to work in England and was arrested and deported from that country. After having challenged the decision in Ireland he was detained in Dublin. He was not told the name of the interviewer and not given any grounds for his expulsion. His case was reconsidered by the Home Secretary at his request, but the decision was not reversed. He questioned whether his case had been considered by a "competent authority", especially in view of the fact that the interviewer had been appointed by the Home Secretary. The European Court found (as it had done in *Dzodzi*[33] and *Adoui and Cornuaille*[34]) that the essential requirement was that it should be clearly established that the authority should perform its duties in absolute independence and not be subject to direct or indirect control by the deciding authority. That authority was required (as in *Dzodzi*) to follow a procedure enabling the persons concerned, on the terms laid down by the Directive, effectively to present his defence. The ECJ said that it was for the national courts to determine in each case whether these requirements were fulfilled.

The Court also held that whilst the decision of the competent authority must be notified to the person concerned, there was no requirement that he should be informed of the identities or professional status of the members of the competent authority. The question arises whether the fundamental rights of the addressees of expulsion decisions are fully respected in Article 9. Advocate General Ruiz-Tarabo Colomber expressed some doubts as to this in his Opinion in *Shingara and Radiom*.[35]

If a person is expelled, and he or she seeks permission to re-enter, it follows from *Adoui and Cornuaille* that he or she may apply for a residence permit and if a reasonable period of time has elapsed since their expulsion, the authorities must consider the contentions advanced by them that there has been a material change in circumstances.

---

33. See paragraph 15 of the Court's judgment.
34. See paragraph 16 of the judgment.
35. See paragraph 17 of his opinion.

8 European Citizenship

I. INTRODUCTION

It appears useful to have some idea of the historical development of the concept of European citizenship in order to comprehend the reasons for the conclusion, and the significance, of its constituent elements, which are discussed below. Furthermore, an elementary knowledge of this background is necessary to obtain some notion of the questions considered and the possible developments suggested in the context of the ongoing debate on citizenship which took place before the incorporation of the relevant provisions in Part 2 of the EC Treaty by the Treaty of Maastricht. Certain of these suggestions, relating for example to a passport union and to a Community Charter on Citizens' Rights remain topical and, in the former case at least, somewhat controversial at the present time. It seems unlikely that any single or common passport system, as opposed to a new standard format for national passports, will be brought into effect in the near future.

It is interesting to note that as early as in 1991, when passing a resolution on European citizenship, the European Parliament mentioned the possibility of extending rights to resident third country nationals.[1] This may eventually come about in the future as the result of secondary legislation made under Title IV of Part III of the EC Treaty.

II. DEVELOPMENTS BEFORE THE MAASTRICHT TREATY

1. Passport union and special rights

The concept of European citizenship was first placed on the political agenda by the Belgian and Italian Heads of Government at the Paris Summit in October 1972,[2] and received further expression in the Tindemans Report on European Union.[3] This Report suggested that the concept of European citizenship would be developed through two main elements, a passport union, and through the granting of special (in other words political) rights which would include the right to vote, to stand for election and to become a public official in the Member

---

1. OJ 1991 C183/473.
2. See Handoll, *Free Movement of Persons in the EU*, (Wiley, 1995), p. 269. There is a helpful account of the evolution of the idea of European citizenship in chapter 9 of Handoll's book, and also in the article by Closa, 'The Concept of Citizenship in the Treaty of European Union' (1992) 29 CML Rev. 1137.
3. The European Union, *Report of the Commission of the European Communities*, EC Bulletin Supplement, 7/75, p. 26.

States. It is interesting to note that evolution towards a passport union would still probably be highly controversial.

It was contended by some writers that the concept of European citizenship would be developed on the basis of certain characteristic features. These would be a class of persons defined by a common European criterion, the enjoyment of certain privileges, including that of free movement through European territory by such persons, and the abolition of discrimination between them on grounds of nationality.[4]

Ten years after the Paris Summit of December 1974 had issued a communique providing for the setting up of working parties on the introduction of a common passport and the establishment of a passport union, and the grant of special rights to the citizens of the Member States. Little or nothing has been accomplished since the Paris Summit in these areas except to the extent that in 1981 a resolution was passed by the Council on a uniform passport, by which Member States resolved to introduce a uniform format or scope for their national passports.[5] Thus, there had been little progress since 1974 towards removing passport controls and harmonising aliens legislation, or in the field of special rights.

2. The Two Adonnino Committee Reports

The two reports from the ad hoc committee on a "People's Europe", set up by the Fontainbleau European Council in June 1984 under the chairmanship of Mr. Adonnino made certain important recommendations. These reports were presented to the Brussels and Milan European Councils in March and June 1985.

The first of these reports dealt, *inter alia*, with freedom of movement for Community citizens, and increased opportunities for employment and residence. The second one was concerned with the special rights of citizens, and also proposed action in a number of areas for the purpose of creating a European identity.[6]

3. Commission Communication on a People's Europe

This communication was made in 1988,[7] three years after the Adonnino Reports. It examined measures promoting awareness of European identity and identified priorities for future action. These included following up the Adonnino Reports, encouraging the recognition and exercise of citizens' rights and accession of the Community to the European Convention on Human Rights. Interestingly, the Report also suggested the introduction of a Community Charter on Citizen's Rights, which did not actually take place until much later.

---

4. Plender, 'An Incipient Form of European Citizenship', in Jacobs (ed.), *European Law and the Individual* (1976) at p. 41.

5. ONJ 1981 C 241/1; see Denza, 'Le passeport européen' (1982) RMC 489.

6. Both these reports can be found in EC Bulletin Supplement 7/75.

7. COM (88) 331 final; Bull. Supp. 2/88.

4. Voting rights in local elections

The question of voting rights in local elections regardless of nationality was already considered in the second Adonnino Report, and such voting rights were advocated by the Commission in its proposal for a Council Directive on voting rights for Community nationals in local elections in the Member States.[8]

III. EUROPEAN CITIZENSHIP AND THE INTERGOVERNMENTAL CONFERENCE

1. Early contributions to the elaboration of the concept

The question of European citizenship was discussed in the Intergovernmental Conference on European Union which preceded the conclusion of the Maastricht Treaty on European Union. The Dublin Council of June 1990 included European citizenship in the framework of the objective of political union. The Council was requested to examine "how will the Union include and extend the notion of Community citizenship, carrying with it specific rights (human, political, social, the right of complete free movement and residence etc.) for the citizens of the Member States by virtue of those states belonging to the Union".

The first important contribution to the elaboration of the concept consisted of the Spanish Memorandum on European Citizenship.[9] The Spanish memorandum envisaged European citizenship as involving a third set or nexus of rights and duties, in addition to those rights and duties originating from national citizenship and from the Community treaties for citizens of Member States. The third set of rights and duties would, according to the Memorandum, have the effect of converting the Community citizen who was no more than a privileged foreigner into a Union citizen.[10] Two other contributions mentioned the concept of citizenship before the opening of the IGC. These were made by the Commission[11] and the Danish delegation[12] and placed less emphasis than the Spanish text had done on the autonomous character of Union citizenship. It is interesting to note in view of recent developments that the Commission proposed as a basis for citizenship a statement of rights and obligations, emphasising basic human rights, reference being made to the ECHR.

---

8. COM (88) 371 final, 11.7.1988. OJ 1988 C246/3.
9. *Towards a European Citizenship*, Council Doc. SN 3940/90, 24 Sept. 1990.
10. For a detailed account of the Spanish Memorandum, see Handoll, *Free Movement of Persons in the EU*, (Wiley, 1995), pp. 275–6. The memorandum also included a proposal for a higher degree of assistance and diplomatic and consular protection by the Member States to citizens of other Member States, and the possibility of making complaints to a European ombudsman.
11. Commission Opinion of 21 October 1990 in the proposal for amendment of the Treaty establishing the European Economic Community with a view to political union, COM (90) 600 final; Bull. EC Supp. 2/91, p. 69.
12. Danish Memorandum on the IGC and political union, Council Doc. SM 9046/1/90.

The Commission suggested that the rights of citizens should be included in the Treaty, and should include the right to residence and movement apart from economic activity; voting rights in European and local elections; and the establishment of targets for the definition of the individual's civic, social and economic rights and obligations at a later stage.

The Danish Memorandum proposed the right to vote in local elections to citizens residing in a Member State other than their own and the introduction of an ombudsman system.

The conclusions of the Presidency after the Rome European Council of December 1990 took note of the consensus between Member States as to the necessity of considering the concept of European citizenship at the forthcoming IGC.[13] The Conference was asked to consider including a number of rights in the Treaty. The first group of these were civil or political rights (participation in elections to the European Parliament in the country of residence and possible participation in municipal elections). The second were social and economic rights (freedom of movement and residence irrespective of economic activity and equality of opportunity and treatment). The third consisted of the joint protection of Community citizens outside Community borders. The European Council also suggested that consideration might be given to the appointment of an ombudsman to defend citizens' rights in relation to the Community. It did not, however, take the view that the basic rights granted by the European Convention on Human Rights should also be included.

2. The approach taken by the European Parliament

The European Parliament took a different approach to the above matters, as is particularly manifested by the Resolution on Union citizenship which it passed in June 1991.[14] This resolution stipulated that such citizenship, viewed as being additional to national citizenship, should be placed firmly in the framework of the human rights and fundamental freedoms mentioned in the ECHR, as well as in that of social, economic, political and cultural rights. It should also be viewed in the context of granting rights to resident third-country nationals. The latter question remains of importance at the present time.

3. The Commission's proposals

The Commission's proposals on Union citizenship were formulated in some detail at the beginning of the Intergovernmental Conference. The Commission adopted the view in its proposal that everyone having the nationality of a Member State should be Union citizen. Union citizens would be able to assert

---

13. Bull. EC 12–1990, point 1.7.
14. OJ 1991 C183/473.

rights under the ECHR, the right to vote in European and local elections, as well as certain other rights.[15]

4. The Agreement on the Draft Treaty on European Union

The Intergovernmental Conference, which began in December 1990, began to discuss the question of citizenship on the basis of a text drawn up by the Spanish delegation, which developed the ideas put forward in the Spanish memorandum,[16] and on that of the contribution of the Commission, mentioned in the above paragraph. Basic agreement was found to be possible on the basis of the final text drawn up by the Luxembourg Presidency,[17] and the provisions on citizenship which now appear in the EC Treaty were in substance contained in the Final draft established by the Presidency in June 1991.[18]

IV. DEFINITION OF UNION CITIZENSHIP

The provisions contained in Article 17–22 of the EC Treaty (as amended by the Treaty of Amsterdam) concerning citizenship of the Union display little alteration from those contained in Articles 8–8c EC (as amended by the Treaty of Maastricht). It should be clear from the short historical introduction to this chapter that the concept of European citizenship had been in existence for some time before its incorporation into the EC Treaty. Union citizenship is now defined in Article 17(1) EC, which provides that:

"Citizenship of the Union is hereby established. Every person holding the nationality of a Member State shall be a citizen of the Union. Citizenship of the Union shall complement and not replace national citizenship."

As indicated above, a Declaration in the Final Act of the Maastricht treaty stipulates that the question whether an individual possesses the nationality of a Member State shall be settled solely by reference to the national law of that Member State. However, in *Micheletti*,[19] the Court emphasised that this competence had to be exercised so as to respect Community law.[20] The emphasis

---

15. See 'Union citizenship: Contribution by the Commission to the Intergovernmental Conference', SEC (91) 500 Bull. EC Supp. 2/1. For a detailed account of the Commission's proposals, see Handoll, *Free Movement of Persons in the EU*, (Wiley, 1995), pp. 279–80.
16. Spanish delegation, Intergovernmental Conference on European Union, 21 Feb. 1991 CONF 1731/91.
17. Non-paper, Luxembourg Presidency, 12 April 1991, SN 1919/91.
18. Draft Treaty on the Union, Luxembourg Presidency reference document Luxembourg 18 June 1991, Europe Documents No. 1722/1723, 5.7.1991.
19. Case C-369/90, [1992] ECR I-4239.
20. See also the High Court's decision in *ex parte Manjit Kaur*, in which this Court referred certain questions to the ECJ concerning the extent of the freedom given to Member States to define citizenship and the limitation which might be imposed by the need to respect fundamental rights. Advocate General Léger took the view that it was not necessary for

placed upon the nationality of a Member State means that qualifications for citizenship will differ widely between different Member States.

The final sentence of Article 17(1) reminds one of the terms of the Danish Declaration on citizenship of the Union, which was taken cognisance of by the Edinburgh European Council in December 1992,[21] which emphasised the distinction between citizenship of the Union and citizenship of a nation state. Although some envisage the concept of Union citizenship as a dynamic one, it does not appear to be a specially rigorous concept at present and can be regarded as a synonym for certain rights, which are described below.[22]

1. The provisions of Article 17(2) EC

According to Article 17(2), the citizens of the Union shall enjoy the rights conferred by the EC treaty and shall be subject to the duties imposed thereby. This provision does not appear to create any new rights or obligations and can even be thought of as having a restrictive effect preventing progress towards a Union modelled to some extent on the existing nation state, which might eventually supersede the Member States. However, it will be noted that it appears to go beyond the rights specifically referred to in Part Two of the EC Treaty (Citizenship of the Union).

The Court made use of Article 17(2) in its somewhat questionable decision in *María Martínez Sala*.[23] Ms Sala, a Spanish national living in Germany, had been refused a child-raising allowance because, although she had been allowed to reside in Germany, she had no residence permit. Certain questions were referred to the European Court of Justice by the Bavarian Regional Social Court (*Bayerisches Landessozialgericht*). The Court found that as far as the material scope of the case was concerned, the benefit in question fell within the scope of the Treaty. Article 17(2) EC entitled a citizen of the Union to protection from discrimination on the grounds of nationality within the material scope of the Treaty,[24] including access to benefits provided for by Community secondary legislation. The interpretation placed upon Article 12 by the Court appears too wide. It is thought, as Tomuschat[25] suggests, that it should have been treated as

---

the Court to answer these questions. He said that although fundamental human rights do form an integral part of the general principles with which the Court must ensure compliance, this is subject to the condition that the area to which the case before it relates falls within the scope of Community law. The ECJ adopted a similar view to that of the Advocate General.

21. See OJ 1992 C348/1.
22. Note in this sense, Bernitz and Bernitz, 'Human Rights and European Identity', in chapter 15 of Alston (ed.), *The EU and Human Rights* (OUP, 1999), pp. 503–527.
23. Case C-85/96, *María Martínez Sala v. Freistaat Bayern* [1998] ECR I-209.
24. See Article 12 EC.
25. Case note (2000) 37 CML Rev. 449, 453. Tomuschat also criticises the total separation between aspects *ratione materiae* and *ratione personae* suggested by the Court.

being related to Article 18(1) EC, which stipulates that the right to reside and move freely is subject to the limitations and conditions laid down in the Treaty and the measures adopted to give it effect. The three Directives[26] which have extended freedom of movement to citizens of the Union who are not pursuing an economic activity all require that in order to benefit from such freedom, such persons must have adequate financial resources and benefit from sickness insurance. It would seem to follow from those three Directives that persons who are not economically active are thought of as being required by Community law to rely upon their own resources to provide for their necessities, without having the right of recourse to public funds in their state of residence. However, a more liberal interpretation of Article 18(1) EC is advocated by some authorities.[27]

It remains to be seen whether the Court will extend its reasoning in *María Martínez Sala* to other benefits, for example in the field of education.

2. Rights of movement and residence

According to Article 18 EC:

> Every citizen of the Union shall have the right to move and reside freely within the territory of the Member States, subject to the limitations and conditions laid down in this Treaty and by the measures adopted to give it effect.

> The Council may adopt provisions with a view to facilitating the exercise of the rights referred to in paragraph 1, save as otherwise provided in this Treaty, the Council shall act in accordance with the procedure referred to in Article 251. The Council shall act unanimously throughout this procedure.[28]

It has been held that Article 18(1) EC does not give any right of free movement within a Member State,[29] and is inapplicable to internal situations which have

---

26. Directive 93/96 (governing students exercising the right to vocational training); Directive 90/365 (governing employed and self-employed persons who have ceased to work) and Directive 90/364 (governing the residual category of persons).

27. See, for example, O'Keefe and Horspool, 'European Community Law and the Free Movement of Persons', in *Essays in Honour of G. J. Hand*, (Sweet and Maxwell, 1996), pp. 145, 159–63.

28. The Treaty of Nice provides for the deletion of this final sentence and for the inclusion of a new Article 18(3) EC, which will stipulate that Article 18(2) EC does not apply to provisions on passports, identity cards, residence permits or any such documents, or to provisions on social security or social protection.

29. Case C-299/95, *Kremzow v. Austria* [1997] ECR I-2629. Note also Advocate General Léger's opinion in Case C-192/99, *R. v. Secretary of State for the Home Department ex parte Manjit Kaur* in which he held that Article 18(1) EC is inapplicable to a situation where a person who holds the nationality of one Member State and is not present in the territory of another Member State challenges the refusal by the first Member State to grant her entry. Note in particular paragraphs 33–40 of his opinion, [2001] ECR I-1237. The Court adopted the view that Kaur was not a British national.

no link with Community law.[30] There remains some doubt as to whether Article 18(1) EC has direct effects. The mere fact that it envisages the enactment of secondary legislation would not, according to such cases as *Reyners*[31] and *Van Binsbergen*,[32] prevent it from having such effects. However, the provisions of Article 62(1) EC appear to militate against the notion of such effects.[33] The Court of Justice has tended to avoid answering the question whether Article 18(1) EC creates a direct right for Union citizens. It was able to do so in *María Martínez Sala*,[34] because in that case Ms Sala had actually been authorised to reside in Germany.[35]

The question of the direct effect of what is now Article 18(1) EC also arose for consideration in *Wijsenbeek*,[36] in which the Commission maintained it had such effect, and the Netherlands, Finnish and United Kingdom Governments maintained that it did not do so. The Court held that there is no reason for it to decide this question. This was because even if what are now Articles 14(2) and 18(1) EC did have direct effects and granted individuals in the Member States an unconditional right to move freely within their territories, such Member States reserved the right to carry out identity checks at the internal frontiers, requiring persons to present a valid identity card or passport in order to be able to determine whether the person concerned was a national of a Member State.

The exact scope of Article 18(1) EC is unclear and it is a matter of controversy whether it has a merely declaratory effect, representing a consolidation of the pre-existing position in relation to free movement, or whether it has direct effects, and may be relied on by individuals to claim a right of movement and residence independently of the other Treaty provisions. The leading English case on this matter is the decision of the Court of Appeal in *Vitale*,[37] in which the Court

---

30. Joined Cases C-64/96 and 65/96, *Land Nordrhein Westfalen v. Hecker and Jacquet v. Land Nordrhein Westfalen* [1991] ECR I-3171 in which the third country national spouses of German nationals resident in Germany failed to persuade the Court of Justice to use the Treaty provisions on Union citizenship, and in particular Article 18(1) EC (ex Article 84(1)) as a basis for extending the ambit of Community law to cover such situations. See also Case C-193/94, *Skanavi and Chryssanthakopoulos* [1996] ECR I-929, in which the Court refused to rule on the effect of Article 18 EC where the case could be decided by applying Article 42 EC (now Article 43 EC).

31. Case 2/74, *Reyners v. Belgian State* [1974] ECR 631.

32. Case 33/74, *Van Binsbergen v. Bestuur van de Bedrifsvereniging voor de Metaalnijverheid* [1974] ECR 1299.

33. Article 62(1) EC provides for the abolition of controls on Union citizens and third country nationals when crossing internal borders within five years of the entry into force of the Amsterdam Treaty.

34. Case C-85/96, *María Martínez Sala v. Freistaat Bayern* [1998] ECR I-269.

35. Advocate General La Pergola showed himself willing to consider whether Article 18(1) EC has direct effect; see also Tomuschat, Case note, in (2000) 37 CML Rev. 449, 452–3.

36. Case C-378/97, [1999] ECR I-6207.

37. *R. v. Secretary of State for the Home Department ex parte Vitale* [1996] All ER (EC) 461. The High Court referred the question of the direct effect of Article 18(1) to the ECJ in *R.*

rejected the view that Article 8a (now Article 14(1) EC) had direct effects and gave rise to an unconditional right of residence. It is unfortunate that this Court did not make a reference of this matter to the ECJ. The Commission, (like Advocate General La Pergola in *Wijsenbeek*), has taken a broader view of the meaning of Article 18(1) EC in its first report on citizenship provisions in 1993,[38] and possibly in its recent Communication on Directive 64/221/EEC.[39] However, the views of the Commission on a matter of interpretation, unlike those of the Court, are clearly not decisive.

No secondary legislation has yet been enacted pursuant to Article 18(2) EC in accordance with the co-decision procedure as revised by the Treaty of Amsterdam. However, the making of such legislation has been envisaged in the Action Plan for the Single Market of 4 June 1997.[40]

3. Voting and candidature at local elections

The above matter is governed by Article 19(1) in accordance with the following provisions:

> Every citizen of the Union residing in a Member State of which he is nor a national shall have the right to vote and stand as candidate in municipal elections in the Member State in which he resides, under the same conditions as nationals of the state. That right shall be exercised subject to detailed arrangements adopted by the Council, acting unanimously on a proposal from the Commission and after consulting the European Parliament; arrangements may provide for derogations where warranted by problems specific to a Member State.

The above provision gave rise to the need for constitutional reform in certain states such as France and Spain which have approved constitutional amendments to give voting rights to non-nationals. The mention of derogation where warranted by problems specific to a Member State would seem to have been largely the result of special problems existing in Belgium and Luxembourg connected respectively with multi-ethnicity and the comparatively large percentage of residents who are non-nationals.

It should be noted that in the Council of Europe Convention on the Participation of Foreigners in Public Life at Local Level,[41] the rights of foreign

---

v. *Secretary of State for the Home Department, ex parte Manjit Kaur* [2001] ECR I-1237. Advocate General Léger took the view that it was unnecessary for the Court to answer this question, because Community law was inapplicable to an internal situation, in his Opinion of 7 November 2000. The ECJ also found it unnecessary to consider a possible direct effect of Article 18.

38. COM (1993) 702 final 21 December 1993.
39. COM (1999) 372.
40. CSE (97) 1 final, 4 June 1997.
41. European Treaty Series 144.

residents to vote and stand in local elections is in accordance with Articles 6 and 7, conferred on all foreign nationals who have complied with a five year residence period. The right to vote and stand in municipal elections is governed by the provisions of Council Directive 94/80,[42] which was amended by Council Directive 96/30[43] by reason of the accession of Austria, Sweden and Finland. It has sometimes been suggested that, as is the case with the Council of Europe Convention, the former rights should be extended to third country nationals who have completed a certain residence period.[44] Such an extension may take place in the future. However, no such extension is suggested in the Charter of Fundamental Rights of the EU, Article 40 of which mentions the right of citizens of the Union to vote and stand as a candidate in municipal elections.

4. Voting and candidature in European Parliament elections

Article 19(2) provides as follows:

> Without prejudice to Article 190(4),[45] every citizen residing in a Member State of which he is not a national shall have the right to vote and stand as a candidate in elections to the European Parliament in the Member State in which he resides under the same conditions as nationals of that state. This right shall be exercised subject to detailed arrangements adopted by the Council, acting unanimously on a proposal from the Commission and after consulting the European Parliament; these arrangements may provide for derogations where warranted by problems specific to a Member State.

The above provision makes possible the establishment of multinational constituencies. The detailed arrangements for the exercise of the rights to vote and stand as a candidate are set out in Council Directive 93/109.[46] According to Article 4(1) of this Directive, voters may exercise the right to vote either in the Member State of residence or, if they are allowed to do so, in their home Member State. If a Member State refused to grant the right to vote in the state of residence, its action would, following *Matthews v. UK*,[47] appear to constitute a violation of

---

42. [1994] OJ L368. A detailed account of this Directive may be found in Handoll, *The Free Movement of Persons in the EU*, (Wiley, 1995), pp. 290–5. Article 12 of this Directive contains three derogations, which appear designed to cover the special circumstances of Belgium, Luxembourg, the United Kingdom and Ireland. Belgium was found not to have complied with the requirements of this Directive in Case 323/97, *Commission v. Belgium* [1998] ECR I-4281.
43. [1996] OJ L122/12.
44. Note, in this sense, Handoll, *op. cit.*, pp. 295–6.
45. This provision relates to proposals drawn up by the EP for elections by direct universal suffrage in accordance with a uniform procedure in all Member States.
46. OJ 1993 L329/34.
47. European Court of Human Rights, judgment of 18 February 1999. See the note by B. Rudolf, (1999) 93 AJIL pp. 682–4 and also Steiner and Woods, *Textbook on EC Law*, (7th edn, Blackstone Press, 2000), p. 128.

Article 3 of Protocol 1 to the European Convention on Human Rights, which guarantees individuals the right to free and regular legislative elections. This would clearly be the case if no voting right was available to the relevant persons in their home state; even if such a right was available to them, it might depending on the circumstances, be regarded by the European Court of Human Rights as disproportionately burdensome to require them to exercise it.

The rights provided for in Article 19(2) are unavailable to third country nationals. It has been suggested that the relevant qualifications for the purposes of European citizenship and for certain other Community rights might be abode rather than nationality.[48] This suggestion may be rather too radical to gain general acceptance, but the extension of the right to vote at and be a candidate in European Parliament elections to long term residents who are third country nationals may well be worthy of consideration. However, as is the case with municipal elections, no such extension to third country nationals is provided for in Article 39 of the Charter of Fundamental Rights of the EU, which only grants the right to vote and stand as a candidate in European Parliament elections to European citizens.

5. Diplomatic and consular protection

According to Article 20 EC:

> Every citizen of the Union shall, in the territory of a third country in which the Member State of which he is a national is not represented, be entitled to protection by the diplomatic or consular authorities of any Member State on the same conditions as nationals of that state. Member States shall establish the necessary rules among themselves and start the international negotiations required to ensure this protection.

The above provision would seem to owe something to what was proposed by the Adonnino Committee and endorsed by the European Parliament in 1985. It was then proposed that a Community individual in need of assistance during a temporary stay in a third country in which he was not represented should be able to obtain assistance from the local representation of another Member State.[49]

A legislative framework and a set of guidelines has been developed in the present context.[50] The provisions of Article 20 extend to all areas of diplomatic

---

48. See Nascimbo, *Nationality Law in the EU*, (Milan, Guiffreè, 1991), p. 10 and Bernitz and Bernitz, 'Human Rights and European Identity: The Debate about European Citizenship', in P. Alston (ed.), *The EU and Human Rights* (OUP, 1999), pp. 505, 526.

49. See Closa, 'The Concept of Citizenship in the EU', (1992) 29 CML Rev. 1137, 1151 and also EC Bulletin 7/85, p. 24, and OJ 1985 C 345/27.

50. See COM (1997) 230, para. 2. Note in addition Decision 95/533 (1995) OJ L314/13 on protection for EU citizens by means of diplomatic and consular representation and also Decision 96/409 (CFSP) adopted by Member States under the second pillar relating to emergency travel documents.

protection including those of national interests in areas not covered by Community powers.

Although exceptions to this rule have sometimes been permitted in practice, the basic rule of public international law is that a state may usually only exercise protection against third states in respect of their own nationals. Such states have a discretion whether or not to exercise such protection. In the *Nottebohm* Case, the International Court of Justice held that a state might refuse to exercise such protection where the national seeking it did not have a genuine and effective link with it based on such considerations as habitual residence, centre of interests, family ties, or participation in public life.[51] Protection may be asserted against third states in the absence of such a link only in accordance with the provisions of suitable bilateral or multilateral agreements between the protecting state or states, and the third state or states against which protection is asserted, except where the third state assented to such protection.

As Handoll indicates, Article 20 EC is worded as to convey the impression that diplomatic protection is an individual right, governed by Community or national law and not, as usually envisaged, a discretionary right belonging to the state.[52] The sentence of Article 20 EC uses the words 'on the same conditions as nationals of that Member State' which is capable of leading to the conclusion that the right is only available where the nationals of that Member State are entitled to insist that it exercises diplomatic protection. However, it is also possible to treat the right of diplomatic protection as being conferred by Community law, which grants the same right to protected persons as that enjoyed by nationals when the home state exercises its discretion to assert that right in their favour. There are defects with both interpretations. If the first one is accepted, it leads to the conclusion that the protection envisaged would only be available in limited circumstances. The principal defect of the second interpretation is that it does not conform with the generally accepted principle that a state is entitled, but not bound, to exercise its right of diplomatic protection.

6. Miscellaneous rights

Additional rights are conferred on European citizens by Article 21 EC. These comprise the right to petition the European Parliament, in accordance with Article 194 EC, to apply to the Ombudsman established in accordance with Article 195 EC, and to write to any of the institutions or bodies referred to in Article 21 or in Article 7,[53] in any one of the twelve languages mentioned in Article 314 EC, and to receive an answer in the same language.[54] The first two

---

51. See *Liechtenstein v. Guatemala* (1993) ICJ Reports 4, 22.

52. *Free Movement of Persons in the EU*, p. 303.

53. These are the European Parliament, the Council, the Court of Justice, the Commission and the Court of Auditors.

54. These languages are Dutch, French, German, Italian, Danish, English, Finnish, Greek, Irish, Portuguese, Spanish and Swedish.

rights are enjoyed in common with natural or legal persons residing or having its registered office in a Member State.

7. Right to petition the European Parliament

According to Article 194 EC the right to petition the European Parliament is one enjoyed individually or in association with other citizens or persons. The petition must be on a matter which comes within the Community's fields of activity, and must affect him, her or it directly. This right of petition was recognised in the European Parliament's Rules of Procedure before the entry into force of the Treaty of Maastricht.

8. Applications to the Ombudsman

The Ombudsman, who is appointed by the European Parliament, is empowered by Article 195(1) EC to receive complaints from any citizen of the Union or any natural or legal person residing or having its registered office in a Member State concerning instances of maladministration in the activities of the Community institutions or bodies, with the exception of the Court of Justice or the Court of First Instance acting in their judicial role. The regulations governing the Ombudsman[55] prevent his or her intervention in cases before courts or questioning the soundness of a court ruling.[56] By Article 41(1) of the Treaty on European Union, the Ombudsman has jurisdiction over matters falling within the reformed Third Pillar.

The first Ombudsman was appointed in 1995. When an investigation has been completed, the Ombudsman is required to send a report to Parliament and the institution under investigation. The Ombudsman is also required to notify the complainant of the result of his inquiry, and to make an annual report to Parliament. Complaints have frequently related to such matters as lack of transparency and availability of information.

9. Strengthening of and addition to the citizenship rights

The Commission is required by the first sentence of Article 22 EC to report to the Council and the Economic and Social Committee every three years on the application of the provisions on European citizenship. Its second report in 1997 gives particulars of the implementation of the relevant provisions in the Member States. This report recommended that because the rights of European citizens

---

55. For Parliament's regulations and conditions governing the performance of the Ombudsman's duties, which were approved by the Council in 1994, see [1993] OJ C329/136 and Council Decision 94/114 [1994] OJ L54/25.

56. This may apply to national courts as well as to the Community courts: see Craig and de Burca, *EC Law: Texts, Cases and Materials*, (2nd edn, OUP, 1998), p. 73.

were to be found in a number of different legal provisions setting out rather different rights, the relevant instruments should undergo revision.

The second sentence of Article 22 EC empowers the Council, acting unanimously and on proposal from the Commission and after consultation with the European Parliament to adopt provisions to strengthen or add to the rights contained in Part Two, which shall be recommended for adoption to the Member States in accordance with their constitutional provisions.

V. CONCLUDING REMARKS

Part Two of the EC Treaty fails to describe what is meant by Union citizenship, although it stipulates that a number of rights and duties attach to it. However, the relationship between Union citizenship and national citizenship is not defined. It is unfortunate that there has not been a more significant extension of the rights of citizenship to third country nationals.

Although the rules governing European citizenship display some interesting features, the rights attached to such citizenship are not generally very significant, and they are not accompanied by any duties. It is not clear whether Article 18(1) EC is directly applicable. The Court did not find it necessary to answer this question in *Kaur*. Apart from its controversial decision in *María Martínez Sala*,[57] the Court has not shown any significant inclination to employ the citizenship provisions to enhance the legal protection of individuals.[58]

It has been pointed out that rights akin to citizenship may be provided by other provisions of Community law, for example the non-discrimination provision set out in Article 12 EC; perhaps the same may be true of the fundamental rights contained in the Charter of Fundamental Rights of the European Union.[59] This document has declaratory rather than binding status. However, the Court may well make reference to it in appropriate circumstances. It is not entirely clear how it will relate to the ECHR. The rights contained therein would seem in general to be applicable to third country nationals as well as Community citizens, but there are some exceptions to this principle, as in the case with the right to vote and stand as a candidate in municipal and European Parliament elections.

---

57. Case C-85/96, [1998] ECR I-2691. See also Case C-274/96, *Bickel and Franz* [1998] ECR 7637 in which the Court found that the exercise of the right to move and reside freely under Article 8a EC (now Article 14(1) EC) was enhanced if citizens of the Union were able to use a language to communicate with the judicial authorities of a state on the same footing as nationals. However, this finding seemed to reinforce their earlier conclusion that Article 6 EC (now Article 12 EC) forbade discrimination against recipients of services.

58. See J. Shaw, 'European Union Citizenship: The IGC and Beyond', (1997) 3 European Public Law 413.

59. Communication from the Commission of 11.10.2000, COM (2000) 544 final.

9   The Rights of Third Country Nationals in the EC

I. INTRODUCTION

It is not possible to give a detailed account of the above matter, on which there is a considerable amount of Community material often partaking of the nature of "soft" law which is not strictly binding, such as recommendations, resolutions and draft conventions in addition to a very considerable amount of doctrinal writing. However, certain recent developments in the relevant areas, particularly in relation to immigration and asylum,[1] will be considered in outline in this chapter.

Although third country nationals make up several millions of the Community, because they do not have the nationality of a Member State they are not granted, except to a limited extent in certain particular situations (e.g. if they are members of the family of a national of a Member State established or working in another such state) the rights granted in accordance with the principle of free movement of persons in the EC. Thus, the general position is that third country nationals who are legally admitted to a Member State have no rights when they move to other such states. However, certain categories of third country nationals may be said to be in a privileged position in so far as they do enjoy certain rights or liberties in relation to freedom of movement within the EC. In addition to the family members mentioned above in chapter 3, these include posted workers, refugees and stateless persons, and nationals of third countries associated with the Community by means of an international agreement.

The limits on the rights given to third country nationals who are members of the family of a citizen working in a Member State other than his own have been mentioned above in chapters 2 and 3, where particular attention was given to the possible and often burdensome requirement of the provision of a visa on entering the territory of a Member State, and the probable non-existence of a right of residence in the territory of the host state for the divorced spouse.[2] The parties to extra-marital, polygamous or same sex relationships may sometimes be placed in a precarious position.

The anomaly exists under Article 11 of Regulation 1612/68 that a third country national who is the spouse or child of a national of a Member State, who pursues a professional activity in the host state as an employed or self-employed person,

---

1. There is an Asylum Protocol attached to the Amsterdam Treaty which governs asylum applications from nationals of EU Member States. It obliges Member States to regard one another as same countries of origin, but the presumption can be rebutted on the grounds set out in paragraphs (a)–(d) of the sole article of the (binding) Asylum Protocol.
2. See Report of High Level Panel, pp. 73–75.

can only pursue such a professional activity as an employed person in that state. The Veil Panel (High Level Panel) suggested that this gap or anomaly should be removed.[3] Under Article 2(2) of the 1990 and 1993 Directives on the right of residence,[4] the third country national spouse or child of a national of a Member State who is studying, has retired, or is lawfully resident in another Member State may pursue an employed or self-employed activity in that state. There seems little justification for this difference in treatment.

II. EFFECT OF INTERNATIONAL AGREEMENTS

The situation which has come about as the result of the large number of association, cooperation and other agreements entered into by the Community is very complex. There are now agreements of different kinds with a very considerable number of countries. They frequently contain provisions governing the mobility of persons, and relating to such matters as employed persons, social security, the right of establishment and the supply of services. The agreements are diverse in character, and affect different rights and for this reason it is difficult to construct general principles about them.[5] Such agreements may contain directly effective rights which may be invoked by individuals.[6] There is a considerable body of jurisprudence of the Court of Justice concerning the EC-Turkey Association Agreement. The Court of Justice has rather controversially done a great deal to assimilate the position of Turkish workers in the Community to that of EC nationals.[7] The various types of agreements mentioned in this paragraph receive fuller consideration in the following chapter.

III. PROPOSALS AND RESTRICTIONS BEFORE THE ENTRY INTO FORCE OF THE TREATY OF AMSTERDAM CONCERNING THE IMMIGRATION OF THIRD COUNTRY NATIONALS

1. Introductory remarks

The above matter cannot be considered in detail in a book of the present scope. Until the Maastricht Treaty came into force, legal competence in the field of

---

3. See Report of High Level Panel, pp. 70–1.
4. Council Directive 90/364/EEC, OJ 1990 L120/26; Council Directive 90/365/EEC, OJ 1990 L120/28; Council Directive 93/96/EEC OJ 1993 L317/59.
5. See Report of High Level Panel, p. 77.
6. Note, for example, Case C-18/90, *ONEM v. Kziber* [1991] ECR I-199, in which a non-discrimination provision concerning social security in an agreement between the EEC and Morocco was said to have direct effects. This decision should be contrasted with that in Case C-37/98, *R. v. Secretary of State for the Home Department, ex p. Savas* [2000] ECR I-2927, in which the Court held that although a provision in the EC-Turkey Association Agreement relating to freedom of establishment had direct effects, it could not in itself confer rights of establishment and residence on a Turkish citizen who had remained and set up business in breach of domestic immigration law.
7. See Hailbronner, *Immigration and Asylum Law and Policy of the EU*, (Kluwer Law International, 2000), pp. 222–234.

immigration remained principally with the national authorities.[8] However, since 1993, the Council, which based itself largely on Article 21 of the Treaty of European Union (formerly Article K3) has passed a number of resolutions concerning third country nationals, which are likely to undergo certain alterations if and when submitted in the form of draft regulations or directives under Title IV of the EC Treaty.[9] These include the Council Resolution of 1 June 1993 on the harmonisation of national policies on family reunification;[10] the Council Resolution of 20 June 1994 on limitation of admission of third country nationals to the territory of the Member States for employment;[11] and the Council Resolution of 30 November 1994 relating to the limitations on the admission of third country nationals to the territories of the Member States for the purpose of pursuing activities as self-employed persons. Furthermore, the Commission has submitted a proposal[12] under Article K3(2)(c) of the Treaty of European Union for a Council Act establishing a Convention on Rules for the Admission of Third Country Nationals on 30 July 1992.

The above proposals distinguish between different categories of persons. The draft convention applies to a number of such categories of third country nationals including self-employed persons, trainees, students, family members and long-term residents. It is inapplicable to applicants for refugee status (and presumably to those granted such status), displaced persons granted admission to stay for temporary protection in a Member State and persons granted exceptional authorisation to stay in the territory of a Member State. The draft convention is informed by the view that immigration is not to be encouraged, but it permits immigration for the purposes of employment in certain circumstances. It appears more liberal in this regard than the relevant Council resolution which permits such immigration in exceptional circumstances only. There now appears to be an increasing recognition of the fact that certain EU Member States may benefit from immigration, especially of skilled workers.

A number of other draft instruments exist concerning the free movement of third country nationals within the Community. Three proposals, which it has been contended are over-ambitious, aimed at abolishing controls on persons at the Community's internal frontiers, were adopted by the Commission on 12 July 1995. The most important of these, which was amended, was a proposal for a Council Directive aimed at eliminating controls on all persons crossing internal frontiers, irrespective of their nationality, or whether they were economically

---

8. Note in this sense, Cases 281, 283–5 and 287/85, *Germany, France, Netherlands, Denmark and the United Kingdom v. Commission* [1987] ECR 3203; see also Weatherill and Beaumont, *EU Law*, (3rd edn, Penguin Books, 1999), pp. 276–7.

9. The Maastricht Treaty came into force on 1 November 1993, Germany being the last state to ratify it.

10. SN 2828/1/1993 WGI 1497.

11. OJ 1996 C274/7.

12. COM(97) 387 final; OJ 1997 C 337/9.

active.[13] A further proposal[14] which was amended, made on the same date was for a Council Directive on the right of third country nationals to travel within the Community. Such nationals would have been entitled to cross internal borders and remain within the territory of a Member State, or proceed onwards without a visa.

As indicated in chapter 2, Part IV of Title III of the EC Treaty confers a considerable degree of competence on the Community in the fields of immigration and asylum, as well as in other fields. Although it should be obvious that the eventual introduction of common policies concerning third country nationals are necessary if internal borders restricting the free movement of citizens and third country nationals are to be removed into accordance with Article 62(1) EC, one must hope that the external border controls brought into being do not have too harsh an impact.[15]

2. The Action Plan and its implementation

The Action Plan of 3 December 1998[16] which was drawn up by the Council and Commission, is concerned with the best method of implementing the provisions of the EC Treaty, as amended by the Treaty of Amsterdam, on an area of freedom, security and justice. Some of the more important features of this plan, insofar as they relate to the free movement of persons, are considered in the following paragraphs, in order to indicate the areas in which the Community institutions will work in the near future. Both the provisions of the Action Plan concerning immigration and those concerning asylum are considered immediately below for the sake of convenience. Certain of the relevant stipulations of the Action Plan, for example those relating to the adoption of minimum standards on procedures in Member States for granting or withdrawing refugee status, and minimum standards for giving temporary protection to displaced persons from third countries who cannot return to their county of origin have already given rise to draft legislation which is considered later in the section, concerning post-Amsterdam developments in refugee and asylum law. More work may be expected in all the relevant fields; some measures are, according to the Action Plan, to be taken within two years, whilst others are to be taken within five years, of the entry into force of the Amsterdam Treaty.

According to paragraph 36 of the Action Plan, a number of measures concerning asylum, including the adoption of minimum standards on procedures in

---

13. OJ 1995 C 289/16; COM (95) 347 final. The amended proposal may be found in OJ 1997 C 140/21; COM (97) 106 final.
14. OJ 1995 C 306/5; COM (95) 346 final. For the amended proposal, see OJ 1997 C139/6; COM (97) 106 final.
15. This fear has been expressed particularly in relation to measures concerning refugees: see Hathaway, 'Harmonising for Whom? The Devaluation of Refugee Protection in the Era of European Economic Integration', (1993) 26 Cornell International Law Journal 719.
16. OJ 1999 C 19/1, 22.1.1999.

Member States for granting or withdrawing refugee status must be taken within two years of the entry into force of the Amsterdam Treaty. Within the same two periods studies must be undertaken with a view to establishing the merits of a common single European asylum procedure. The implementation of the Dublin Convention and the transformation of its basis is also to be the subject of measures adopted within the two year time period.

Certain measures on immigration are also to be taken within this period. These include the adoption of an instrument on the lawful status of legal immigrants, and the establishment of a coherent EU policy on readmission and return. Furthermore, within two years of the entry into force of the Amsterdam Treaty, illegal immigration must be combated through *inter alia*, information campaigns in transit countries and countries of origin,[17] and practical proposals must be brought forward for combating it more effectively.

Cooperation to discourage illegal immigration has also been discussed at the European Council in the summits at Tampere, Feira and Nice, as well as at a meeting of Balkan and EU states in Zagreb in November 2000.[18] The British and Italian Prime Ministers have recently said that their countries would take certain steps against illegal immigration and would encourage other Member States to combat it, especially insofar as it involves trafficking in human beings.[19] The subject of illegal immigration has also been dealt with in certain other proposals made by Mr Straw[20] (which have some dubious features), and has been further considered by the EU at a Ministerial meeting in Stockholm and subsequently.

Paragraph 36 of the Action Plan requires certain measures to be taken in relation to external borders and the free movement of persons within two years of the entry into force of the Treaty of Amsterdam. These include particular measures on visas and further harmonisation of Member States' rules on carriers' liability.

By paragraph 37, measures have to be taken as quickly as possible on the temporary protection of displaced persons. A draft Directive has been prepared in this area which is considered below. According to paragraph 38, certain other measures in the fields of external borders, and the free movement of persons, have to be adopted within five years. The measures in the field of asylum include the adoption of minimum standards with respect to the qualification of nationals

---

17. Action plans, which are not based exclusively on Title IV EC, have been prepared by the High Level Working Group on Asylum and Migration set up by the Council, for the most important countries of origin and transit. The European Parliament has passed an initial resolution which chiefly concerns these plans. See OJ 2000 C378/75, 29.12.2000.

18. Much trafficking in illegal immigrants seems to take place in Turkey and the Balkans.

19. See "The Observer", 4 February 2001, p. 31 (joint contribution by Mr. Blair and Signor Amato).

20. See "The Guardian", Feb.7 2001, p. 7. The UN High Commissioner for Refugees has adopted a sceptical attitude to these proposals, which aim at the processing of claims for asylum near to the applicant's home state.

of third countries as refugees. In the field of immigration they include the preparation of rules on the conditions of entry and residence, and standards and procedures for the issue of long-term visas and residence permits, including those for the purpose of family reunion.

The European Council meeting in Tampere agreed upon a number of important measures to realise an area of freedom, security and justice. One of these was the development of a common immigration and asylum policy; possible progress with its implementation is discussed in the communication from the Commission to the Council and the European Parliament of 22 November 2000 on a Community Immigration Policy.[21] Certain recent proposals in the fields of immigration and asylum are discussed below, together with some earlier initiatives in the field of refugee and asylum law, some of which remain of importance.

3. Some recent proposals and initiatives on immigration

Certain recent Commission proposals, including that of 1 December 1999, which is concerned with the right of family reunification,[22] as well as a recent French initiative based on Article 63(3) EC on mutual recognition of decisions on the expulsion of third country nationals, have been inspired by the European Council meeting at Tampere in Finland on 15 and 16 October 1999. A more positive approach to immigration policy within the EU was taken at this meeting than might have been feared, partly perhaps because of the recognition of the need of business for skilled and qualified staff, and of the realisation that the population of the EU is ageing. The European Council adopted the view that a common European policy on immigration and asylum would aim at the fair treatment of third country nationals and better management of migration flows. It asked the Council to rapidly adopt decisions on the basis of Commission proposals concerning the admission and residence of third country nationals in EC states.

(1) Proposal for a Directive on family reunification

As already pointed out, before the proposal for a Council Directive on the right of family reunification was published in December 1999, the Council and Commission had already worked on the topic of family reunification. Entry and residence for the purpose of family reunification is the chief form of immigration into the EU states, as well as into Canada and the United States at the present time. The right of family reunification is mentioned in a number of international instruments and Articles 8 and 12 of the European Convention on Human

---

21. COM (2000) 757 final. The Communication emphasises the need for migrants in certain sectors of the economies of the EU states, and the fact that such migrants generally have a positive effect on economic growth and do not impose a burden on the welfare state. It also emphasises the need for positive admissions policies concerning economic migrants, and for the gradual integration of third country national migrants into Member States.
22. COM (1999) 638 final; for the amended proposal see COM (2000) 624 final.

Rights are specially relevant to it. Article 8 secures the right to respect for personal and family life and Article 12 secures the right to marry and found a family. Although the European Court of Human Rights has decided a number of relevant cases, it has not yet deduced the existence of any unlimited right to family reunification of the members of the family of a third country national lawfully settled in a Member State. It has also not granted absolute protection against separation from members of the family in the event of an expulsion, unless a normal family life is impossible in the country of origin. However, the decisions of the ECHR place limits on the discretionary exercise of the powers of public authorities regarding controls on entry into the territory, and in the event of expulsion. It has been suggested that because of the provisions of Article 8 of the European Convention on Human Rights it is very difficult to deport certain long-term resident third country nationals.[23]

The purpose of the proposed Directive is to establish a right to family reunification for the benefit of third country nationals[24] residing on the territory of the Member States, and for citizens of the Union who (as in *Morson and Jhanjan*)[25] do not exercise their right of free movement. The Preamble to the proposal states that the proposal, which contains a number of common rules, confines itself to the minimum necessary to comply with the requirements of subsidiarity and proportionality. The proposal is based upon Article 63(3) EC, which provides that the Council is to adopt certain measures in the field of immigration policy, which comprise conditions of entry and residence and standards and procedures for the issue by Member States of long term visas and residence permits, including those for the purpose of family reunion.

(2)   General provisions of the proposed Directive

The proposed Directive attempts to harmonise the legislation of the Member States such that third country nationals would be broadly subject to the same reunification conditions, irrespective of the state to which they were admitted for residence purposes. Article 2 of the proposed Directive is a definitions section. Article 5 is concerned with the scope of the Directive. It would be applicable where the applicant for reunification was:

(a) a third country national residing lawfully in a Member State[26] and holding

---

23. See Sherlock, 'Deportation of Aliens and Article 8 ECHR', (1998) 23 EL Rev. HR 62–75; but note on the contrary *Baghli* v. *France*, Case 34374/97, 30 November 1999, in which the ECHR permitted the deportation of an Algerian national who had been resident in France for 17 years since the age of 2.

24. A third country national is defined in Article 2(a) of the proposed Directive as any person who is not a citizen of the EU.

25. Cases 35 and 36/82, *Morson and Jhanjan* v. *Netherlands* [1982] ECR 3723.

26. The reason for such residence is not spelt out: they might be employed or self-employed persons or students according to the Commission's commentary on Article 2.

a residence permit issued by that state for a period of at least one year;

(b) a refugee,[27] irrespective of the duration of his residence permit;

(c) a citizen of the Union not exercising his right of free movement, and the applicant's family members were third party nationals, irrespective of their legal status. They might thus be refugees or persons governed by a temporary protection scheme.

The Directive would not apply where the applicant for reunification was:

(a) a third country national applying for recognition of refugee status, where application had not yet given rise to a final decision;

(b) a third country national authorised to reside in a Member State on the basis of temporary protection[28] or applying for authorisation to reside on that basis and awaiting a decision on his status;

(c) a third country national authorised to reside in a Member State on the basis of a subsidiary term of protection in accordance with international obligations, national legislation or the practice of Member States, or applying for authorisation to reside on that basis, and awaiting a decision on his status.

The exclusion of the categories of persons mentioned above is explained by the fact that, when the proposal was made further Commission proposals on the status of persons enjoying subsidiary forms of protection were expected in the near future.

The Directive would also be applicable to family members of citizens of the Union exercising their right to free movement of persons. This is obviously because such persons already enjoy the right to be joined by members of their family under the relevant Community legislation. The Directive is said by Article 3(4) to be without prejudice to the more favourable provisions of Community or mixed agreements concluded with third countries, and already in force.

The family reunification of Union citizens who do not exercise their right of free movement has hitherto been subject exclusively to national rules.[29] Article 4 permits the family member of Union citizens who have not exercised this right to benefit from the relevant provisions of Community law.

---

27. The Commission's commentary on Article 2 says that the concept of refugee covers both those who have obtained this status under the Geneva Convention and those who have obtained it under a constitutional provision: note for example Article 16 of the German Constitution.

28. When the proposal on family reunification was first made by the Commission, there were already two proposals in existence on the temporary protection of displaced persons: see OJ C 106/13, 4.4.1987 and OJ C 268/12, 21.8.1998. The most recent proposal on temporary protection is discussed below.

29. Note for example, Cases 35 and 36/82, *Morson and Jhanjan v. Netherlands* [1982] ECR 3723.

a. Family members

Detailed provisions concerning family members who would be eligible for admission and residence are included in Article 5 of the Directive. These would include the applicant's spouse or unmarried partner living in a stable relationship, if the legislation of the Member State concerned treated the situation of unmarried couples as corresponding to that of married ones. They would also include minor children of the applicant and his spouse or unmarried partners, including adopted children. Furthermore, they would include the children of just one of the spouses or partners provided that the spouse or partner applying for reunification had custody and responsibility. Should custody be shared, the other partner's authorisation would be required. In addition the relevant family member would also include relations in the ascending line of the applicant and his spouse or unmarried partner who were dependent on them, and had no other means of support in their country of origin. Finally, children of the applicant or his spouse or partner, of full age, who by reason of their health, were objectively unable to satisfy their needs, would also be entitled to entry and residence.

The age of children admitted for reunification must be below the age of majority set by the law of the Member State, and such children must not be married. Article 5(2) provides that where an applicant has contracted a polygamous marriage and already has a spouse living with him in a Member State, the Member State concerned shall not authorise the entry and residence of a further spouse, nor the children of that spouse; the entry and residence of children of another spouse shall be authorised if the best interests of the child so require. The latter contingency may obviously occur where a child's mother dies, or becomes subject to an incapacity.

Article 6 provides for derogations from Article 5 in the case in which a refugee is an unaccompanied minor, and is based upon Article 22 of the United Nations Convention on the Rights of the Child. Thus, such unaccompanied minors may be joined by their parents without any need to prove that the latter are dependent on them, and have no other means of support in the country of origin. Where the minor has no parents, or it has proved impossible to trace them, other family members (e.g. collaterals) may have their entry and residence authorised for the purposes of family reunification.

b. Submission and examination of the application

By Article 7, the application for family reunification is made to the competent authority of the Member State where the applicant resides, and must be accompanied by documentary evidence of the family relationship. The decision must be notified to the applicant within six months, and reasons must be given if it is rejected. If the applicant is a refugee and cannot produce documentary evidence of the family relationship, Member States are required to have regard to other evidence of the relationship.

c. Practical conditions for the exercise of the right to family reunification

According to Article 8(1) Member States would be entitled to refuse to allow the entry of family members on grounds of public policy, domestic security or public health. It follows from Article 7(3) that if an application is rejected on one of these grounds, reasons must be given. By Article 8(2), the public policy and domestic security considerations which may be taken as a basis for refusing entry must be based on the family member's personal conduct. It follows from Article 8(3) that once a residence permit is issued, its renewal cannot be withheld on the basis of subsequent illness or disability. By virtue of Article 9(1) of the proposed Directive, when the application for family reunification is submitted, the Member State concerned may ask the applicant to provide that he has accommodation at least equal in size to that provided as social housing, and which meets general health and safety standards in the Member State concerned. He may also be asked to prove that he has sickness insurance in respect of all risks in the Member State concerned to himself and the members of his family; and stable resources which are higher or at least equal to the level of resources below which the Member State concerned may grant social assistance.[30] The provisions of Article 9(1) are stated by Article 9(3) to be inapplicable where the applicant is a refugee.

It is difficult to understand the need for Article 10(1), which provides that the Member State may require the applicant to have resided lawfully in its territory for a period not exceeding one year before having his family members join him. The existence of this requirement (which is made inapplicable to refugees by Article 10(2)) would seem to follow already from Article 3(1)(a).

d. Entry and residence

Article 11 governs the admission of family members. Member States are required to grant such persons every facility for obtaining the necessary visas. According to Article 12(1), the applicant's family members would be entitled in the same way as citizens of the Union to access to education (which appears to include university education), access to employment and self-employed activity; and access to vocational guidance, initial and further training and retraining. Article 12(2) contains the somewhat restrictive provision that Member States may restrict access to employment or self-employed activity by relatives in the ascending line or children of full age to which Article 5(1)(d) and (e) applies. These articles apply to dependent relatives and adult children who have health problems. Article 13(1) provides that at the latest after four years of residence, and provided the family relationship still exists, the spouse or unmarried partner, and a child who has reached majority shall be entitled to an autonomous residence permit independent of that of the applicant. Furthermore, Article 13(2) once again displays a more cautious attitude to children of full age and relatives

---

30. Where the latter provision cannot be applied, resources must be higher than or at least equal to the level of the minimum social security pension paid by the Member State.

of the ascending line to whom Article 5(1)(d) and (e) apply. The relevant Member State has a discretion whether or not to grant such persons a residence permit.

e. Penalties and redress

It follows from Article 14 that Member States may impose sanctions in the event of circumventions of the rules and procedures set out in the Directive. These sanctions consist of the rejection of an application for entry and residence for the purpose of family reunification or the withdrawal or refusal to remove a residence permit. Such penalties may be imposed where entry and/or residence was obtained by means of falsified documents or fraud; or a marriage or adoption was contracted for the sole purpose of enabling the person concerned to enter or reside in a Member State. It may prove very difficult to prove the latter contingency. Member States would be permitted to undertake specific checks where there were grounds for suspicion. The Commission's commentary suggests that systematic checks would not be permitted, but it might prove difficult to prevent them from taking place in practice.

The principle of proportionality appears to inspire Article 15 which provides that "Member States shall have proper regard for the nature and validity of the person's family relationships and the duration of his residence in the Member State and to the existence of family, cultural and social ties, with his country of origin where they withdraw or refuse to renew a residence permit or decide to order the removal of the applicant or members of his family."[31]

According to Article 16, the applicant and the members of his family have the right to apply to the courts of the Member State concerned where an application for family reunification is rejected or a residence permit is either not renewed or withdrawn, or removal ordered. Such recourse to judicial procedures appears desirable and would apply, for example, where entry was refused on one of the grounds set out in Article 8.

Article 17 is a standard provision under Community law, providing for effective, proportionate, and dissuasive penalties. It gives the Member States the discretionary power to determine the penalties applicable in the event of infringement of national provisions for the application of the Directive.

f. Final provisions

The Member States would be required by Article 19 of the proposal to transpose the Directive by 31 December 2002 at the latest, and to inform the Commission of changes to their laws, regulations and administrative provisions. It seems

---

31. The Commission's commentary says that account should be taken of the jurisprudence of the European Court of Human Rights on the interpretation of Article 8 ECHR (notably in *Moustaquin v. Belgium* (18.2.1991) and *Bedjaoui v. France* (26.3.1992), and account must be taken of family relationships, the duration of residence, and the existence of links in the country of origin.

unrealistic to assume that the proposed Directive could be adopted by the latter date. There does not seem any question of the United Kingdom or Ireland "opting in" to the provisions of the proposed Directive at present. According to Article 18, not later than two years after the deadline set in Article 19, the Commission would be required to report to the European Parliament and the Council on the application of the Directive in the Member States and will propose such amendments as may appear necessary.

(3) French initiative on illegal immigration

A French initiative was published in the Official Journal for 24 August 2000.[32] It is once again based upon Article 63(3) EC, which permits the taking of measures against illegal immigration and illegal residence, including the repatriation of illegal residents. It should be remembered that Article 67(1) EC permits proposals to be made within the areas covered by Title IV on the initiative of a Member State. The objective of this proposal is to make possible the enforcement of an expulsion decision issued by a competent authority (the "issuing Member State") against a third country national present within the territory of another Member State ("the enforcing Member State"). The European Parliament's Committee on Citizens and Freedoms and Rights (Justice and Home Affairs) contended in its Report on the French initiative that the latter does not seem to have a proper basis in Article 63(3) EC, which it said concerns repatriation and not the mutual recognition of expulsion decisions.[33] There seems considerable force in this contention.

(4) Adoption of the proposals mentioned above

The above proposals would have to be adopted in accordance with Article 67 EC, whereby, during a transitional period of five years, the Council is to act unanimously on a proposal from the Commission, or on the initiative of a Member State, after consulting the European Parliament. The subjects of the entry and residence of third country nationals for the purpose of family reunification and temporary protection in the event of a mass influx of displaced person, which is discussed below, have been discussed within the Community for a number of years, and there may be difficulties in securing unanimous agreement about them, as is required by Article 67.

It will be remembered that the United Kingdom and Ireland do not take part in the adoption by the Council of measures under Title IV, and such measures are not binding on them, although they may agree to a specific proposal, or to a measure which has actually been adopted. Denmark is in a similar position to the United Kingdom and Ireland, except that Denmark does not have the

---

32. OJ 2000 C243/1. There have been further French initiatives on defining and preventing the facilitation of unauthorised entry and residence: see OJ 2000 C 253/1 and C253/6.
33. EP, Session Documents, Final A5-0394/2000, 11.12.2000, pp. 8–9.

ability to opt into relevant measures. One can envisage that whatever the position might be in relation to temporary protection and family reunification, there might be a certain reluctance on the part of the United Kingdom and Ireland to opt into measures providing for the enforcement of expulsion decisions of other Member States.

(5) Possible further Commission work on immigration

Further Commission work on legal immigration and in particular on the entry and residence of third country nationals is likely in the near future.[34] It is intended that the Commission will pursue work on such matters as entry and residence for the purposes of study or vocational training, and of salaried and self-employed persons. It has also been expected to examine the legal position of third country nationals holding a long term residence permit,[35] as well as the rights of third country nationals residing lawfully in one Member State to reside in another Member State.[36] There has been a recent French initiative with a view to adopting a Council regulation on freedom of movement with a long stay visa.[37]

5. Certain earlier instruments providing for favourable treatment of refugees

Although the EC Treaty did not contain any provisions governing these matters until its revision by the Treaty of Amsterdam, "soft law" instruments have sometimes provided for favourable treatment to be given to refugees and stateless persons. Thus, for example, in 1964 the representatives of the Member States adopted Declaration 64/305, according to which "the admission into their territory to pursue an activity as an employed person of refugees recognised as such under the 1951 Convention[38] and established on the territory of another Member

---

34. Recent or intended Commission proposals related to immigration policy are set out in the Commission communications to the Council and the European Parliament on a common immigration policy, COM (2000) 757 final.

35. See the Commission proposal for a Council Directive concerning the status of third-country nationals for long term residence, COM (2001) 127 final, which aims at a common status for certain long term residents who have resided in a member state for five years.

36. See page 29 of the Communication from the Commission to the Council and the EP on a Community Immigration Policy, COM (2000) 757 final for an account of some planned proposals in the field of immigration.

37. OJ 2000 C200/4. It is not entirely clear from Article 67 whether this initiative has the effect of preventing the Commission from submitting its own proposal. The French initiative is based in part upon Article 63(3)(a) EC, and is intended to represent a development of the Schengen *acquis*. It is designed as a first step in the harmonisation of the conditions for the issue of long term visas.

38. The Convention mentioned is the Geneva Convention on the Status of Refugees. A refugee is defined in Article 1A(2) of the Convention as any person who: "As a result of events occurring before 1 January 1951, and owing to well founded fear of being persecuted by

State must be given especially favourable consideration, in particular in order to allow refugees the most favourable treatment possible in their territories". Furthermore, it should be noted that refugees, and stateless persons, as well as EEA citizens, are often entitled to benefits under Regulation 1408/71, which governs social security matters.[39]

IV. SOME DEVELOPMENTS IN THE FIELDS OF REFUGEE AND ASYLUM LAW BEFORE THE ENTRY INTO FORCE OF THE TREATY OF AMSTERDAM

1. Preliminary remarks

Although there was no basis for such harmonisation in the EC Treaty until it was amended by the Treaty of Amsterdam, Member States began the harmonisation of asylum and refugee law in the 1980s by means of preparing and concluding agreements and conventions, and by means of the adoption of non-binding instruments as well as through the creation of a number of committees. The Palma document[40] aimed at the harmonisation of asylum law in accordance with the Geneva Convention and was adopted by the European Council in 1989. It identified as essential measures: (a) the preparation of a Convention on the determination of the state responsible for the application for asylum; (b) rules on the free movement of asylum seekers between Member States; (c) recourse to a simplified procedure in accordance with national legislation for manifestly unfounded applications: (d) the acceptance of identical international obligations with regard to asylum.

2. The Dublin Convention

This Convention, which was concluded in June 1990, made provision for exclusive competences in determining asylum claims, but did not come into force until September 1997. When it did so, it supplanted the generally similar rules contained in the section of the Schengen Implementation Convention on asylum.

---

reasons of race, religion, nationality, membership of a particular social group or political opinion, is outside the country of his nationality and is unable or owing to such fears is unwilling to avail himself of the protection of that country; or who, not having a nationality and being outside the country of his former habitual residence, as a result of such events, is unable or, owing to such fear, is unwilling to return to it." The time limitation is inapplicable to parties to the 1967 Protocol. The phrase "membership of a particular social groups" has been treated in certain national jurisprudence as capable of being applied to women or homosexuals.

39. The Commission made a proposal in 1998 to extend the personal scope of Regulation 1408/71 to third country nationals: see OJ 1998 C6/15.
40. See Hailbronner, *op. cit.*, p. 360.

Article 3 of the Dublin Convention (to which all the EC states are parties[41]) contains the general principle that Member States should examine applications for asylum. By virtue of Article 3(2), the Member State responsible for such an application is determined in accordance with criteria set out in Article 4–8. Member States preserve the right under their national laws to send an applicant for asylum to a third state, in accordance with the 1951 Geneva Convention and its 1967 Protocol. Article 3(7) makes provision for the taking back during the process of determining the responsible state, of an applicant who has made an application for asylum in another Member State, by a Member State in which an application for asylum has been made, but subsequently withdrawn.

The criteria set out in Articles 4–8 apply in the order in which they appear. First of all, the Member State in which certain members of the family already have refugee status will be the responsible state, provided the persons affected so wish.[42] Secondly, the Member State issuing the asylum seeker with a residence permit or valid visa (in some cases) will be the responsible state.[43] Thirdly, where irregular entry has taken place from a third country, the Member State entered will be responsible; but where an application has been made in a Member State where the applicant has been living for at least six months, that state will be responsible.[44] Fourthly, the Member State responsible for controlling the entry of the alien into the territory of the Member State will be the responsible state; nevertheless, if the need for a visa is waived after legal entry, and the alien lodges an application in another Member State where the requirement for a visa is also waived, the latter state will be responsible.[45] Fifthly, a Member State will be responsible where the application is made in transit in one of its airports.[46] Finally, if after applying the foregoing criteria no Member State can be designated as the responsible one, the first Member State with which the application for asylum is lodged is treated as being the responsible state.[47]

The consequences of such responsibility are set out in Articles 10–13 of the Convention. Both the Dublin Convention and the Schengen Implementation Convention are applicable only to asylum seekers who request refugee status under the Geneva Convention, and do not usually apply to persons who are victims of wars or natural disasters. The provisions of the Dublin Convention will obviously be influential when the Council enacts measures pursuant to Article 63(1)(a) EC, which is concerned with the determination of the Member State responsible for considering an asylum application from a third country

---

41. See Handoll, *Free Movement of Persons in the EU*, (Wiley, 1995), pp. 419–425, and Hailbronner, *op. cit.*, pp. 382–93 for useful brief accounts of this Convention.
42. Dublin Convention Article 4.
43. Dublin Convention, Article 5.
44. Dublin Convention, Article 6.
45. Dublin Convention, Article 7(1).
46. Dublin Convention, Article 7(3).
47. Dublin Convention, Article 8.

national. However, the Dublin Convention system has proved somewhat disappointing in practice. It has frequently proved difficult to determine the responsible Member State, especially where countries have requested proof of an applicant's earlier movements. Such proof sometimes fails to exist, because the applicant has destroyed all the relevant documents. In consequence, an EU country in which a refugee has applied for asylum has often had to accept responsibility, even if it was not the first state in which the refugee entered. Furthermore, it has often been asserted that the Dublin Convention does not ensure a fair distribution of requests for asylum.

3. Actions by the Commission and the immigration ministers

In October 1991, the Commission issued an important communication to the Council and Parliament[48] emphasising the need for the taking of common action to counter abuse, and in the long run, for the harmonisation of the procedural and substantive law of asylum. The Commission took the view that future common action might include the harmonisation of conditions of refoulement (sending back to the state of origin) at the external frontier of the EU; and of the provisions and practices relating to *de facto* refugees; and of the conditions of entry of asylum seekers. Such harmonisation might also include the establishment of machinery for mutual information exchange, and of a common system of legal remedies.

A report for the European Council meeting in Maastricht on immigration and asylum policy dealing with the harmonisation of the immigration and asylum policies of the Member States was adopted by the ministers responsible for immigration on 3 December 1991.[49] This report mentioned six areas in which harmonisation might take place.[50] The Community immigration ministers also adopted four instruments on asylum procedures at their London meeting from 30 November–1 December 1992. Their Resolution on Manifestly Unfounded Applications for Asylum and their Conclusions on Safe Third Countries, have received some criticism in the literature.[51]

4. The meaning of the term "refugee"

The Member States of the EU and their courts interpret the meaning of the term "refugee" rather differently. The 1996 Joint Position defined by the Council

---

48. SEC/9D1857.

49. Document WGI 930; see Guild and Niessen, *The Developing Immigration and Asylum Policies of the European Union* (1996) 449 et seq.

50. See Hailbronner, *op. cit.*, pp. 362–3.

51. Note in particular Noll and Vedsted, 'Non-Communitarians: Refugee and Asylum Policies', ch. 11 in Alston (ed.), *The EU and Human Rights*, (OUP, 1999), at pp. 395–9. These two writers contend that "manifestly unfounded" applications are defined in a broad and vague way and that low standards are required for safe third countries, which standards take

on the basis of the former Article K3 of the Treaty on European Union attempted to solve the problems arising from this disparity, but it is clear from paragraph 3 of the preamble to Joint Position 96/196/JHA that it has no binding force.[52] However, reference may be made to it when the Council takes measures under Article 63(1) EC which is concerned with minimum standards for the qualification of third party nationals as refugees. Furthermore, the Joint Position might be regarded as subsequent practice which, in accordance with Article 31(3)(b) of the Vienna Convention on the Law of Treaties, may be of value for the purposes of interpretation of the Geneva Convention. According to paragraph 5.2 of the Joint Position:

> "Persecution by third parties will be considered to fall within the scope of the Geneva Convention where it is based on one of the grounds in Article 1A, is individual in nature, and is encouraged or permitted by the authorities. Where the official authorities fail to act, such persecution should give rise to individual examination of each application for refugee status, in accordance with national judicial practice, in the light in particular of whether the failure to act was deliberate. The persons concerned may be eligible in any event for appropriate forms of protection under national law."

Thus, where state agents deliberately fail to prevent persecution by third parties, such persecution is treated as falling within the ambit of the Convention. When a state is incapable of protecting its citizens, Member States appear able (but not bound) to treat relevant acts done by persons other than state agents as constituting persecution falling within the Convention. Some would argue that they should be bound to treat such acts as persecution. In its decision in *Adan v. Secretary of State for the Home Department*,[53] the House of Lords held that Article 1A(2) of the Convention offered protection to persons subject to persecution by factions within the state if for whatever reason the state is unable to offer protection against such factions. France and Germany apparently do not adopt the same approach to the interpretation of Article 1A(2).

The Joint Position covers a number of other matters, such as the effect of

---

inadequate account of the positive obligations which have to be fulfilled under international law by a country to which an asylum applicant might be transferred.

52. OJ 1996 L 63/2 paragraph 3 thereof provides: The joint position is adopted within the limits of the constitutional powers of the governments of the Member States; it shall not bind the legislative authorities or affect the decisions of the judicial authorities of the Member States.

53. [1999] 1 AC 293. See also in the same sense *R. v. Secretary of State for Home Department, ex parte Adan* and *R. v. Secretary of State for the Home Department ex parte Aijsegur* (HL), "The Times", 20 December 2000, p. 22, and *Horvat v. Home Secretary* [2000] 3 All ER 577 (HL). In the latter case, their Lordships were dealing with a situation of alleged persecution by non-state agents, and found that the protection by the Slovakian state against alleged attacks was sufficient to prevent those discriminatory actions from constituting persecutions.

internal armed conflict (which is not in itself regarded as sufficient to justify refugee status according to paragraph 6), the fear of punishment for conscientious objection or desertion and the effect of the possibility of obtaining protection in another part of the relevant country's territory.[54] The provisions of the Joint Position relating to internal armed conflict and the possibility of internal flight are considered below.

If an internal armed conflict takes place fear of persecution on one of the grounds set out in Article 1A of the Geneva Convention must be shown to exist. Such persecution may result from the action of legal authorities or from any third parties encouraged or tolerated by them, or from *de facto* authorities in control of part of the territory in which the state has lost its power of protection. The Joint Position further provides that the use of armed force does not in itself constitute persecution if it is in accordance with international rules of war. However, it will do so if the authorities in a particular area attack political opponents or the general population in a manner rendered serious by the nature of such attacks, or by virtue of their repetition, and such attacks are based on one of the grounds mentioned in Article 1A of the Geneva Convention. Paragraph 8 of the Joint Position adopts the approach that when it seems that persecution is clearly confined to one part of a country's territory, it may be necessary to determine whether the putative victim of such persecution cannot obtain effective protection in some other part of the country, to which he might reasonably be expected to move. It will obviously sometimes be difficult to decide whether persecution is clearly confined to one part of a country; whether "effective" protection in another part of the country is available; and whether a person might reasonably be expected to move to another part of his native country. The necessary information with which to decide these matters may well be lacking, especially in a state of civil war, and might lead to conflicting interpretations.

V. INSTRUMENTS ADOPTED BEFORE THE ENTRY INTO FORCE OF THE AMSTERDAM TREATY CONCERNING THE TEMPORARY PROTECTION OF DISPLACED PERSONS

The influx of displaced persons from Yugoslavia in the early 1990s, many of them from Bosnia-Herzegovina, formed the occasion for the adoption of two instruments, a Council Resolution of 25 September 1995 on burden sharing with regard to the admission and residence of displaced persons on a temporary basis, based on the former Article K1 of the Treaty of Union[55] and a Council Decision of 4 March 1996 on an alert and emergency procedure for burden sharing with regard to the admission and residence of displaced persons on a temporary basis, based upon the former Article K3(2)(a) of the Treaty of

---

54. A fuller discussion of the Joint Position may be found in Hailbronner, *op. cit.*, pp. 377–381.
55. OJ 1995 C262/1.

European Union.[56] Neither of these instruments was ever implemented, even at the time of the crisis in Kosovo. On 26 April 1999, the Council, acting on the basis of former Article K3 of the Treaty of European Union adopted a joint action "establishing projects and measures to provide practical support in relation to the reception and voluntary repatriation of refugees, displaced persons and asylum seekers, including persons who have fled as the result of recent events in Kosovo".[57] However, certain other Commission proposals for joint actions concerning the temporary protection of displaced persons put forward by the Commission on 5 March 1997 and 24 June 1998 failed to be adopted and lapsed when the Treaty of Amsterdam came into force.

VI. DEVELOPMENTS IN REFUGEE AND ASYLUM LAW AFTER THE TREATY OF AMSTERDAM

1. Recent Commission proposals

As new Commission proposals for a Council Directive[58] on temporary protection in the case of a mass influx of displaced persons from third countries based on solidarity between the Member States and made pursuant to Articles 63(2)(a) and (b) EC, is part of a series of recent and forthcoming Commission initiatives on asylum policy. In July 1999, the Commission proposed a draft Council Regulation concerning the Eurodac system for comparing the fingerprints of asylum seekers and other foreign nationals, the object of which is to improve the effectiveness of the Dublin Convention.[59] On 14 December 1999, the Commission presented a proposal under Article 63(2) EC for a Council Decision establishing a European Refugee Fund. This was designed to assist in the integration of refugees into Member States and to support their repatriation when they so wished. The Council Decision was adopted on 28 September 2000.[60] The Commission proposal for a Council Directive on family reunification of the same month, which has been considered above, contains certain provisions which govern the situation of refugees. In March 2000, a document was tabled to facilitate strategic discussion on the replacement of the Dublin Convention by Community legislation. A proposal for a Community Directive on minimum standards on procedures in Member States for granting and withdrawing refugee status was put forward by the Commission on 20 September 2000.[61] A proposal

---

56. OJ 1996 L63/10.
57. OJ 1999 L114/2.
58. COM (2000) 303 final of 24 May 2000.
59. COM (1999) 260 final – CNS 99/0116. The draft Regulation was based in substance on the earlier draft Eurodac Convention and Additional Protocol which it was intended to adopt as intergovernmental instruments under Title VI of the Treaty of European Union. This intention was abandoned when the Treaty of Amsterdam came into force. The Eurodac Regulation was adopted by the Council on 11 December 2000.
60. Council Decision 2000/596/EC establishing a European Refugee Fund, OJ 2000 L 252/12.
61. COM (2000) 578 final.

on the criteria and mechanisms for determining which Member State is responsible for an asylum application is expected shortly. This proposal will be intended to replace the Dublin Convention and will be followed by further proposals governing asylum.[62]

2. The proposed Directive of May 2000 on temporary protection

(1) Basis and general provisions

The purpose of the proposed Directive of 24.5.2000[63] is, according to Article 1 thereof, to establish minimum standards for giving temporary protection in the event of a mass influx of displaced persons from third countries (i.e. countries outside the EU) who are unable to return to their country of origin, and to promote a balance of effort between Member States in receiving and bearing the consequences of receiving such persons. The proposed Directive is based upon Articles 63(2)(a) and (b) EC,[64] and must be adopted under the Article 67 procedure. It will not be applicable in the United Kingdom and Ireland unless those countries decide otherwise. It will also be inapplicable in Denmark.

Article 2 of the proposed Directive contains a number of definitions. Thus for example "displaced persons from third countries who are unable to return to their country of origin" are said to be third-country nationals or stateless persons who have had to leave their country of origin, and who are unable to return in safe and humane conditions, because of the situation prevailing in that country, who may fall within the scope of Article 1A of the Geneva Convention, or other international or national instruments giving protection, in particular persons who had fled areas of armed conflict or endemic violence; and persons at serious risk of or who have been the victims of systematic and generalised violations of their human rights.

The above definition seems to be illustrative rather than exhaustive but is of some considerable help. That of "temporary protection in the event of a mass influx" is similarly lengthy. This is said to mean "exceptional measures to provide, in the event of a mass influx of displaced persons from third countries who are unable to return to their country of origin, immediate and temporary protection for such persons, where there is a risk that the asylum system will be unable to process that influx without adverse effects for its efficient operation, in the

---

62. A detailed account of these proposals appear in the Commission's Communication to the Council and Parliament on a common asylum procedure and a uniform status valid throughout the Union, for persons granted asylum: COM(2000) 755 final.
63. For which see COM (2000) 303 final.
64. Article 63(2)(a) provides for the adoption of criteria and mechanisms for determining which Member State is responsible for considering an application for asylum submitted by a national of a third country in one of the Member States. Article 63(2)(b) requires the adopted of minimum standards for the reception of asylum seekers in the Member States.

interests of the persons concerned and other persons requiring protection, hereinafter referred to as "temporary protection"." Nothing is said in this definition
how the risk to the asylum system will be determined, or what is deemed to
constitute a man influx.

By virtue of Article 3(1) of the proposed Directive, temporary protection does
not prejudice the grant of refugee status. The establishment, implementation and
termination of temporary protection shall, according to Article 3(3), be subject
to regular consultations with the UNHCR and other organisations involved.[65]

(2) Duration and implementation of temporary protection

According to Article 4, the maximum duration of protection is two years. This
period of time may be the maximum it is reasonable to anticipate agreement on
but may prove inadequate in some circumstances. By virtue of Article 3(1) of
the proposals a mass influx of displaced persons shall be established by a Council
decision adopted by qualified majority on a proposal from the Commission,
which must also examine a request by a Member State that it submits a proposal
to the Council. The role of Parliament is unfortunately limited to that of being
informed of the Council Decision.

The conditions governing the expiry of temporary protection, the procedure
for adopting the Council decision terminating the protection, the basis for such
a decision and its extent, are set out in Article 6. Temporary protection ends
after the expiry of the two year period mentioned in Article 4(1) or by reason
of a Council decision taken by qualified majority on a proposal from the
Commission. The Commission must examine any request from a Member State
that it should submit such a proposal. It must be established that the persons
receiving temporary protection must be able to return on a long term, safe and
dignified basis, in accordance with the provisions of Article 33 of the Geneva
Convention and the ECHR.[66]

By Article 7, Member States may extend temporary protection to additional
categories of persons who are displaced for the same reasons and from the same
country of origin where such categories are not included in the Council Decision
provided for in Article 5.

---

65. The UNHCR has a mandate in relation to refugees and, in accordance with Declaration
    No.17 on former Article 73K of the EC Treaty, consultations must be established with
    the UNHCR and other relevant international organisations on matters relating to
    asylum policy.
66. According to Article 1 of the proposals the "Geneva Convention" means the Convention
    of 1951 relating to the status of refugees, as amended by the New York Protocol of 1977.
    Article 33(1) of the Geneva Convention provides that no contracting state shall expel or
    return a refugee in any manner whatsoever to the frontiers of territories where his life may
    be threatened on account of his race, religion, nationality, membership of a particular
    social group or political opinion. By Article 33(2) the benefits of Article 33(1) cannot be
    claimed by a refugee whom there are reasonable grounds for regarding as a danger to the

(3) Obligation of the Member States towards persons enjoying temporary
    protection

Member States are required by Article 8(1) to provide persons enjoying temporary protection with residence permits for the whole duration of the temporary
protection. Article 8(2) allows Member States to decide on the period of validity
of the residence permits. Whatever such period may be, the treatment granted
by Member States to persons enjoying temporary protection must be no less
favourable than that set out in Articles 9–15. Member States are required, where
necessary, by Article 8(3) to provide persons admitted to their territory for the
purpose of temporary protection, with every facility for obtaining the necessary visas.

According to Article 9, persons enjoying temporary protection must be
informed of the rules governing such protection. This was requested by the
European Parliament in its resolution on temporary protection of November
1999. Member States are required by Article 10 to authorise persons enjoying
temporary protection to engage in employed and self-employed activities under
the same conditions as refugees. Article 11(1) provides that persons enjoying
temporary protection shall have access to suitable accommodation or if necessary
receive the means to obtain housing. This provision does not impose very well
defined obligations upon Member States: some may properly deem that accommodation in dormitory premises or in special accommodation centres is "suitable", this would seem to be the case from the Commission commentary on this
provision.[67] Article 11(2) stipulates that Member States shall make provision
for persons enjoying temporary protection to receive the necessary assistance in
terms of social welfare, and means of subsistence, if they do not have sufficient
resources, as well as for medical care. This provision does not state what form
this assistance must take, and it may thus be that a voucher system could be
regarded as adequate. The provision of appropriate medical or other assistance
to persons enjoying temporary protection who have special needs is provided
for by Article 11(4), which envisages in particular unaccompanied minors and
persons who have undergone torture, rape, or other serious forms of psychological, physical or sexual violence.

By virtue of Article 12(1), Member States must grant minors enjoying temporary protection access to the education system under the same conditions as
nationals of the host state. Such access may be restricted to the state education
system. Minors must be younger than persons who have reached the age of legal
majority in the relevant Member State. Thus, access to the university system
would rarely be available under Article 12(1). If access is not limited to the state
system, it is not clear whether such access is intended to cover the payment of
fees. Article 12(2) requires Member States to allow adults enjoying temporary

---

security of the country in which he is or having been convicted by a final judgment of a
particularly serious crime, constitutes a danger to the community of that country.
67. COM (2000) 303 final, p. 18, in this sense.

protection access to the general education system as well as to vocational training, further training and retraining.

Article 13 provides for the conditions of maintaining the family unit during the period of temporary protection. It does not provide for a right to family reunification as defined in the Proposal for a Council Directive on the right to family reunification, as amended.[68] The family circle is defined more broadly than in the latter proposal, but it covers the case of families already established in the country of origin, and excludes the establishment of a family. It also fails to cover the reunification of a family member lawfully resident in a third country other than that of origin with members of the family enjoying temporary protection in one of the Member States. Spouses or unmarried partners in a stable relationship will be admitted, if the legislation of the Member State concerned treats unmarried couples in the same way as married ones.[69]

Furthermore, Article 13(1)(b) provides that the children of a married or unmarried couple will be admitted, provided they are unmarried and dependent. By Article 13(1) family members not already covered are included if they are dependent on the applicant, or have undergone particularly traumatic experiences or need special medical treatment. According to Article 13(2), families may be reunited at any time up to two months before the end of the two year maximum protection period. Furthermore, Article 13(3) provides that the application for reunification shall be lodged by the applicant in the Member State where he resides. The Member State must establish that the various members of the family agree to the reunification. Article 13 does not permit the exclusion of family members on such grounds as public policy, public security or public health.

Article 14 provides for particular obligations to unaccompanied minors under the temporary protection scheme. By Article 14(1) such a minor must be represented. By virtue of Article 14(2) Member States must provide for the placement of unaccompanied minors with adult relatives; or with a foster family; or in accommodation suitable for minors. Nothing is said about the consultation of the minor in connection with such placement. Article 14(3) contains further provisions concerning the placing of an unaccompanied minor whose family has not been located, which provide for such placement with a person or persons who looked after the child when fleeing. In this case Member States must establish that the unaccompanied minor and the person or persons concerned agree to the reunificaiton. Article 14 is based upon the Council Resolution of 26 June 1997 on unaccompanied minors who are nationals of third countries.[70]

Under Article 15, Member States are required to implement their obligations under Articles 1–14 without discriminating between persons enjoying temporary

---

68. COM (1999) 638 final, as amended by COM (2000) 624 final.
69. Article 13(1)(a), *ibid.*, which seems also to apply to same sex partners.
70. OJ 1997 C221/23.

protection on grounds of sex, race, ethnic origin, nationality, religion or convictions, or on that of a handicap, age or sexual orientation.

(4) Access to the asylum procedure in the course of temporary protection

According to Article 16(1) persons enjoying temporary protection will be granted access to the procedure for determining refugee status (i.e. the asylum procedure) if they so desire. By Article 16(2), such access must be granted not later than the end of the period of temporary protection. Where access to the asylum procedure has already been granted before or during temporary protection and consideration of the application has been suspended, such suspension shall not extend beyond the end of the temporary protection. Article 17 provides that the criteria and mechanisms for deciding which Member State is responsible for considering asylum applications shall apply. At present these are set out in the Dublin Convention, but are expected to be governed by a Community instrument in the near future. It is hoped that such an instrument will not include all the provisions of the Convention: the safe country exception contained in this Convention has been subject to some apparently justified criticism, especially on the ground that it may not make possible the proper consideration of individual cases in accordance with the requirements of international law.

According to Article 18(1), Member States may provide that temporary protection may not be enjoyed concurrently with the status of asylum seeker when applications are under consideration. This provision may have an unfortunate impact on asylum seekers, especially where they wish members of their family to join them. The situation where, after an asylum application has been examined, refugee status is not granted to a person eligible for temporary protection is dealt with in Article 18(2). This draft provision stipulates that, in this situation, Member States shall, without prejudice to Article 29 (which provides for exclusion from temporary protection in certain circumstances, e.g. where there are serious grounds for believing that the person in question has committed a war crime or a crime against humanity), provide for such persons to enjoy temporary protection for the remainder of the period of protection.

(5) Return and measures after temporary protection

Articles 19–23 which govern the above matters seem to be generally informed by a liberal and humanitarian spirit, which unfortunately may not always recommend itself to the Member States. Article 19 provides that when the temporary protection period ends, the ordinary law on entry and residence of nationals in the Member States shall apply. By Article 20, the Member States are required to consider any compelling humanitarian reason which may make return impossible or unrealistic in specific cases. Such compelling humanitarian reasons may arise in the context of persistent armed conflict or persistent violation of human rights.

It follows from Article 21(1) that the voluntary return of persons benefiting or having benefited from temporary protection is thought of as the preferable solution. Thus, Member States are required to facilitate such return. Because voluntary return may take some time to implement, Article 21(3) provides that Member States may extend protection to individuals benefiting from a voluntary return programme until the actual date of return. Article 22 is concerned with the position of particular individuals who have enjoyed special protection and have special needs, after the end of the protection period. Member States are required to take the necessary measures governing the residence conditions of such persons, who may need psychological or medical treatment, or if they are school children, to cover the current school period. The definition of such period is within the competence of the Member States.

Article 23 provides that the Member States shall take appropriate measures, in agreement with the person concerned and in cooperation with the international organisations responsible, to facilitate any resettlement programmes which may be necessary.

(6) Solidarity

As with its revised proposals for joint action of 1998, the Commission has taken account of the link between temporary protection in the event of a mass influx of displaced persons and Community solidarity.[71] The relevant provisions are contained in Articles 24–27 of the proposal. Article 24 provides that the European Refugee Fund, which is likely to be established by a Council Decision, will finance emergency measures in the event of an influx of displaced persons into the European Union.[72] It appears unfortunate that there appears to be no way to make states responsible for such an influx contribute to the financing of such measures.

By Article 25(1), Member States are required to receive persons in a spirit of Community solidarity, and must indicate either in figures or in general terms, their capacity to receive such persons, or state the reasons for their incapacity. This indication must be set out in a declaration by the Member States to be annexed to the Decision referred to in Article 5. According to Article 25(2), the Member States acting in cooperation with the competent international organisations shall ensure that the beneficiaries defined in the Decision referred to in Article 5 who are not yet on their territory are willing to be received on their territory. it appears that Member States might encounter considerable practical difficulties in trying to fulfil this obligation. Article 26(1) provides for cooperation between the Member States for the duration of the temporary protection where

---

71. COM (97) 93 final, OJ 1997 C106/13.
72. For the original proposal for such a decision, see COM (1999) 686 final; for the amended proposal, see COM (2000) 533 final.

appropriate, with a view to transferring the residence of persons enjoying temporary protection from one Member State to another. The consent of the beneficiaries must be obtained. It is rather surprising that no other limits are placed by Article 26(1) on the circumstances in which such a transfer may be contemplated or take place. However, it is clear from Article 27 that the provisions of Articles 25 and 26 shall be without prejudice to the Member States' obligations regarding non-refoulement (expulsion or return of refugees).

Article 26(2) provides for the method of making transfer requests, whilst Article 26(3) sets out the consequences of the transfer of residence for the persons involved in terms of residence permits and entitlements to temporary protection.

(7) Special provisions

In accordance with Article 29 of the proposed Directive, a Member State may exclude a person from temporary protection if they are regarded as a danger to the national security; or if there are serious reasons for thinking they have committed a war crime or a crime against humanity; or if during the consideration of the asylum application it is found that the exclusion clauses in Article 1F of the Geneva Convention apply.[73] Rather unsurprisingly in the circumstances, Article 29 makes no reference to public health or public policy reasons as grounds for exclusion. The reference to Article 1F of the Convention on the Status of Refugees appears somewhat tautologous, as certain of the grounds stated in this provision already appear in Article 29. It is also unclear under what circumstances the serious reasons mentioned in Article 29 can be said to exist.

Article 29 also provides that the grounds for exclusion must be based exclusively on the personal conduct of the persons concerned. Exclusion decisions (as in the case under Directive 64/221) must be based upon the principle of proportionality. The person concerned will be entitled to seek redress in the courts of the relevant Member States.

(8) Final remarks

Article 30 is a standard penalty clause providing that Member States must provide for effective proportionate and dissuasive penalties for infringement of the Directive. The duty of the Commission concerning the drawing up of reports on the application of the Directive is set out in Article 31. The provisions of Article 32, which would require the Member States to transpose the Directive

---

73. This provision stipulates that the provisions of the Geneva Convention do not apply to any person in respect of whom there are serious reasons for thinking he has committed a crime against peace, a war crime or a crime against humanity as defined in the relevant international instrument; or that he has committed a serious non-political crime outside the country of refuge; or that he has been guilty of an act contrary to the purposes and principles of the United Nations.

by 31 December 2002 seem unrealistic. There have already been two abortive attempts to enact Community legislation in this area. Because of the need for unanimity, it may well prove to be the case that protracted negotiations are necessary before the adoption of the above proposals which would seem capable of imposing meaningful and possibly onerous burdens on the Member States which would be bound by it.

VII. THE REGULATION ON THE ESTABLISHMENT OF EURODAC

It is not proposed to give a very detailed account of the provisions of this Regulation.[74] The proposal suggests the setting up of a central unit within the Commission, which will be a computerised central database, in which the data are processed for the purpose of comparing the fingerprints of applicants for asylum and certain other third country (i.e. non-EU) nationals. Data may be transferred between the unit which operates the database (central unit) and the Member States. The proposal derives from earlier models, and the United Kingdom and Ireland propose to 'opt in' to it in accordance with Article 3 of the Protocol governing that position, attached to the Amsterdam treaty. The processing of personal data within the Eurodac system is governed by the requirements of the Data Protection Directive.[75] Article 2(2) of the proposed Regulation provides that the terms defined in Article 2 of that Directive (e.g. "personal data" and "processing of personal data") have the same meaning in the Regulation.

According to Article 1(1) of the Regulation, the Eurodac system may be used to establish which Member State is responsible for examining an application for asylum lodged in a Member State, and otherwise to facilitate the application of the Dublin Convention under the conditions laid down in the application. Data kept by the Central Unit may not be used for the purposes of criminal investigations or administrative control. However, as is recognised in Part 4.5 of the Explanatory Memorandum to the proposed Regulation, and as is apparent from Article 2(3) of the Regulation, fingerprints which a Member State takes and communicates to the Central Unit may be used in databases set up by the relevant states for another purpose.

1. Data on applicants for asylum and illegal immigrants

Every Member State is required by Article 4(1) to fingerprint every asylum applicant aged at least 14 years, and to transmit this fingerprint data together

---

74. For the draft proposal see COM (99) 260 final – CNS 99/0016; for the amended version of 16 October 2000, see Document 500 PCO 100; for the actual Regulation see OJ 2000 L 310/1.

75. Directive 95/46/EC This follows from Article 286 EC. A regulation of the Council and Parliament has been proposed which would establish a data processing body for the European Community: see COM (1999) 337 final.

with certain other data specified in Article 5 to the Central Unit. The procedure for taking fingerprints is required to be determined in accordance with the national practices of the Member State concerned and in accordance with the safeguards laid down in the European Convention on Human Rights,[76] and the United Nations Convention on the Rights of the Child.[77] Such fingerprinting is, of course, necessary to determine responsibility under the Dublin Convention.

The Central Unit is required by Article 4(3) to compare the data transmitted to it by any Member State with that transmitted by other Member States and already stored in the central database. This procedure is obviously intended to identify multiple asylum applicants. Furthermore, Article 4(5) requires the Central Unit to transmit the "hit"[78] or negative result of the comparison to the Member State of origin. If there appears to be a "hit", that Member State has to check it. Should the check appear to confirm the findings of the Central Unit, Article 4(6) provides that the final identification has to be made by the state of origin, in cooperation with the other Member States concerned, pursuant to Article 15 of the Dublin Convention (which deals, *inter alia*, with exchanges of information). Article 4(6) also provides that information received from the Central Unit regarding data found to be unreliable shall be erased or destroyed by the Member State of origin as soon as the mismatch or unreliability of the data is established.

By virtue of Article 6, the data which is kept on asylum applicants may be stored in the central database for ten years form the date on which the fingerprints were taken. Upon expiry of this period, the Central Unit is required to automatically erase the data from the central database. It has been suggested that this period is too long, but on the other hand it may sometimes take a very considerable period of time before an asylum applicant obtains the status of a refugee or that of a national of a Member State, such that multiple applications for asylum would usually be of little interest to him. According to Article 7 of the Regulation, if a person acquires the citizenship of a Member State, and the Member State of origin becomes aware of this before the expiry of the ten year period, then the data relating to the former applicant for asylum must be immediately erased from the database.

By Article 8 of the Regulation third country nationals over 14[79] who are

---

76. See Article 8 of this Convention which enjoins respect for private and family life. Article 8(2) contains a number of exceptions to the above requirement.

77. Article 16 of this Convention provides that children shall not be subjected to arbitrary or unlawful interference with their privacy.

78. According to Article 2(e) (Article 2 is the definitions section of the Regulation) a hit means the existence of a match or matches established by the Central Unit by comparison between fingerprint data recorded in the databank and those transmitted by the Member State, with regard to any one person, subject to the requirement that the Member States shall immediately check the results of the comparison.

79. The safeguards contained in the ECHR and in the United Nations Convention on the Rights of the Child must be observed.

apprehended in connection with an irregular border crossing and not having been turned back, must be fingerprinted by the relevant Member State, and particulars of them, including such fingerprints sent to the Central Unit. Such data is only required by Article 10 to be stored in the central database for two years. There was no obligation under the draft Regulation to take fingerprints of persons who are found illegally within the territory of a Member State. However, it appears from Article 11 that Member States may transmit to the Central Unit any fingerprint data relating to fingerprints it may have taken of a third country national of at least fourteen years of age found illegally present in its territory, with a view to checking whether that person has claimed asylum in another Member State. Once the results of the comparison have been transmitted by the Member State, Article 11(5)(a) requires that the Central Unit shall erase the fingerprints.

2. Rights, obligations and supervisory authorities

According to the Commission's commentary on Article 13, within the context of the Eurodac system the Member States act as controllers, i.e. the entities which determine the purposes and means of the processing of personal data. The Central Unit processes personal data on behalf of the Member States (note in this connection Article 3) and as such is a processor. Most of the obligations under Directive 95/46/EC (the Data Protection Directive) are addressed to the controller. Those of the processor are more specific and it must act only on the instructions of the controller. For the purpose of the proposed Regulation, the processor is the Central Unit.

Article 13(1)–(3) sets out the responsibilities of the Member State of origin, in its role as a controller, at the moment of collection, transmission and reception of personal data. Article 13(4) sets out the requirements for the processor (i.e. the Central Unit) in relation to confidentiality and security. Article 14 is an application of Article 17 of Directive 95/46, and determines which measures have to be implemented to ensure the security of processing. The provisions of Article 15 concern access to and correction or erasure of data recorded in the central database. These matters are reserved for the Member State of origin, except where the Central Unit is required to erase data automatically at a certain point, or is instructed to amend or erase data by the Member State of origin. According to Article 16, the Central Unit is required to keep records of all data processing operations within the Central Unit. Such records must be protected by appropriate measures against unauthorised access and erased after a period of one year.

Article 17 is concerned with liability for damages. Paragraph 1 thereof is based upon Article 23 of Directive 95/46/EC. In principle, the controller (the Member State responsible) will be held liable for any unlawful processing operation or any act incompatible with the provisions laid down in the Regulation, but will be wholly or partly exempted from such liability if it proves that it is not responsible for the event giving rise to the damage. Thus, if it can be shown that the processor, i.e. the Central Unit, is responsible for the damage, the Member State concerned escapes liability.

The rights of the data subject are set out in Article 18. These rights must be read together with the Data Protection Directive 95/46, and in particular with Articles 10, 12, 22, 28(4) and 28(6) thereof. Article 18(1) contains a list of things he or she should be informed about, and when such information should be provided. By article 18(3), the data subject may require correction and erasure in any Member State. According to Articles 18(5) and (6), he or she must receive a written reply to his request without undue delay. Furthermore, by Article 18(11) the data subject is given the right to apply to a supervisory authority or a court if he is denied access, or if he or she wishes to have their data amended or deleted.

By virtue of Article 19 which refers to Article 28(1) of the Data Protection Directive, the national supervisory authorities are competent to monitor the legality of all data processing operations performed by Member States. Article 20 which provides for the establishment of an independent joint supervisory authority which will be responsible for the monitoring of personal data by the Central Unit was intended only to have effect if the Eurodac Regulation came into force before the proposed Regulation on the protection of individuals in the processing of personal data by the institutions and bodies of the Community, which has been referred to above.[80] This contingency has now occurred.

3. Some criticism of the Regulation

There does not appear to be a great deal written by academics on the above topic apart from what is presented in Hailbronner's textbook.[81] The latter writer emphasises that the words used "apprehended in connection with an irregular crossing by land, sea or air of the border of that Member State" is not entirely clear. As he recognises, human rights objections may well be raised to the fingerprinting of adolescents, and indeed to that of adults. However, such fingerprinting seems essential if the Dublin Convention or any successor instrument is to work properly, and unfortunately a number of adolescents, and even unaccompanied children younger than 14, seek asylum in states belonging to the EU. Problems associated with multiple asylum applications may well arise in relation to such persons, as well as in relation to adults. Such fingerprinting would seem to be permissible under Article 8 ECHR and under Article 17 of the UN Convention on the Rights of the Child provided that certain safeguards are respected. However, some would argue that the fingerprinting of illegal immigrants is excessive and undesirable.

---

80. The supervisory body will be disbanded when the proposed Regulation on the protection of individuals in the processing of data by the institutions comes into effect.
81. *Immigration and Asylum Law and Policy of the EU*, pp. 407–410.

VIII. MINIMUM STANDARDS ON PROCEDURES OF MEMBER STATES FOR GRANTING AND WITHDRAWING REFUGEE STATUS

The proposal for a Directive governing the above matter, which will not be discussed in detail, is said in the relevant Commission document to constitute a first measure to build the common European asylum system.[82] It will, as already indicated, be followed by other proposals in the same field, including one providing for a clear and workable determination of the state responsible for the examination of an asylum application. This proposal would undoubtedly be influenced by the Dublin Convention but would hopefully remedy certain of its perceived defects. Later proposals will concern such matters as the recognition and content of refugee status, reception conditions for asylum seekers, and subsidiary means of protection.[83]

The present proposal basically consists of three groups of provisions. The first sets out procedural guarantees for asylum applicants, which relate to all situations found throughout all stages of the asylum procedure, and are designed to approximate concepts of procedural fairness among Member States.[84] Special guarantees are provided for persons with special needs, such as unaccompanied minors. The second group of provisions concerns minimum requirements regarding the decision making process.[85] The third group of provisions contain common standards for the application of certain concepts and practices, i.e. "inadmissible applications", "manifestly unfounded applications", "safe country of origin" and "safe third country".[86] These notions are familiar in many Member States,[87] but

---

82. COM (2000) 578 final – 2000/0238 (CNS).
83. See the proposal for a Council Directive laying down minimum standards for the reception of asylum seekers in Member States presented by the Commission on 3/4 April 2000, COM(2001) 181 final.
84. Note in particular, Articles 7–10 of the proposal.
85. Note in particular, Articles 6, 11–17, 24–26 and 27–31.
86. Note, in particular, Articles 18–23 and Articles 27–31. The cases in which an asylum application may be dismissed as inadmissible or manifestly ill founded are set out in Articles 18 and 28. The concept of a safe third country is explained in Annex 1 (principles with respect to the designation of safe third countries) and that of a safe country of origin in Annex II (principles with respect to the designation of safe countries of origin) Articles 11–17, 24–26, 32–40.
87. The concept of safe third countries was examined critically by the House of Lords in *Regina v. Secretary of State for the Home Department, ex parte Adan* and *Regina v. Secretary of State for the Home Department, ex parte Aitsegur,* "The Times", 20 December, 2000, p. 22, in which it was found that in the particular circumstances, France and Germany were not such countries. Note also *Regina v. Secretry of State for the Home Department, and Another, ex parte Javed, Regina v. Secretary of State for the Home Department, ex parte Zulfakar Ali* and *Regina v. Secretary of State for the Home Department, ex parte Abid Ali,* "The Times", 9 February, 2001, p. 22, in which Mr. Justice Turner held that declarations could be granted in all three cases and that the Home Secretary had erred in designating Pakistan as a safe country of origin. Emphasis was placed by the judge on Article 3 of the European Convention on Human Rights. An appeal against this judgment,

their application and interpretation varies considerably between different states, and in order to limit secondary movements between them, the Commission has proposed that they be made subject to common standards.

One may doubt whether, given the special position of the United Kingdom, Ireland and Denmark, the general requirement for unanimous votes in the Council and the considerable differences of the laws and practices of Member States in the relevant areas, the goal of a common EU immigration and asylum policy will be fully achieved, although a considerable degree of harmonisation in these areas may be attained.

---

which was heard by the Court of Appeal on 17 May 2001 was unsuccessful: see "The Times", 24 May 2001.

10   International Agreements and Free Movement

This chapter examines the free movement provisions under certain bilateral agreements, specifically the partnership and cooperation agreements with Russia, Ukraine and other former members of the Soviet Union and certain association agreements as well as the multilateral General Agreement on Trade in Services (GATS). The object is to analyse the relationship between the restrictions imposed by these agreements on trade.

I. Introduction: Types of International Agreement

With the exception of the Partnership and Cooperation agreements with Russia, Ukraine and other former members of the Soviet Union, all the association agreements mentioned in this chapter are based upon what is now Article 310 EC (ex Article 238 EC).[1] The procedure for negotiating and concluding such agreements is set out in Article 300 EC (ex Article 228 EC).[2] There are many different types of such agreement: the most far reaching type of economic cooperation is to be found in the European Economic Area (EEA) Agreement between the Community and three of its neighbours, Norway, Iceland and Liechtenstein. The free movement provisions of this agreement are considered below. The Europe Agreements with Poland, the Czech Republic, Slovakia, Hungary, Bulgaria, Romania, Slovenia and the three Baltic states, Estonia, Latvia and Lithuania, enshrine a rather less significant degree of economic cooperation. However, they are generally envisaged as pre-accession agreements, and are designed to establish a free trade area over a period of time as well as to make progress in achieving other economic freedoms between partners as well as establishing a political dialogue between them.[3] The agreements contain a common provision expressing these and other aims.[4] They have been reorientated by means of accession partnerships in order to assist in making them vehicles for accession. However, this alteration in their context has not caused any substantial changes in the contents of the agreements.

---

1. Article 310 EC provides: "The Community may conclude with one or more states or international organisations agreements establishing an association involving reciprocal rights and obligations, common action and special procedure".
2. The assent of Parliament is necessary before such agreements can be concluded: see Article 300(3) EC.
3. See Kapteyn & Verloren van Themaat, *Introduction to the Law of the European Communities*, (3rd edn, Gormley (ed.), Kluwer Law International, 1998), p. 1329. See also the helpful article by Inglis, 'The Europe Agreements Compared in the Light of their Pre-Accession Orientation', (2000) 37 CML Rev. 1173.
4. Note for example, Article 1(2) of the Poland Europe Agreement, OJ 1993 L348/2.

The provisions of the agreement with Poland relating to the free movement of persons will be considered below: the provisions in the Europe Agreements concerning the free movement of workers are substantially the same, but there are some differences between the provisions of the earlier agreements and the later ones with the Baltic States and Slovenia as far as establishment and services are concerned. Certain of the Community agreements with third countries concern themselves with development, as do the bilateral agreements between the Community and the Maghreb states (Algeria, Morocco and Tunisia) and the Mashreq states (Egypt, Syria, Lebanon and Jordan). New agreements with Mediterranean countries now take the form of Euro-Mediterranean Agreements, and certain provisions for a political dialogue as well as financial, economic and cultural cooperation. The Euro-Mediterranean Agreement with Tunisia receives brief discussion below. This discussion is preceded by one of the pre-accession agreements with Turkey which was concluded in 1963 and which had to be supplemented by an additional protocol in 1970. The discussion of the agreement with Tunisia is followed by one of the Europe Agreement with Poland. The chapter concludes with consideration of the Partnership and Cooperation Agreement (PCA) with Russia and of the GATS. The PCAs with the former members of the Soviet Union (apart from the Baltic States and Tajikistan) establish this contractual relationship between the EC and these states. The PCAs are based upon Article 133[5] and 308 EC (ex Article 113 and 235 EC) and on certain other provisions of the EC Treaty. They represent a significant level of cooperation and contain provisions expressing respect for human rights and democratic principles as well as the movement provisions and provisions concerning free trade and intellectual property. A brief account will be given of the EC-Russia Agreement which is in many respects similar to that with Ukraine.

II. Jurisdiction of the ECJ

Association Agreements together with decisions of the different councils of Association directly connected with the agreement to which they give effect form an integral part of the Community legal order, and the Court of Justice has jurisdiction to give a preliminary ruling as to their meaning.[6] Such jurisdiction also extends to mixed agreements,[7] which are agreements concluded by the Community and the Member States, each within their sphere of competence, where the relevant provisions come within an area covered by the EC Treaty.

---

5. This article is concerned with the Common Commercial Policy, and provides for the conclusion of agreements between the EC and states or international organisations.
6. See Case 181/73, *Haegeman v. Belgian State* [1974] ECR 449, paragraphs 5–6; Case 12/86, *Demirel v. Stadt Schwäbisch Gmünd* [1987] ECR 3719, paragraph 73; Case 30/88, *Greece v. Commission* [1989] ECR 3711, paragraph 12 and Case C-192/89, *Sevince v. Staatssecretaris van Justitie* [1990] ECR I-3461, paragraph 8. Note also Handoll, *Free Movement of Persons in the EU*, (J. Wiley, 1995), pp. 315–6.
7. See Case 12/86, *Demirel*.

Most of the agreements mentioned in this present chapter are mixed agreements: this is true of the agreements with Poland and Turkey, the Europe Agreements and Participation and Cooperation Agreements (PCAs) with states formerly forming a part of the Soviet Union.

III. DIVISION OF COMPETENCES TO CONCLUDE AGREEMENTS

The Community sometimes has an expressly conferred external competence in accordance with one of the provisions of the EC Treaty,[8] or an implied external competence resulting from other provisions of the Treaty, or measures adopted to give effect to them. However, such implied competence only becomes exclusive where internal common measures are enacted or the conclusion of an international agreement is necessary to fulfil treaty objectives which cannot be attained by the enactment of Community rules.[9] Where such common measures have not been enacted thus giving rise to an internal transfer of powers to the Community, and the conclusion of an international agreement is not otherwise necessary, each Member State remains competent to enter into international agreements in the relevant areas. Thus many agreements entered into by the Community are of a mixed kind, certain areas covered by them being within the competence of the Community, and certain others within that of Member States.

IV. THE AGREEMENTS

1. The EEA Agreement

The aim of the above agreement is stated in Article 1(1) thereof to be the promotion of a continuous and balanced strengthening of trade and economic relations between the contracting parties with equal condition of competition, and respect for the same rules, with a view to creating a homogeneous European Economic Area, referred to as the EEA. Article 1(2) of the Agreement provides that in order to attain the former objectives, the association shall entail, in accordance with the provisions of the agreement, the free movement of goods, persons, services and capital. Furthermore, Article 1(2) also provides that it shall entail the setting up of a system ensuring that competition is not distorted and that the rules thereon are equally respected, as well as closer cooperation in other fields, such as research and development, the environment, education and social policy.

The original signatories of the Agreement were the twelve Member States of

---

8. Note for example Articles 133, 170, 174(4), 302–4 and 310 EC. The Community's exclusive competence under Article 133 (Common Commercial Policy) is limited to trade in goods and the cross border supply of services. This limitation, together with limitations in certain other fields, helps to explain the need for mixed agreements.

9. See Opinion 1/94, *Opinion pursuant to Article 228(6) of the EC Treaty* [1994] ECR I-5267 at 5411 and 5413–4.

the EC and the six states belonging to the European Free Trade Association (EFTA), i.e. Norway, Sweden, Finland, Iceland, Austria and Switzerland. It takes the form of a mixed agreement, which had to be ratified by the contracting parties in accordance with their constitutional rules. Switzerland failed to ratify the Agreement, which caused difficulties for Liechtenstein; the Agreement did not enter into force as regards the latter country until 1 May 1995.[10] As far as the other participants were concerned, the Agreement came into force on 1 January 1995. On that date Austria, Finland and Sweden became members of the European Union, and as from that time, the EEA Agreement had to be regarded as being between the 15 EU states and the three members of EFTA which did not become members of the EU, i.e. Norway, Iceland and Liechtenstein.

The Agreement is a mixed one. The EEA lacks a common external trade regime and thus, unlike the EC, it is not a customs union, although it is a common market. The Agreement does not provide for the abolition of border controls between the three EFTA states, and between these states and those belonging to the EU.[11]

The rules relating to free movement of persons, freedom of establishment and freedom to provide services contained respectively in Articles 28–30, 31–35 and 36–39 of the Agreement are identical with, subject to certain minor provisos, those contained in the corresponding provisions of the EC Treaty. Articles 28, 31 and 36 of the EEA Agreement all of which refer to the market freedoms of nationals of the EEA, make reference to a number of Annexes. Annexes V–VIII contain detailed provisions governing the scope of application of the relevant secondary EC law on freedom of movement. This legislation includes Council Directives 64/221,[12] 68/360[13] and 75/34[14] and Council Regulations 1612/68[15] and 1251/70.[16] Retired persons benefit from the rights conferred on them by Regulation 1251/70 and Directive 75/34. They may also benefit from Council Directive 90/365.[17] Students may rely on the provisions of Council Directive 93/96.[18] Other persons may benefit from Council Directive 90/364.[19]

Provisions of the Agreement identical with the corresponding norms contained in the EC Treaty and the ECSC Treaty and secondary legislation adopted thereunder must be interpreted in accordance with relevant rulings of the

---

10. Decision 1/95 of the EEA Council of 10 March 1995, OJ L 86, 20.4.1995.
11. The Member States of the EC and the EFTA states (but not the Community itself) have made a Joint Declaration on the Facilitation of border controls.
12. OJ Spec. Ed. 1964, No. 850/64, p. 117.
13. OJ Spec. Ed. 1968, No. L257/13, p. 485.
14. OJ 1975 L14/10.
15. OJ Spec. Ed. 1968, No. L237/2, p. 475.
16. OJ Spec. Ed. 1970, OJ 142/24, p. 402.
17. OJ 1990 L180/28.
18. OJ L317/59.
19. OJ 1990 L180/26.

European Court of Justice made before the date of signature. No such binding obligation applies in relation to subsequent developments in EC law. However, the EEA Joint Committee, which consists of representatives of the contracting parties and the Commission of the EC, has the task of monitoring legal developments within the Community and adapting EEA law to relevant developments in EC secondary legislation.[20] It is also given the task of keeping the development of the case law of the ECJ and the EFTA Court (the judicial body set up under the EEA Agreement) under constant review, and of acting so as to preserve the homogeneous interpretation of the Agreement.[21]

2. The special position of Liechtenstein under the EEA Agreement

Protocol 15 to the EEA Agreement provides for a transitional period for achieving free movement of persons for Liechtenstein.[22] This transitional period expired on 1 January 1998, but sectoral adaptations have been made to Annexes VIII (right of establishment) and V (free movement of workers) by a Decision of the EEA Joint Committee of 17 December 1999, to take account of the special geographical position of Liechtenstein, which had been emphasised by the Government of the Principality in a Declaration on its specific situation.[23] The adaptations, which are very similar both for the right of establishment and the free movement of workers, will have effect until 31 December 2006, and will be reassessed before that date by the Joint Committee which will determine whether, and to what extent, such measures will be maintained.

Nationals of Iceland, Norway and the EU Member States may take up residence in Liechtenstein only after having received a permit from the Liechtenstein authorities. Their right to obtain such a permit is subject to detailed restrictions. No such permit is needed for a period of less than three months per year, provided no employment or other permanent economic activity is taken up, nor for persons providing cross-border services in Liechtenstein. The conditions regarding Iceland, Norway and the EU Member States may be less restrictive than those which apply to third country nationals.

3. The Association Agreement with Turkey

(1) Introductory remarks

The Association Agreement between the EC and Turkey was signed in September 1963; the Additional Protocol was signed in November 1970.[24] Like the Europe

---

20. Article 162(1) EEA.
21. Article 105(2) EEA. See also Articles 111 and 113 EEA, which relate respectively to dispute settlement and safeguard measures.
22. See Martin and Guild, *Free Movement of Persons in the EU*, (Butterworths, 1996), paragraphs 12.17–12.20.
23. Article 9(2) of Protocol 15 required a joint review of the transitional measures to be undertaken; the Decision of 17 December 1999 is a result of that review.
24. Both these instruments may be found in OJ 1977 L361/2. According to Article 62 of the Protocol, the instrument forms an integral part of the Association Agreement.

Agreement, the Association Agreement contemplates the accession of the relevant third country state to the EC. However, this may, as has been recognised in the Commission's Report on Turkey's Progress towards Accession of 29 November 2000, be inhibited by political reasons and reasons connected with lack of economic development in certain areas as well as Turkey's failure to respect the human rights of the Kurdish minority in the near future. The Agreement is a mixed one, and certain EC Member States took the view that the provisions thereof and of the Additional Protocol concerning the movement of persons came within their competence. In *Demirel*,[25] the Court decided that this was the case. The Court held that because the agreement was an association agreement creating certain privileged links with Turkey, it must to some extent operate within the Community system. Article 310 (ex Article 237) EC must necessarily empower the Community to guarantee commitments towards non-Member States in all fields contained in the EC Treaty. The free movement of workers was one of these fields, and hence obligations in the field of freedom of movement came within the powers conferred on the Community by Article 310 EC.

The Agreement contains a number of provisions on workers, establishment and the provision of services. Further detailed provisions on these matters are contained in Title II of the Additional Protocol.[26] The access of Turkish workers to the labour market in the EC states is governed by Decision 1/80 of the Council of Association.[27] Certain residence rights have been somewhat controversially implied by the Court of Justice on the basis of Article 6(1) and 7(1) and (2) of this Decision,[28] which Articles have been held to be directly effective.

(2) Relevant provisions of the Agreement and the Additional Protocol
    concerning workers

Article 9 of the Association Agreement provides that the contracting parties recognise within the scope of this agreement and without prejudice to any special provisions laid down by Article 8, any discrimination on the grounds of nationality shall be prohibited in accordance with the provisions laid down in Article 12 EC. Article 12 of the Agreement provides that the contracting parties agree to be guided by Articles 48, 49 and 50 of the EC Treaty for the purpose of

---

25. Case 12/86, *Demirel* [1987] ECR 3719, paragraphs 8–9.
26. See Articles 36–40 on workers and Articles 41–2 on the right of establishment, services and transport.
27. According to Article 23(1) of the Agreement, the Council of Association is made up of members of the governments of the Member States, members of the EC Council and Commission and members of the Turkish government.
28. The Decision is based upon Article 12 of the Agreement and Article 36 of the Protocol together with Article 7 of the Agreement. The latter provision has direct effect, but this is not true of the first two provisions.

progressively securing freedom of movement of workers between them. Because of its programmatic nature, Article 12 has been held to lack direct effects.[29]

Article 36 of the Additional Protocol provides for the attainment of freedom of movement of workers in progressive stages and stipulates that the Council of Association shall decide on the rules necessary to that end. Member States are required by Article 37 not to discriminate against Turkish workers on comparison with workers of other Member States in relation to conditions of work and remuneration. Because workers of other Member States must be treated in the same way as national workers by virtue of Article 39(2) EC, the comparison also relates to the host Member State's own nationals.[30] The clear and precise wording of Article 37 leads to the conclusion that it has direct effect.

The Council of Association is granted competence to examine questions relating to the mobility of Turkish workers and to make recommendations to other Member States by Article 38 of the Protocol. Article 39 is concerned with the adoption of social security measures for Turkish workers moving within the Community and family members residing there. The Council of Association is empowered by Article 40 to make recommendations to the Member States and Turkey in order to encourage the exchange of young workers. Article 41, which contains provisions concerning establishment and the provision of services, is considered below.

(3) Decision 1/80 of the Council of Association, and workers

a. Scope

The above decision contains a number of detailed provisions governing the employment rights of Turkish workers and members of their families, as well as rules governing the rights of children of such workers to education, apprenticeship and vocational training. However, as the Court of Justice has repeatedly reiterated, Decision 1/80 does not interfere with the competence retained by the Member States to regulate the entry into their territory of Turkish nationals; and to determine the conditions under which they may take up their first employment, and to regulate the conditions under which they work for the first year.[31] It follows from *Kadiman* that Member States are also empowered to regulate the entry of family members of Turkish workers.[32]

---

29. Note in this sense Case 12/86, *Demirel v. Stadt Schwäbisch Gmünd* [1987] ECR 3719. The Court of Justice also held in *Demirel* that Article 36 of the Additional Protocol lacked direct effect.
30. Note in this sense Martin and Guild, *The Free Movement of Persons in the EU*, (Butterworths, 1996), paragraphs 13.28–13.30.
31. Note, in this sense, Case C-171/95, *Tetik v. Land Berlin* [1997] ECR I-379, paragraph 21 and Case C-37/98, *R. v. Secretary of State for the Home Department, ex parte Abdulnasir Savas* [2000] ECR I-2927, paragraph 18.
32. See Case C-351/95, *Kadiman v. Freistaat Bayern* [1997] ECR I-2133, paragraph 31.

b. Effects of Article 6(1) of Decision 1/80

According to the above provision, subject to Article 7 on free access to employment for members of his family a Turkish worker duly registered as belonging to the labour force of a Member State is entitled, according to procedures established by national rules: (i) after one year's legal employment to the renewal of his permit to work for the same employer; (ii) after three years of legal employment and subject to the priority of Community workers, take up another offer of employment with an employer of his choice, made under normal conditions and registered with the employment services of that state, for the same occupation; (iii) after four years of legal employment, access to any legal employment of his choice.

Article 6(1) is phrased in clear, precise and unconditional terms, and was held to have direct effects in *Sevince*.[33] Furthermore, in paragraph 29 of that decision the Court held that the situation of a Turkish worker in relation to employment and residence were closely linked and that "by granting to such a worker, after a specific period of legal employment, access to any paid employment of his choice, the provisions in question necessarily imply since otherwise the rights granted by them to a Turkish worker would be deprived of any effect – the existence, at least at that time, of a right of residence for the person concerned." The Court has reaffirmed its approach in *Sevince* in a number of other cases,[34] and has treated Article 6(1) as establishing a system of gradual integration of Turkish workers in the host country's labour force.[35] Thus, Turkish workers are not only entitled to a work permit for the Member State in which they are working, but, because of the direct effect of Article 6(1), they also enjoy a concomitant residence status in that country; that rights governing employment are treated as necessarily implying a right of residence. This goes beyond the position accorded to third country national workers under the Europe Agreements,[36] or under the partnership and cooperation agreements with the successor states to the Soviet Union. However, Turkish workers, unlike workers belonging to Member States of the EEA, do not enjoy freedom of movement between Member States.

---

33. Case C-192/89, *Sevince v. Staatssecretaris van Justitie* [1990] ECR I-3491; note especially paragraphs 21–24 of the decision.
34. See Hailbronner, *Immigration and Asylum Law and Policy of the EU*, (Kluwer Law International, 2000), p. 223, note 354.
35. See Case C-386/95, *Eker v. Land Baden-Württemberg* [1997] ECR I-2697, paragraph 23; Case C-36/96, *Günaydin v. Freistaat Bayern* [1997] ECR I-5143, paragraph 37; Case C-98/96, *Ertanir v. Land Hessen* [1997] ECR I-5197, paragraph 35 and Case C-1/97, *Birden v. Bremen* [1998] ECR I-7747, paragraph 37.
36. This was recognised by Advocate General Alber in paragraph 66 of his Opinion in Case C-63/99, *R. v. Secretary of State for Home Department ex parte Gloszczuk and Gloszczuk*, 14.9.2000, n.y.r., and in paragraph 15 of his Opinion in Case C-235/99, *R. v. Secretary of State for Home Department ex parte Kondova*, 14.9.2000, n.y.r.

A Member State cannot unilaterally alter the scope of the system of gradually integrating Turkish workers into the host state's labour force, and may not adopt measures impeding the exercise of the rights granted by Article 6(1) and the other rights expressly granted by Decision 1/80[37] (certain of which are directly effective).

Administrative documents such as a residence permit issued by the authorities of the host state have been treated by the European Court of Justice as only having a declaratory or probative value, and not as having a constitutive effect,[38] i.e. as not being a condition for their existence. The Court's use of the concept of implied residence in its jurisprudence on Article 6(1) and its apparent restriction of the competence of Member States in the field of immigration in certain decision, such as *Günaydin* and *Ertanir*, have received considerable criticism from German writers.[39] However, it seems probable that the Court will continue to adopt its present approach to the Association Agreement with Turkey, but may be reluctant to extend it to other such agreements.

Member States may prevent rights from arising for Turkish nationals and their families under Articles 6 and 7 of Decision 1/80 if they do not admit such nationals as workers. Thus, in *Günaydin*, in which the status of a Turkish engineer who was in paid employment with the same employer for a period of three years after having undergone a period of vocational training was in question, the Court of Justice held, in paragraph 32 of its judgment that "there is nothing to prevent a Member State from permitting Turkish nationals to enter and reside there only in order to enable them to follow within its territory specific vocational training, in particular in the context of a contract of apprenticeship." The Court held that Günaydin had been fully employed for three years in a genuine and effective economic activity for the same employer, and that his employment status was not different from that of other employees employed by the same employer. He was thus treated by the Court of Justice as duly registered as belonging to the German labour force, and legally employed within the meaning of Article 6(1). He thus had implied residence rights in Germany, and could apply for the renewal of his residence permit there. This was despite the fact that he only had work and residence permits for the purpose of taking up employment temporarily with a particular employer.[40] Günaydin wife and two

---

37. Note in this sense Case C-340/97, *Nazli v. Stadt Nürnberg* [2000] ECR I-957, paragraphs 30, 31.

38. See Case C-434/93, *Bozkurt v. Staatssecretaris vn Justitie* [1995] ECR I-1475, paragraphs 29 and 30; Case C-36/96, *Günaydin v. Freistaat Bayern* [1997] ECR I-5143, paragraph 49; Case C-98/96, *Ertanir v. Land Hessen* [1997] ECR I-5197, paragraph 55; Case C-1/97, *Birden v. Bremen* [1998] ECR I-7747, paragraph 65, and Case C-329/97, *Ergat v. Stadt Ulm* [2000] ECR I-1487, paragraphs 62 and 63.

39. Note, for example, Hailbronner, *Immigration and Asylum Law and Policy of the EU*, (Kluwer Law International, 2000), pp. 229–231.

40. A similar approach to the renewal of a residence permit was taken by the Court of Justice in *Ertanir*, in which a specialist chef working in Germany was advised when the work and residence permits were granted that they were for a maximum period of three years.

minor children would seem to have been entitled to benefit from Article 7(1) of Decision 1/80, which is discussed below.

c. Certain concepts used in Article 6(2)

(i) Persons duly registered as belonging to the labour force

The meaning of the concepts of "being duly registered as belonging to the labour force" and being "legally employed" were in question in *Günaydin* and *Ertanir* and have been discussed in a number of other decisions,

The concept of being duly registered as belonging to the labour force has been liberally interpreted by the European Court of Justice, which seems to have been partially influenced by its jurisprudence on the definition of a worker in such interpretation. According to the two cases mentioned in the above paragraph,[41] in order to fulfil this requirement, the legal relationship of employment of the person concerned must be located within the territory of a Member State, or retain a sufficiently close link with that territory, account being taken of the place where the Turkish national was hired, the territory on or from which the paid employment is pursued, and the applicable national legislation in the field of employment and social law. It is a matter for the courts of Member States to determine whether the former requirements are fulfilled.[42] It appears that anyone who complies with the above mentioned criteria and who is bound by an employment relationship covering a genuine and effective economic activity is treated as being duly registered as belonging to the labour force.[43] In the somewhat controversial decision of the Court in *Nazli*, a Turkish worker who had been convicted of trafficking in heroin, detained in custody for over twelve months prior to such conviction, and subsequently paroled, was held not to have left the labour force. The Court also held that Article 14(1) of Decision 1/80, which provides that the provisions of the section on workers is to be applied subject to limitations justified on grounds of public policy, public security and public health was formulated in a similar way to Article 48(3) EC, and should thus be interpreted in a similar manner as had been interpreted in the

---

41. *Ertanir*, paragraphs 29–31; *Günaydin*, partagraphs 28–43; see also Case C-434/93, *Bozkurt v. Staatsecretaris van Justitie* [1995] ECR I-1475, paragraphs 22 and 23; and Case C-1/97, *Birden v. Bremen* [1998] ECR I-7747, paragraph 33.
42. See *Bozkurt*, in which the Court held that a Turkish worker who had become incapacitated as the result of an accident at work, and who had worked in the Netherlands for nine years, had no right to remain there.
43. See Case C-98/96, *Ertanir v. Land Hessen* [1997] ECR I-5179, paragraph 43. The requirement of a genuine and effective economic activity is, of course, derived from the Court's jurisprudence on the definition of a worker for the purpose of EC law: see in this connection, Craig and de Burca, *EU Law: Texts, Cases and Materials*, (2nd edn, Oxford University Press, 1998), pp. 673–681.

relevant cases relating to the free movement of workers who are nationals of a Member State of the EC.[44]

According to the Court's decision in *Birden*, a person may be treated as "duly registered as belonging to the labour force" even though his employment depends on public funding, and its purpose is to enable unemployed persons to enter the general labour market. The Court held that the latter concept must be regarded as applying to all workers who have complied with the requirements laid down by law and regulation in the Member State concerned, and are thus entitled to pursue an occupation in its territory.[45] It appears that the Court of Justice has given a liberal interpretation of the concept of being duly registered as belonging to the labour force, and has been considerably influenced by the jurisprudence of the European Court of Justice concerning the free movement of workers who are nationals of Member States.

(ii) The concept of legal employment
The above concept has been examined in a number of decisions, including the recent one of *R. v. Secretary of State for the Home Department ex parte Savas*,[46] in which the principles underlying this concept, which had been established in the context of the EC-Turkey Association Agreement for the progressive achievement of free movement of Turkish workers in the Community, were applied by way of analogy to the right of establishment. This matter receives further discussion in this section.

According to *Sevince*,[47] the legality of employment within the meaning of the third indent of Article 6(1) of Decision 1/80, even assuming it is not necessarily conditional on the possession of a properly issued residence permit, nevertheless presupposes a stable and secure situation as a member of the labour force. In the same case the Court of Justice held that legal employment cannot be said to exist where a Turkish worker is authorised to reside and be employed on a temporary basis pending the outcome of an appeal against a judgment refusing a residence permit.[48] Furthermore, the concept of "legal employment" does not cover the situation of a person on whom the right of residence in the host country had been conferred pending completion of the procedure for the grant

---

44. The Court, which made reference to Case 30/77, *R. v. Bouchereau* [1977] ECR I-999, paragraph 25, held that Nazli's expulsion could not be justified on grounds of general prevention: see paragraphs 556–64 of its judgment.
45. Case C-1/97, *Birden v. Bremen* [1998] ECR I-7747, paragraph 51. The Court interestingly made reference to Case 344/87, *Bettray* [1989] ECR 1621, which it distinguished. In that case the Court held that work that constitutes merely a means of rehabilitation or reintegration the persons concerned cannot be considered as a genuine and effective activity. And the Court pointed out the position of Birden differed considerably from that of Bettray, who was undergoing treatment as a drug addict.
46. Case 37/98, [2000] ECR I-2927.
47. Case C-192/89, *Sevince v. Staatssecretaris van Justitie* [1990] ECR I-3461, paragraph 30.
48. See paragraph 3 of the judgment in *Sevince*.

of a residence permit, on the ground that he had been given the right to work and remain in that country only on a provisional basis pending a final decision on his right of residence.[49] However, it follows from Article 6(1) of Decision 1/80, which does not make recognition of the rights stated therein subject to the requirement that Turkish nationals must establish that their employment is legal by means of any specific administrative document, that a Turkish worker may establish that he is in a stable and secure situation as a member of the labour force of a Member State, although he has not been required to obtain a residence permit or a work permit.[50]

In *Kol*[51] the Court of Justice held that the periods in which a Turkish national was employed under a residence permit which was issued to him only as the result of fraudulent conduct which led to his conviction, were not based upon a stable situation, in view of the fact that during the period in question the person concerned was not entitled to a residence permit.

As already indicated the Court of Justice applied certain of the principles established in the above cases in *Savas*,[52] in which it found that a Turkish national who remained in the United Kingdom in breach of immigration law and who started business without being authorised to do so was not entitled either to a right of establishment or a right of residence derived directly from Community provisions. This Court mentioned in paragraph 5 of its judgment that a Turkish national's first admission to the territory of a Member State is governed exclusively by that state's own domestic law and the person concerned may claim certain rights under Community law in relation to holding employment or exercising self-employed activity, and correlatively in relation to residence, only insofar as his position in the Member State concerned is regular.

d. Transposition of rules of Community law

Certain of the cases mentioned above assimilate the position of Turkish workers to that of EU citizens. This is not, however, true of all relevant decisions. Thus, a Turkish worker who becomes permanently incapable of working may be required to leave the host state: there is nothing in the EC-Turkey Association Agreement comparable to Regulation 1251/70/EC and the Court has refused to

---

49. See Case C-237/91, *Kus v. Landeshauptstadt Wiesbaden* [1992] ECR I-6781, paragraphs 12, 13 and 22.
50. Case C-434/93, *Bozkurt v. Staatssecretaris van Justitie* [1985] ECR I-1475, paragraphs 26, 29 and 30. See also Case C-36/96, *Günaydin v. Freistaat Bayern* [1997] ECR I-5143, paragraph 49 and Case C-98/96, *Ertanir v. Freistaat Bayern* [1997] ECR I-5197, paragraph 55, in the same sense.
51. Case C-285/95, *Kol v. Land Berlin* [1997] ECR I-3069, paragraph 27.
52. Case C-37/98, *R. v. Secretary of State for the Home Department, ex parte Savas* [2000] ECR I-2927.

interpret the EC-Turkey Association Agreement in an analogous manner[53] so as to grant persons permanently incapable of working the right to continue residence. Article 6(2)[54] of Decision 1/80 only provides for temporary intermissions of work, and assumes capacity to continue working. However, the Court took a different view in *Tetik*,[55] which was not concerned with a permanent incapacity, but voluntary termination of work by Mr Tetik, a Turkish national who had been employed as a seaman for more than eight years on German seagoing vessels. The Court held that a Turkish worker who had already been employed for more than four years in the host state and who voluntarily left such employment, but who did not enter into a new employment relationship immediately had the right to continue residence for a reasonable period or time to seek further employment. The Court found that it followed from Article 6(3) of Decision 1/80[56] that it was for the national authorities to determine how long this period should be; however, it must be sufficient not to deprive the right accorded to the worker by the third indent of Article 6(1) of its substance.[57]

The reference made to Article 48(3) EC and to its decision in *Bouchereau*[58] in the Court's decision in *Nazli*[59] has already been mentioned above. The Court also referred to certain other of its decisions involving the expulsion of Community nationals on general preventive grounds, and expressing the need for deportation on public policy grounds to be justified by conduct constituting a present threat to one of the fundamental interests of society.[60]

e. Article 7 and its effects

Article 7 of Decision 1/80 provides:

The members of the family of a Turkish worker duly registered as belonging to the labour force of a Member State who have been authorised to join him:

---

53. Case C-434/93, *Bozkurt v. Staatssecretaris van Justitie* [1995] ECR I-1475, paragraph 38.
54. Article 6(2) is concerned with the treatment of periods of short absence from work, involuntary unemployment and long absences on account of sickness.
55. Case C-171/95, *Tetik v. Land Berlin* [1997] ECR I-329, paragraphs 27–30 and 35–39.
56. Article 6(3) provides that the procedures for applying paragraphs 1 and 2 shall be those established under national law.
57. According to Hailbronner, *op. cit.*, p. 229, the appropriate period may be extended up to six months. This is the period suggested by the European Court of Justice as probably not too short for Community nationals seeking employment in Case C-292/89, *R. v. IAT ex parte Antonissen* [1991] ECR I-745, paragraph 4. Article 10 of Decision 1/80 provides that there must be no discrimination between Turkish and Community workers on grounds of nationality as regards remuneration and conditions of work.
58. Case 30/77, [1977] ECR 1999.
59. Case C-340/97, *Nazli v. Stadt Nürnberg* [2000] ECR I-957.
60. See paragraphs 56–58 of the Court's judgment. The cases referred to were Case 67/74, *Bonsignore* [1975] ECR 297, paragraph 7, and Case C-348/96, *Calfa* [1999] ECR I-11, paragraphs 22–24.

shall be entitled – subject to the priority given to Member States of the Community to respond to any offer of employment after they have been legally resident for at least three years in that Member State;

shall enjoy free access to any paid employment of their choice provided they have been resident there for at least five years.

Children of Turkish workers who have completed a course of vocational training in the host country may respond to any offer of employment there, irrespective of the length of time they have been resident in that Member State, provided that one of their parents has been legally employed in the Member State concerned for at least three years.

The above provisions only cover integration into the labour force of the relevant Member State, but the Court of Justice has held in *Eroglu*[61] that the right conferred upon a person by Article 7(2) to respond to any offer of employment gives a person the right to residence in the relevant host state. The Court held that the obligation contained in the second indent of Article 7(1) had direct effect, and also gave rise to a concomitant right of residence in *Ergat*.[62] In that case, the Court held that Member States remained competent to regulate the entry of the family of a Turkish worker and the conditions of his residence during the three years before he had the right to respond to any offer of employment.[63]

Decision 1/80 has been treated by the Court of Justice as allowing the authorities of a Member State to make the right of access to paid employment and the corresponding right of residence which it confers on members of a Turkish worker's family subject to the condition that the person concerned cohabits with that worker for the period of three years prescribed by the first indent of Article 7(1).[64] It should be noted that Article 7 does not include a nationality requirement and contains no definition of family members. In *Eyup*, the wife of a Turkish worker who was authorised to join him in Austria, but who divorced him before the end of the three year qualification period laid down in the first indent of Article 7(1), but who continued to cohabit with him until their remarriage, was held by the Court of Justice to be entitled to reside in Austria. The period of extra-marital cohabitation which had taken place was held not to have interrupted the couple's joint family life in Austria.

Involuntary stays of less than six months by the person concerned in his country of origin are not treated as interrupting the three year period of legal residence required by the first indent of Article 7(1). Shorter voluntary interrup-

---

61. Case C-355/93, *Eroglu v. Land Baden-Württemberg* [1994] ECR I-5113, paragraph 23.
62. Case C-329/97, *Ergat v. Stadt Ulm* [2000] ECR I-1487, paragraphs 58–59.
63. *Ibid.*, paragraph 423; see also Case C-351/95, *Kadiman v. Freistaat Bayern* [1997] ECR I-2133, paragraph 32 in a similar sense.
64. See *Ibid.*, paragraphs 41 and 44; Case C-329/97, *Ergat*, paragraph 37; and Case C-65/98, *Eyüp v. Landesgeschäftsstelle des Arbeitsmarktsservice Vorarlberg* [2000] ECR I-4747.

tions, for example for the purpose of holidays or visiting family members in the country of origin also do not interrupt the relevant period.[65] It was held in *Ergat* that a Turkish national who was authorised to enter a Member State for the purpose of reuniting the family of a Turkish worker belonging to the legal labour force of that state, and who had been legally resident there for five years, having been legally employed there with interruptions in various jobs, did not lose the benefit of the rights given to him by the second indent of paragraph 7(1) and in particular, the right to extend his residence permit, because his residence permit had expired before he applied for its extension.[66] The fact that the children of a Turkish worker are given the right to enter for a reason unconnected with reuniting the family, for example for the purposes of study, does not deprive them of the employment rights mentioned in Article 7(2),[67] which is directly effective in the Member States of the Community.[68] The Court of Justice held in *Akman* that Article 7(2) did not require that the relevant Turkish worker was still employed n the host state when his child was desirous of obtaining access to the labour market in that state.

f. *Priority for Turkish workers*

Article 8 of Decision 1/80 provides that employment authorities shall endeavour to give priority to Turkish workers where positions cannot be filled by Community workers. The use of the world "endeavour" in both paragraphs of Article 8 leads one to the conclusion that this provision lacks direct effect.[69]

g. *Admission of children to educational courses etc.*

According to Article 9 of Decision 1/80, Turkish children residing legally in the Member State with their parents who are or have been legally employed in that Member State will be admitted to courses of general educational, apprenticeship and vocational training under the same educational entry qualifications as the children of nationals of the Member State. They may in that Member State be eligible to benefit from the advantages provided for under the national legislation in this area. Although there are some differences between the relevant provisions,

---

65. See Case 351/95, *Kadiman v. Freistaat Bayern* [1997] I-2133, paragraph 47–49.
66. Case 329/97, *Ergat v. Stadt Ulm* [2000] ECR I-1487, paragraph 67.
67. Case C-355/93, *Eroglu v. Land Baden-Wurttemberg* [1994] ECR I-5113, paragraph 22. Nevertheless, it follows from paragraph 39 of the Court's judgment in Case C-351/95, *Kadiman v. Freistaat Bayern* [1997] ECR I-2133, that the family member must have been authorised to join a Turkish worker residing in a Member State.
68. Case C-210/97, *Akman v. Oberkreisdirektor des Rheinisch-Bergischen-Kreises* [1998] ECR I-7519, paragraph 39.
69. Note in this sense, Martin and Guild, *op. cit.*, paragraph 13.70.

the first sentence of Article 1 is obviously influenced by Article 12 of Regulation 1612/68. The provisions of the first sentence of Article 9 would seem to have direct effect; this may not be true of the second sentence of that provision because of the discretion implied by the use of the word "may".[70]

h. Non-discrimination: the provisions of Article 10

The provisions of Article 10(1) are in very similar terms to those contained in Article 37 of the Additional Protocol. Those of Article 10(2) resemble those in Article 5 of Regulation 1612/68. This article provides that "subject to the provision of Articles 6 and 7, the Turkish workers referred to in paragraph 1 and members of their families shall be entitled, on the same footing as Community workers, to assistance from the employment services in their search for employment". The reference to Articles 6 and 7 makes it clear that only Turkish nationals who are free to take up any paid employment, i.e. those covered by Article 6(1) third indent and Article 7, may benefit from the relevant assistance. Article 12 of Decision 1/80 permits a Member State or Turkey to temporarily desist from automatically applying Articles 6 and 7.

i. Miscellaneous rights

(i) Rights of nationals of EC Member States
According to Article 11, nationals of the Member States duly registered as belonging to the labour force in Turkey and family members authorised to join them, benefit from the rights and advantages granted under Articles 6, 7 and 10 of Decision 1/80.

(ii) Safeguard clause
Article 12 permits an EC Member State or Turkey to refrain temporarily from automatically applying Articles 6 and 7.

(iii) Standstill clause
Member States and Turkey are prohibited from introducing new restrictions on the conditions of access to employment for workers and family members legally resident and employed in their respective territories by Article 13.

(iv) Applicable limitations
By virtue of Article 14 of Decision 1/80, the provisions of the section of workers are to be applied subject to limitations justified on grounds of public policy, public security and public health. However, such provisions are said not to prejudice rights and obligations arising from national legislation or bilateral agreements, when these provide for more favourable treatment.

---

70. Note in this sense, *ibid.*, paragraph 64, at paragraph 13.73. These writers also contend that Article 9 of Decision 1/80 should be interpreted in the light of Regulation 1612/68.

It is arguable that, because the rights granted to Turkish workers under Decision 1/80 are considerably less than those conferred on Community workers by Article 39(3) EC, which include rights of movement and residence, these two provisions cannot be interpreted in the same way. Turkish workers and their family members may, of course, have a concomitant right of residence under Articles 6 and 7 of Decision 1/80 respectively.

It is noteworthy that the Court of Justice held in paragraph 56 of its decision in *Nazli*[71] that when determining the scope of the public policy exception provided for in Article 14(1), reference should be made to the interpretation given to that exception in the field of freedom of movement of workers who are nationals of a Member State of the Community. The Court added that such an approach was all the more justified because Article 14(1) is formulated in almost identical terms to Article 48(3) EC.

(v) Exchange of information
Article 15 provides for the exchange of information by the Association Committee to ensure that the provisions on workers in Decision 1/80 are applied harmoniously, and in such a way as to exclude the danger of disturbance to the employment market.

(vi) Social and cultural advancement of Turkish workers and their families
Article 17 provides that the Member States and Turkey shall cooperate to achieve the above end, which cooperation may involve such schemes as literacy campaigns and courses in the language of the host country, as well as activities to maintain links with Turkish culture and access to vocational training. According to Article 18, recommendations must be made to the Member States with a view to implementing any action that may enable young workers who have received their basic training in their own country to complement their vocational training by participating in in-service training.

4. Provisions of the Agreement and the Additional Protocol concerning establishment and services

Articles 13 and 14 of the Association Agreement respectively contain provisions governing establishment and services according to which the Contracting Parties agree to be guided by Articles 52 to 56 and 58 EC[72] for the purpose of abolishing restrictions on freedom of establishment, and by Articles 55, 56, 58–65 EC[73] for the purpose of abolishing restrictions on freedom to provide services. The programmatic language of Articles 13 and 14 make it clear that these two articles

---

71. Case C-340/97, *Nazli v. Stadt Nürnberg* [2000] ECR I-957, paragraphs 57–60.
72. Now Articles 42–46 EC.
73. Now Articles 55, 56 and 48–54 EC.

do not have direct effect. The fact that Article 13 does not have direct effect was recognised by the Court of Justice in *R. v. Secretary of State for the Home Department ex parte Savas.*[74]

The direct effect of Article 41(1) of the Additional Protocol, which provides that the contracting parties shall refrain from introducing between themselves any new restrictions on the freedom of establishment and freedom to provide services, was recognised by the Court in *Savas.*[75] In that case the Court of Justice also held that Article 41(2), which is concerned with the establishment of a timetable and rules for the progressive abolition by the contracting parties between themselves, of restrictions on freedom of establishment and on freedom to provide services, was held not to be directly effective.[76]

In his written observations in the Court of Justice in the latter case, Savas contended that Article 41(1) was capable of conferring on him a right of establishment and a corresponding right of residence in the United Kingdom, whose territory he had been authorised to enter, even though he had remained there and carried on activities there as a self employed person in breach of the United Kingdom's immigration law. As Article 41(1) is a standstill clause, it appears clear that a Turkish national would not necessarily achieve rights of establishment and residence from it. As the Court of Justice observed, whether he could do so would be dependent on whether the rules of United Kingdom law applied to the applicant in the main proceedings were less favourable than those which were applicable at the time when the Additional Protocol entered into force.[77] Although it does not appear that it was strictly necessary for the Court to answer the contentions put forward by Savas in his written observations, because he subsequently abandoned them, the Court found that Article 41(1) of the Additional Protocol was not of itself capable of conferring upon a Turkish national a right of establishment and as a corollary, a right of residence, in a Member State in whose territory he had remained and carried on business as a self-employed person in breach of domestic immigration law.[78] The Court seems to have felt it necessary to emphasise that what was applicable to Turkish workers was also applicable to Turkish nationals wishing to establish a business in a Member State.

---

74. Case C-37/98, [2000] ECR I-2927, paragraph 42.
75. Case C-37/98, paragraph 48. The Court found that Article 41(1) laid down a clear and unconditional principle that is sufficiently operational to be applied by a national court.
76. Case C-37/98, paragraph 48.
77. Case C-37/98, paragraphs 69–71.
78. Case C-37/98, paragraph 71.

5. The Euro-Mediterranean Agreement with Tunisia

(1) Introductory remarks

This Agreement, which is called an Association Agreement,[79] has quite extensive aims, which are set out in Article 1(2) thereof. It also contains provisions governing establishment and services, and the legal status of workers, which provisions together with certain related ones, are briefly considered below. Its ambit is more extensive than was the case in former agreements between the EC and Maghreb states.

(2) Employment, establishment and services

According to Article 31(1) of the Agreement, "the parties agree to widen the scope of the Agreement to cover the right of establishment of one party's firms on the territory of the other and the liberalisation of the provision of services by one party's firms to consumers of services in the other. The above provision has no application to natural persons, and my not have direct effect. The use of the words "agree to widen the scope" do not seem to impose a precise obligation. Furthermore, the wording of Article 31(2), which stipulates that the Association Council shall make recommendations to the achievement of the objective described in paragraph 1 also seems to militate against the conclusion that Article 31(1) has direct effect.[80] According to Article 32(1) of the Agreement, the parties reaffirm their obligations under the General Agreement on Trade in Services (GATS) and in particular the obligation of granting reciprocal most favoured nation treatment in the areas covered by that obligation.

The provisions of Title VI of the Agreement, which is entitled "Cooperation in social and cultural matters", deal with a number of matters arising from the migration of workers and others. Chapter 1 of Title VI, which comprises Articles 64–68, is entitled "workers". By Article 64(1) workers are to be granted national treatment in relation to working conditions and remuneration and dismissal. The same principle is applicable according to Article 64(2), to Tunisian workers allowed to undertake paid employment in a Member State on a temporary basis. It does not appear that such workers have any right to undertake such temporary employment. Furthermore, it follows from the Joint Declaration relating to Article 64(1) of the EC-Tunisia Agreement that the rights granted under Article 64(1) are without prejudice to the residence status enjoyed by Tunisian workers. This Declaration stipulates as follows:

With regard to the absence of discrimination as regards redundancy, Article

---

79. For which, see OJ 1998 L97/1.
80. However, in Case C-18/90, *ONEM v. Kziber* [1991] ECR I-199, the existence of such a provision in Article 42(1) of the Morocco Agreement of 1976 was held not to prevent this provision from having direct effect.

64(1) may not be invoked to obtain renewal of a residence permit. The granting, renewal or refusal of a residence permit shall be governed by the legislation of each Member State and the bilateral agreements and conventions in force between Tunisia and the Member State.

Family members of Tunisian workers are not granted access to the labour market of the Member States. A Joint Declaration between the contracting parties concerning Article 64 provides as follows:

> Without prejudice to the conditions and procedures applicable n each Member State, the parties shall examine the matter of access to a Member State's labour market of the spouse and children, legally resident under family reunification arrangements, of Tunisian workers legally employed on the territory of a Member State, except for seasonal workers, those on secondment or on placement, for the duration of the worker's authorised stay. It seems quite clear from this Joint Declaration that the parties did not intend the agreement to provide for family reunification.

A similar Joint Declaration may be found in the 1996 EC Agreement with Morocco,[81] which also fails to contain a provision on access to employment for family members. However, Article 65 of the Tunisia Agreement contains detailed provisions governing the social security rights of Tunisian workers, and in principle grants such persons equal treatment to nationals of the Member States in which they are employed in the field of social security. Nevertheless, a Joint Declaration relating to Article 65 of the Agreement stipulates "it is understood that the term 'members of the family' shall be defined in accordance with the legislation of the host country concerned".

Article 66 of the Tunisia Agreement, which is paralleled by Article 66 of the Morocco Agreement, stipulates that "the provisions of this chapter shall not apply to nationals of the parties residing or working illegally in the territory of their host countries".

The new Euro-Mediterranean Agreement calls for a dialogue in the social field. According to Article 69(1) of the Tunisia Agreement, the parties shall conduct regular dialogue on any social matter which is of interest to them. Article 69(2) provides that such dialogue shall be used to find ways to achieve progress in the field of movement of workers and equal treatment and social integration for Tunisian and Community nationals residing legally in the territories of their host countries. Such dialogue is, according to Article 69(3), to cover in particular all issues connected with:

(a) the living and working conditions of the migrant communities;
(b) migration;
(c) illegal immigration and the conditions governing the return of individuals

---

81. COM (95) 740 final.

who are in breach of the legislation dealing with the right to stay and the right of establishment in their host countries;

(d) schemes and programmes to encourage equal treatment between Tunisian and Community nationals, mutual knowledge of cultures and civilisations, the furthering of tolerance and the removal of discrimination.

No particular framework is provided for such dialogues, and it remains to be seen how successful it will prove to be in practice. In a Unilateral Declaration concerning Article 69, Tunisia has expressed the wish for family reunification to be the subject of in depth discussion with the Community. A proposal for a directive on family reunification was adopted by the Commission in 1999,[82] and an amended version of this proposal was published in 2000.[83] It is now based upon Article 63(3)(a), and lays down the conditions for the entry and residence of family members who are nationals of third countries. Full consideration has been given to the proposed directive in the ninth chapter. However, it is clear from Article 31 of the Protocol on the position of the United Kingdom and Ireland that these countries will not be bound by a directive whose basis is in Part IV of the EC Treaty, unless they have duly notified the President of the Council that they wished to take part in its adoption and application. It appears that the United Kingdom and Ireland did not take the latter step, and will thus not be bound by the Directive. However, it is conceivable that they might be bound by measures similar to those included in the Directive if such measures were proposed in the course of carrying on the dialogue under Article 69(3)(a) of the EC-Tunisia Agreement, which mentions migration. Although such measures would have to be implemented in accordance with Title IV, it is conceivable that the United Kingdom and Ireland would be bound to implement the results of the dialogue.[84]

The need for a dialogue on anti-discrimination would seem to have been reduced by the enactment of the major anti-discrimination Directives in accordance with Article 13 EC in the year 2000.[85] Member States are given a period of three years to implement these Directives. However, under Council Directive 2000/78/EC they are given an additional period of three years, if necessary, to implement the provisions on age and disability discrimination. This period ends on 2 December 2006. As is clear from paragraph 13 of the Preamble of Council Directive 2000/43/EC and paragraph 12 of the Preamble to Council Directive

---

82. COM (1999) 638 final.
83. COM (2000) 0258 (CMS).
84. Note in a similar sense, Hailbronner, *op. cit.*, p. 236.
85. See Council Directive 2000/41/EC on the principle of equal treatment between persons irrespective of racial or ethnic origin, OJ 2000 L190/22; and Council Directive 2000/78/EC, establishing a general framework for equal treatment in employment and occupation. The former Directive has a different scope than the latter one, the purpose of which is to lay down a general framework for combating direct or indirect discrimination on grounds of religion or belief, disability, age or sexual orientation as regards employment or occupation.

2000/78/EC, the prohibition of discrimination in both the two Directives applies to nationals of third states but does not cover differences of treatment on grounds of nationality and is without prejudice to provisions governing the entry of third country nationals and their access to employment or occupation.

In addition to the provisions considered above, the Tunisia Agreement also contains certain provisions, in particular those of Article 71, concerning cooperation in the social field. According to Article 73 of the Agreement, a working party set up by the Association Council shall be responsible for the continuous and regular implementation of Chapters 1–3 of Title VI, which respectively concern workers' cooperation in social matters, and in the social field.

6. The Europe (CEEC) Agreement with Poland

(1) Introductory remarks

The above agreement[86] is one of three third generation agreements concluded with Poland, Hungary and Czechoslovakia before its partition in 1991. It is one of the Europe Agreements which are in general based upon a uniform approach to Central and Eastern European countries and their nationals as far as the free movement of persons is concerned. The Polish Agreement, in common with other Europe Agreements, is expressly aimed at:

providing an appropriate framework for the political dialogue, allowing the development of close political relations between the parties

promoting the expansion of trade and harmonious economic relations between the parties and so as to foster the dynamic economic development and prosperity in the associated states

providing a basis for the Community's technical and financial assistance to those states

providing an appropriate framework for their gradual integration into the Community on the basis that they work towards fulfilling the necessary conditions

promoting cooperation in cultural matters.

Title IV of the Poland Agreement, in common with the other Europe Agreements, contains rules governing the movement of workers, establishment and the supply of services. These Agreements do not expressly provide for a protected residential status for CEEC workers. The right of establishment is granted under Article 44(3) of this Agreement to self-employed Polish nationals, but, according to the opinion of Advocate-General Alber in *R. v. Secretary of State for Home*

---

86. OJ 1993 L348/2.

Department ex parte Gloszczuk and Gloszczuk,[87] it is not accompanied by any concomitant right of residence. The Agreement is a long and complex document and it is only possible to make brief reference to its relevant provisions.

(2) The legal position of Polish workers

The rules contained in the Poland Agreement concerning the status of Polish workers are paralleled by the corresponding provisions of the other Europe Agreements. According to Article 31(1) of the former agreement, subject to the conditions and modalities applicable in each Member State, Polish national workers legally employed in the territory of a Member State shall be free from any discrimination based on nationality as regards working conditions, remuneration or dismissal. According to a Joint Declaration annexed to the Final Act, "it is understood that the concept 'conditions and modalities applicable in each Member State' includes Community rules, where appropriate". Furthermore, Article 41(1) provides that "taking into account the labour market situation in the Member State, subject to its legislation and to the respect for rules in force in that Member State in the area of mobility of workers:

the existing facilities for access to employment for Polish workers accorded by Member States under bilateral agreements ought to be preserved and if possible improved;

the other Member States shall consider favourably the possibility of concluding similar agreements.

Article 37(1) may be regarded as directly effective,[88] despite the use of the words "subject to the conditions and modalities applicable in each Member State" in the agreement. Whether or not this is the case, it is clear that the Poland Agreement, like the other Europe Agreements, does not grant any rights of entry and residence to workers. Thus, Article 41(3) of the Agreement makes it clear that Member States are only required to consider a grant of a work permit to a Polish national, even if such a national already has a residence permit in the Member State concerned.

---

87. Case C-63/99, Opinion delivered on 14.9.2000, n.y.r. Advocate General Alber had a similar view of Article 45(1) of the Association Agreement with Bulgaria in Case C-235/99, *R. v. Secretary of State for Home Department ex parte Kondova*, opinion delivered on 16.9.2000, n.y.r.

88. See the discussion of the matter in Martin and Guild, *Free Movement of Persons in the EU*, (Butterworths, 1996), paragraphs 16.5–16.7. The French Administrative Court of Nancy held that Article 37(1) was sufficiently clear to have direct effect without making any reference to the ECJ in *Malaja*, decision of 5 February 1999 N99 NBC 00282. The decision which concerned the rights of a Polish basketball player legally employed in France has been said to extend the ambit of the ruling in Case C-415/93, *Bosman* [1995] ECR I-4921 to association agreements with the EC. See in this sense Inglis, *op. cit.*, p. 1173, fn.3; p. 1202, fn.125.

Furthermore, although unilateral declarations are of questionable value, a similar conclusion may be reached from the Declaration of the European Community annexed to the Final Act on Chapter 1 of Title IV of the Poland Agreement (similar Declarations occur in other Europe Agreements). This Declaration stipulates that "nothing in the provisions of Chapter 1 'movement of workers shall be construed as impairing any competence of Member States as to the entry and stay on the territories of workers and their families." Although this Declaration should have been made by the Community Member States (which at the time of the Poland Agreement had sole competence on immigration matters), it may possibly reflect their intentions, and more certainly those of the Community, with regard to the provisions governing workers and their families.[89] The conclusion that Member States remain free to regulate the residence of Polish workers appears to, as Advocate General Alber suggested in relation to self-employed persons in *Gloszczuk and Gloszczuk*,[90] receive further support from Article 58 of the Poland Agreement, which is considered below under the heading "Provisions granting discretionary powers to Poland and the Member States".

(3) Families of Polish workers

The Poland Agreement, like the other Europe Agreements, only deals with the position of the family members of workers. According to Article 37(1) indent 2 of the Poland Agreement, the legally resident spouse and children of a worker legally employed in a Member State with the exception of seasonal workers, or workers coming within the scope of the special provisions of bilateral agreements, shall have access to the labour market of that state during th period of that worker's authorised stay of employment. Article 37(1) makes the reunification of family members subject to national law. According to a joint declaration annexed to the Final Act, contracting parties have provided that "it is understood that the notion of 'children' is defined in accordance with the national legislation of the host country."

There seems little possibility of Polish workers and their children obtaining an implied right of residence comparable to that available to them under the Turkish agreement. This right was derived solely and exclusively from Decision 1/80 of the Council of Association of 19 September 1980, and no rules similar to this decision exist in the Poland Agreement.[91] In fact as far as workers are concerned, the powers of the Council of Association, set up in Article 41(2) of

---

89. Note, in the latter sense, Martin and Guild, *op. cit.*, note 86, paragraphs 16.29–16.31. However the authors suggest that because competence to interpret a Community agreement belongs exclusively to the Court of Justice, it might be possible for the Court to ignore the Declaration.

90. Case C-63/99, *R. v. Secretary of State for Home Affairs ex parte Gloszczuk and Gloszczuk*, 14.9.2000, n.y.r.

91. Note in this sense, Opinion of the Advocate General in Case C-63/99, *Gloszczuk and Goloszczuk*, paragraph 66.

the Agreement, seem more circumscribed than those conferred upon the Council of Association set up under the EC-Turkey Agreement.[92]

(4) Freedom of establishment

The provisions of Article 44 of the Agreement, which are concerned with establishment, are lengthy and sometimes quite complex. The meaning of "establishment" for the purposes of the Agreement is defined in Article 44(4)(a)(i) and (ii) thereof. It is said to mean, as regards nationals, the right to take up and pursue economic activities as self-employed persons and to set up and manage undertakings, which they effectively control. The right of establishment granted does not give Polish nationals the right to provide services in another Member State, in the absence of any specific provision in the Agreement so permitting them. Self-employment and business undertakings by nationals are said not to extend to seeking or taking employment in the labour market or to confer a right of access to the labour market of another party. The provisions of the chapter (Chapter II of Title IV) on establishment are said to be inapplicable to those who are not exclusively self-employed. As is pointed out by Martin and Guild, the latter wording cannot be treated as excluding from Chapter II Community nationals who have taken advantage in the Community of Articles 39 and 43 EC, and been both employed and self-employed. It must be interpreted as applying in Poland to Community nationals who have exercised in that country self-employed activities only.[93]

As far as companies are concerned, establishment is defined as the right to take up and pursue economic activities by means of the setting up of subsidiaries, branches and agencies.[94]

The above provisions are clearly modelled on those of Articles 43 and 44(2)(f) EC. Article 44(1) of the Poland Agreement provides that "Poland shall during the transitional period referred to in Article 6,[95] facilitate the setting up of operations on its territory by Community companies and nationals ... and to this end grant for the establishment of Community companies and nationals ... treatment no less favourable than that accorded to its own nationals in accordance with the following timetable".[96] Article 44(1) also requires that "Poland

---

92. Note in particular Article 36 of the Additional Protocol to that Agreement.
93. Martin and Guild, *op. cit.*, paragraph 16.44.
94. "Community companies" and "Polish companies" are defined in Article 48. The basic elements of this definition are similar to those in Article 48 EC.
95. The total length of these two periods is ten years, and they thus expire on 31.1.2004. It is hoped that Poland and certain of the other CEECs will accede to the Community by that time.
96. The timetable for various sectors is made clear in a number of annexes to the Agreement. For a detailed account, see Martin and Guild, *op. cit.*, paragraph 16.36. The provisions of the Europe Agreement are inapplicable to air transport, inland waterways and maritime cabotage transport services.

shall grant from entry into force of this Agreement in the operation of Community companies and nationals established in Poland, a treatment not less favourable than that accorded to its own companies and nationals". Similar obligations to these, contained in Article 44(1), are imposed on Member States in respect of the establishment and operation of Polish companies and nationals by Article 44(3). The language in Article 44(1) and (3), despite the use of the word "facilitate" in the earlier provision, appears to be sufficiently clear and precise for these provisions to have direct effect.

The latter view was taken by Advocate General Alber of the provisions of Article 44(3)[97] in *Gloszczuk and Gloszczuk*.[98] Article 44(3) stipulates that "each Member State shall grant, from entry into force of this Agreement, a treatment no less favourable than that accorded to its own companies and nationals as defined in Article 48, and shall grant in the operation of Polish companies and nationals established in its territory a treatment no less favourable than that accorded to its own companies and nationals". Advocate General Alber took the view that Article 44(3) of the Agreement provides for a right of establishment but not for a right of residence. This view seems to be correct, even if it has other unfortunately practical consequences. It would appear that a similar view has to be taken of Article 44(1), thereby considerably diminishing the useful effects of this provision.[99]

It is noteworthy, as Hailbronner points out,[100] that the Poland Agreement, in common with the other Europe Agreements, defines the scope of establishment as the pursuit of economic activity. Freedom of establishment has a wider scope in Article 43 EC, where it is defined as including such activity. The Europe Agreements do not contain any express prohibition of restrictions on freedom of establishment, irrespective of whether these restrictions adversely affect such freedom in a direct or indirect manner. Hailbronner thus concludes that freedom

---

97. Note the doubts expressed as to the direct effect of the provisions concerning establishment by Hailbronner, *op. cit.*, pp. 247–8. His doubts are based upon the language of the Agreement. It may well be the case that the contracting parties were somewhat ambivalent about the effect of certain provisions of this Agreement and the other Europe Agreements on establishment when they were included therein.

98. Case C-63/99, paragraph 50. In addition to *Gloszczuk* and *Kondova*, there are two other cases pending before the Court of Justice concerning the direct effect of Article 44 of the Poland Agreement and Article 45 of the Czech Agreement, Case C-268/99, *Jany*, pending and Case C-257/99, *R. v. Secretary of State for Home Department ex parte J. Barkoci and M. Malik*, n.y.r. respectively. In all these cases, the effect of the provisions of Article 58 or 59 of the relevant Agreement enabling the parties to apply their own laws and regulations in certain areas was also referred to.

99. Note the contrary view expressed by Hailbronner, *op. cit.*, p. 245. See also Peers, 'Towards Equality: Actual and Potential Rights of Third Country Nationals in the European Union', (1996) 33 CML Rev., p. 7, 40. See also the cases mentioned by Inglis, 'The Europe Agreements Compared in the Light of their Pre-Accession Orientation', (2000) 37 CML Rev., pp. 1173, 1203.

100. Hailbronner, *op. cit.*, p. 248.

of self-employed activity does not include social rights and claims for family reunification: these matters are not expressly included or referred to in any secondary legislation. Furthermore, restrictions on such rights would only affect freedom of establishment in an indirect manner and not be covered by the relevant texts.

Although the provisions of the Europe Agreements governing establishment are different from those in the EC Treaty, it seems doubtful whether the Court of Justice would necessarily follow such an approach rigorously. The phrase "a treatment no less favourable than that accorded to its own companies and nationals" used in Article 44(1)(ii) and 44(3) of the Poland Agreement could perhaps be used to combat indirect discrimination. A Joint Declaration annexed to the Final Act stipulates that the parties agree that the treatment of nationals or companies of one party shall be considered to be less favourable than that accorded to the other party if such treatment is either formally or de facto less favourable than the treatment accorded to the other party. De facto less favourable treatment would seem to include indirect discrimination.

(5) Derogation from chapter 1 in favour of certain personnel

It has already been indicated that Article 37(1) of Chapter 1 of the Poland Agreement does not provide Polish workers with any right of access to employment in the Member States. Article 52 provides for a derogation from the provisions of Chapter 12 in favour of senior employees of an organisation who primarily direct its management or who possess high or uncommon qualifications or knowledge. Beneficiaries of the rights of establishment granted by Poland and the Community respectively are entitled to employ such persons or have them employed by one of their subsidiaries, in accordance with the legislation in force in the host state of establishment,[101] in the territory of Poland and the Community respectively. The employees must be nationals of Community Member States or of Poland, and have been employed by the organisation for at least one year prior to the detachment therefrom. The residence permits and work permits for such persons must only cover the period of such employment. The present provision would seem to be of considerable use to companies, although it is not limited to them.

(6) The provision of services

By Article 55(1), Poland and the Member States undertake to take the necessary steps to allow progressively the supply of services by Community or Polish companies or nationals who are in a party other than that of the person for whom the services are intended, account being taken of the development of the services sector in the parties. In step with that liberalisation process, and subject

---

101. Note Article 58(1) of the Agreement which sets out what legislation may be applied.

to Article 58(1), which permits the application of national laws and regulations regarding entry and stay, work, labour conditions and establishment of natural persons and supply of services, the parties shall permit the temporary movement of natural persons providing the service or who are employed by the service provider as key personnel. Such movement includes that of natural persons who are representatives of a Community or Polish company or national and are seeking temporary entry for the purpose of negotiating for the sale of services or entering into agreements to sell services for that service provider. However, such representatives must not be engaged in making direct sales to the general public, or in supplying services themselves.[102]

Given the wording of Article 55(1), it does not appear to have direct effects: this would seem to be the case because of the use of the words "undertake" and "progressively" which seem to indicate unconditional obligations are not assumed. Despite the complex nature of Article 55(2), the use of mandatory language in this paragraph suggests that it contains unconditional obligations, and it is couched in clear and precise terms. It would therefore appear to have direct effect.[103]

a. Provisions granting discretionary powers to Poland and the Member States

(i) Restrictions based upon public policy and the exercise of official authority
According to Article 53 of the Poland Agreement:

1. The provisions of this chapter shall be applied subject to limitations based upon grounds of public policy, public security or public health.
2. The provisions of this chapter shall not apply to activities which, in the territory of each party are connected even occasionally with the exercise of official authority.

Article 53(1) constitutes a repetition of Article 39(3) EC and, despite the fact that the two provisions pursue rather different aims, it would seem from *Nazli*[104] to require interpretation in a similar manner. The wording of Article 53(2) resembles that of Article 45(1) EC (ex Article 55(1) EC) rather than that of Article 39(4) EC, According to *Reyners v. Belgium*,[105] Article 45(1) cannot be given a scope which would exceed the objective for which the exception clause was inserted. Furthermore, it is limited to those activities which, taken on their own, constitute a direct and specific connection with the exercise of official authority. It is not clear whether these limitations apply to Article 53(1) of the

---

102. See Articles 55(2) and 52(2) of the Poland Agreement.
103. Note in this sense Martin and Guild, *op. cit.*, paragraphs 16.70–72.
104. Case 340/97, [2000] ECR I-957, paragraph 56. The Court held in that case that Article 14(1) of Decision 1/80 of the Council of Association set up under the EC–Turkey Agreement had to be interpreted in a similar way to Article 39(3) EC, because it was formulated in almost identical terms to the latter provision.
105. Case 2/74, [1974] ECR 631, paragraphs 43 and 45.

Poland Agreement.[106] An exception for the exercise of official authority also occurs in Article 46(2) of the Partnership and Cooperation Agreement with Russia as well as in the other Europe Agreements. As Hailbronner points out, this exception might be applicable to self-employed economic activity privatised on a contractual basis by a competent public authority.[107]

(ii) The provisions of Article 58(1)
The above stipulation, whose effect is controversial, provides as follows:

> For the purposes of Title IV of this Agreement, nothing in the Agreement shall prevent the partner from applying their laws and regulations regarding entry, stay, works, labour conditions and establishment of natural persons, and supply of services, provided that, in so doing they do not apply them in a manner as to nullify or impair the benefits accrued to any party under the terms of a specific provision of this Agreement. This provision does not prejudice the application of Article 53.

A Joint Declaration is annexed to the EC-Poland Agreement, according to which the sole fact of requiring a visa for natural persons of certain parties and not for those of others shall not be regarded as nullifying or impairing benefits under a specific commitment.

It should be noted that both of the above provisions are inapplicable to the establishment of companies. It has been contended that these above provisions run counter to the grant of a right of establishment, and that the meaning of the phrase "nullify" or "impair" is not clear.[108] In his opinions in *Gloszczuk and Gloszczuk*[109] and in *Kondova*,[110] Advocate General Alber took the view that Article 58(1) of the Poland Agreement and Article 59 of the Bulgaria Agreement, which corresponds with the former provision, demonstrate *a fortiori* that Member States continue to be entitled to regulate the entry and residence of Polish and Bulgarian nationals in regard to the right of establishment. The Advocate General did not attempt an exhaustive analysis of Article 58(1) of the Poland Agreement or Article 59 of the Bulgaria Agreement, but correctly pointed out that these provisions are addressed to the Community, its Member States and Poland or Bulgaria, and do not confer any direct rights on Polish or Bulgarian nationals. However, it seems that the provisions in question might be applied

---

106. The contrary view is taken by Martin and Guild, *op. cit.*, paragraph 16.67.

107. Hailbronner, *op. cit.*, p. 252.

108. Guild in Guild (ed.), *The Legal Framework and Social Consequences of Free Movement of Persons in the European Union*, (Kluwer Law International, 1999), 127, 136. For a contrary view, see Hailbronner, *op. cit.*, p. 253. The learned author thinks that the relevant provisions are limited to the legal relationships established between the parties to the Agreement.

109. Case C-63/99, *R. v. Secretary of State for the Home Department, ex parte Gloszczuk and Gloszczuk*, opinion of 14.9.2000, paragraphs 79–83.

110. Case C-235/99, *R. v. Secretary of State for the Home Department ex parte Kondova*, opinion of 14.9.2000, paragraphs 88–91.

by a party to the relevant Agreement in such a way as to cause difficulties for nationals or companies of another party.[111]

7. The PCA with Russia

(1) Introductory remarks

The Partnership and Cooperation Agreements (PCAs) are concluded with states which were former members of the Soviet Union, but which are now independent, but which are not yet thought of as possible candidates for membership of the EU. The Agreement with Russia[112] and Ukraine[113] are supplemented by a number of common strategies, which are based upon Article 13 of Title V of the Treaty of European Union. These common strategies do not amend the PCAs, but are intended to strengthen the partnership originally based on them.[114] The provision of the PCA with Russia in general resembles that with Ukraine, but there are some differences between the two Agreements. Thus, for example, it seems that the provisions of Article 23 of the Russia Agreement concerning the equal treatment of workers may have direct effect; the less compelling language of the corresponding provisions of Article 24 of the Ukraine Agreement, which uses the words "shall endeavour" instead of "shall ensure", which is used in the Russia Agreement, may lead to the conclusion that Article 24 of the Ukraine Agreement does not have such an effect. Article 84 of the Russia Agreement provides that the parties should cooperate for the purpose of preventing illegal activities, including illegal immigration and illegal presence of natural persons of their nationality on their respective territory, account being taken of the principle and practice of readmission.[115] There is no corresponding provision in the Ukraine Agreement, but Article 27 thereof provides that the Cooperation Council[116] shall examine what joint efforts can be made to control immigration, taking into Account the principle and practice of readmission.

The Russia Agreement, like the other PCAs, is a mixed agreement, the parties being the Community and its Member States and Russia. It contains rules on labour, establishment and services in Part IV thereof, which is headed "Provisions on business and investment".

---

111. Note however, the different view taken by Hailbronner, *op. cit.*, p. 253.
112. OJ 1997 L327/1.
113. OJ 1999 L333/1.
114. See C. Hillion, 'International Aspects of the Partnership Between the European Union and the Newly Independent States of the Former Soviet Union: Case Studies of Russia and Ukraine', (2000) 37 CML Rev. 1211.
115. See Handoll, *op. cit.*, pp. 340–1.
116. In the two Agreements the Cooperation Council is made up of members of the Council of the EU, the Commission of the EC, and members of the government of the Ukraine or Russia. See EC-Ukraine Agreement, Article 85 and EC-Russia Agreement, Article 11.

(2) Labour conditions

The above matter is dealt with in Articles 23–27 (Chapter 1 of Title IV) of the Russia Agreement, which in general resemble those of Articles 24–28 of the Ukraine Agreement. Article 23(1) of the former Agreement provides that "subject to the law, conditions and procedures applicable in each Member State, the Community and the Member States shall ensure that the treatment accorded to Russian nationals legally employed in the territory of a Member State shall be free from any discrimination based on nationality, as regards working conditions, remuneration or dismissal, as compared to its own nationals. By virtue of Article 23(2), "Russia shall subject to the conditions and modalities applicable in Russia, accord the treatment referred to in paragraph 1 to nationals of a Member State who are legally employed in its territory.

Despite the use of such language as "subject to the laws, conditions and procedures applicable in each Member State" and "subject to the conditions and modalities applicable in Russia", it would seem that Article 23 may have direct effect. The use of such wording as "shall ensure" and "shall accord" tends to lead to this conclusion. As in the case with Article 37(1) of the Poland Agreement, it is possible to interpret these phrases as making it clear that the same treatment is required as that given to nationals of the Member States, and Russian nationals, in the relevant fields.[117]

Articles 24 and 25 contain provisions on social security. The former Article provides for the conclusion of agreements for the coordination of social security systems to benefit for Russia, and for the Community states, those of its nationals legally employed and family members lawfully resident in the other's territory. According to a Joint Declaration annexed to the Agreement, "members of the family" are defined in accordance with the national legislation of the host country concerned. Article 25 provides that measures taken under the Agreement shall not affect any more favourable treatment arising from bilateral agreements between Member States and Russia.

According to Article 26, the Cooperation Council[118] shall consider what improvements can be made in working conditions for businessmen consistent with the international commitments of the Parties, including those set out in the document of the CSCE[119] Bonn Conference. This provision is the subject of a Joint Declaration in which the parties stipulate that they shall ensure that the issuing of visas and residence permits in conformity with the laws and regulations

---

117. Note in this sense Martin and Guild, *op. cit.*, paragraphs 16.5–16.7 and paragraphs 20.43 and 20.47. The authors say that the reservation may be intended to give substance to what is meant by equal treatment in their discussion of the corresponding provisions of Article 37(1) of the Poland Agreement.

118. This is made up of members of the Council of the EU and the Commission of the EC and members of the government of the Russian Federation; see Articles 90–94 of the Russia Agreement.

119. The acronym is short for Conference on Security and Cooperation in Europe.

of the Member States and Russia respectively is conducted in a manner consistent with the principles of the concluding document of the CSCE Bonn Conference, in particular with a view to facilitating the prompt entry, stay and movement of businessmen in the Member States and Russia. The parties also agree that the timely conclusion of readmission agreements between the Member States and Russia is of importance. The Cooperation Council is required to regularly review the development of the situation in these areas.

By Article 27 the Cooperation Council is required to make recommendations for the implementation of Articles 23 and 26.

(3) Rules governing the establishment and operation of companies

Articles 28–38 (Chapter II of Title IV) contain detailed rules governing the above matter. For reasons of space, the present discussion will be limited, concentrating in particular on the position of individuals. As is also the case with the Ukraine Agreement, the chapter only provides for companies and contains no provisions governing the establishment of individuals.

Article 28(1) requires the Community and its Member States and Russia to guarantee treatment no less favourable than that awarded to companies of third countries with regard to conditions affecting the establishment of companies in their territories. The position of Community subsidiaries of Russian companies under Article 28(2) is better than that granted for the establishment of Russian companies in the Community under Article 28(1). The former provision stipulates that the Community and the Member States are obliged to secure national treatment to the activities of subsidiaries of Russian companies, except those in the sectors listed in Annex 3, which include mining, fishing, telecommunications and audio-visual services, professional services, agriculture, real estate purchase and news agency services. By Article 28(3), except in the sectors listed in Annex 4,[120] Russia is under the same obligations as the Community insofar as the guarantee of national treatment is concerned. However, if it grants better than national treatment to Russian companies which are subsidiaries of any third country companies, it must instead extend this treatment to Community companies.

Article 29 is a complex provision relating to banking and insurance and Article 30 contains a number of definitions and is the subject of a number of Joint Declarations addressed to the Final Act. The provisions of Article 32, which are concerned with the employment of key personnel, appear of considerable interest. By Article 32(1) companies of one party established in the territory of another are permitted to employ, or have employed by one of their subsidiaries, branches or joint ventures in accordance with the legislation of the host state employees

---

120. The relevant sectors are use of the subsoil and natural resources including mining, fishing, real estate (immovable property) purchase and brokerage, telecommunications, mass media services, professional activities, lease of federal property.

treated as key personnel under paragraph 2 who are employed exclusively by such companies or their subsidiaries, branches, or joint ventures. The residence and work permits of such employees must only cover the period of employment. Article 32(1) defines key personnel, who must have been employed by or partners in, the organisation (other than majority shareholders) for at least one year prior to secondment, as (i) senior employees who primarily direct the management of the organisation, receiving general supervision or direction principally from the board of directors or shareholders of the business, or their equivalent; (ii) employees who possess uncommon knowledge essential to the establishment's service, research, equipment, techniques or management.

The key personnel must satisfy the requirements of being an "intra-corporate transferee" as defined in Article 32(1)(i). This provision defines an "intra-corporate transferee" as a natural person working within an organisation within the territory of a party, and being temporarily transferred in the context of the pursuit of economic activities in the territory of the other party; the organisation concerned must have a principal place of business in the territory of a party and the transfer must be to an establishment of that organisation providing like economic activities in the territory of the other party.

Article 33 enables the parties, if they so desire, to move towards the extension of rights of establishment further than they must do under Article 28. It follows from Article 35(1) that Article 28 is inapplicable to air transport, inland waterways transport and maritime transport.

(4) The cross-border supply of services

The cross-border provision of services is governed by Chapter III of Title IV, which is made up of Articles 36–43. The most important of the provisions of Chapter III seem to be Articles 36 and 37. The former article provides that for the sectors listed in Annex 5 of the Agreement, the parties shall grant each other MFN (most favoured nation) treatment with regard to the cross-border supply of services by Community or Russian companies into the territory of Russia or the Community respectively. Annex 5 mentions services in a large number of fields, such as accounting, book-keeping, engineering, architecture, computing, advertising, market research, telecommunications, construction, adult education, franchising, news agencies, insurance and data processing.

According to a Community declaration annexed to the Final Act cross-border services under Article 36 do not "imply the movement of the service supplier into the territory of the country where the service is destined, nor the movement of the recipient of the service into the territory of the country from which the service comes." The Community declaration is interpreted by Russia in the following sense: "the suppliers in Community declarations in relation to Article 36 could not be considered as natural persons, who are representatives of a Community or Russian company and are seeking temporary entry for the purpose of negotiating the sales of cross-border supply services or entering into agreements to sell cross-border services for that company." Given the provisions of Article 37, which are considered below, the need for this Russian declaration appears questionable.

Article 37 provides, subject to Article 48,[121] that as far as the sectors listed in Annex 5 are concerned, the parties shall permit the temporary movement of natural persons, representing a Community or a Russian company, who are seeking temporary entry for the purpose of negotiating for the sale of cross-border services or entering into agreements to sell cross-border services or entering into agreements to sell cross-border services for the companies where those representatives will not be engaged in making direct sales to the public, or in supplying services themselves.

(5) General provisions

a. Article 46

Chapter IV of Part IV of the Russia Agreement consists of a number of general provisions, Articles 44–51, some of which merit consideration. The wording of Article 46 is practically the same as that of Article 53 of the Poland Agreement. Article 46(1) thus provides that the provisions of this Title shall be applied subject to limitations, justified on grounds of public policy, public security or public health. Article 46(2) provides that they shall not apply to activities which in the territory of either country are connected, even occasionally, with the exercise of official authority. A Joint Declaration is annexed to the Final Act, in relation to Article 46(2), in which the

"parties confirm their understanding that the question of whether activities are connected, even occasionally, with the exercise of official authority in their respective territories, depends on the circumstances of each particular case. An examination in each particular case, whether such activities are connected with:

the right to use physical constraint; or

the exercise of judicial functions; or

the right unilaterally to enact binding regulations

will help to determine the answer to such questions."

b. Article 48

The above provision corresponds almost exactly with Article 58(1) of the Poland Agreement, except insofar as it terminates with a mention of Article 46 (instead

---

121. Article 48 corresponds almost exactly to Article 58(1) of the Poland Agreement, which has been considered above. Like Article 42 of the Ukraine Agreement, it permits a party to apply their laws and regulations concerning the establishment of natural persons, although the substantive provisions of the Russia Agreement do not cover this matter.

of Article 53) of the Agreement. Like Article 58(1) of the Poland Agreement, it is the subject matter of a Joint Declaration annexed to the Final Act; this Declaration states that "the sole fact of requiring a visa for natural persons of certain parties and not for those of others shall not be regarded as nullifying or impairing benefits under a specific commitment."

c. Article 50

The need for Article 50 seems at first sight questionable. This provision can only have been inserted from an abundance of caution. The provision stipulates that without prejudice to Articles 32 and 37, no provision of Chapter II, III or IV of Title IV shall be interpreted as giving the right to:

1. nationals of either Party to enter or stay in the territory of the other in any capacity whatsoever, in particular as a shareholder or partner in a company or manager or employee thereof, or as a supplier or recipient of services;
2. Community subsidiaries or branches of Russian companies to employ or have employed in the territory of Russia nationals of Member States. A similar rule is applicable to Russian subsidiaries or branches of Community companies;
3. Russian companies or Community subsidiaries or branches of Russian companies to supply workers who are Russian nationals to act for and under the control of other persons by temporary employment contracts. A similar rule is applicable to Community companies or Russian subsidiaries or branches of Community companies.

A Joint Declaration annexed to the Final Act concerning Articles 26, 32 and 37 provides that the parties are to ensure that the issuing of visas and residence permits in conformity with the laws of host states is conducted in a manner consistent with the concluding document of the CSCE Bonn Conference, particularly with a view to facilitating the prompt entry, stay and movement of businessmen. Such efforts are to apply in particular to key personnel (as defined in Article 32(2), and to sellers of cross-border services referred to in Article 37, and ensure that the administrative procedures do not nullify or impair the benefits accruing to any party under Article 32 or 37. The Joint Declaration also expresses the agreement of the parties that an important element in this context is the timely conclusion of readmission agreements. The Cooperation Council is required to regularly review the situation in these areas. The Joint Declaration appears to be designed to combat obstructionism and unnecessary bureaucratic delay.

8. The General Agreement on Trade in Services (GATS)

(1) Introductory remarks

From the late 1970s, the services sector became recognised as particularly dynamic and critical to a modern economy and as of more economic importance than labour, raw materials, or capital.[122] The General Agreement on Trade in Services (GATS) which provides for the progressive liberalisation of trade in services, reflects that recognition as well as of more economic importance a certain conceptual influence which the EC was able to bring to bear on the drafting of the Agreement.[123]

Nonetheless, the GATS and the EC Treaty have a different scope of application. The GATS applies when both service supplier and service consumer of a particular service in question have specific links with a WTO Member. Thus, a "natural person of another Member" is one residing in the territory of a Member, and who is a national of that Member,[124] while a "juridical person" benefits from the GATS if it is one that is constituted or otherwise organized under applicable law.[125]

Accordingly, a company incorporated in England but conducting all its business, say, in Australia can benefit from the GATS. Under Article 48 EC (ex 58) such a company could also enjoy free movement under Community law, using its incorporation as a connecting factor, provided its registered office or principal place of business or central administration is also in an EC Member State.[126]

(2) Service supply through "natural persons"

The scope of the GATS *ratione materiae* is circumscribed by reference to the concept of 'trade in services' which is defined by four modes of supply of a service (Article I:2). The fourth mode of service supply involves the delivery of a service in the territory of any other Member through the presence of 'natural persons'.[127] These will usually be 'business persons', but the concept also covers natural persons who are themselves service suppliers, as well as natural persons who are employees of service suppliers, e.g. foreign consultants.[128] This mode of

---

122. Today services already account for more than 70 per cent of GDP in many OECD countries and 50 per cent in some DCs and absorb 60 per cent of all foreign investment flows in the world economy, see Francisco Javier Prieto and Sherry M. Stephenson, 'Multilateral and Regional Liberalization of Trade in Services', in Miguel Rodriguez Mendoza, Patrick Low and Barbara Kotschwar (eds.), *Trade Rules in the Making*, (Brookings Institution Press, Washington, D.C.), p. 235, 237.

123. See in particular footnote 5 to Article XIV (a) GATS on a general exception to the GATS "necessary to protect public morals or to maintain public order" which "may be invoked only where a genuine and sufficiently serious threat is posed to one of the fundamental interests of society", language reminiscent of Case 30/77, *R.v.Bouchereau* [1977] ECR 1999.

124. Article XVIII(k) GATS.

125. Article XVIII(l) GATS.

126. Such companies are, for the purposes of the relevant chapter of the EC Treaty, treated in the same way as if they were natural persons who were nationals of Member States.

127. Article I:2(d); see Friedl Weiss, 'The General Agreement on Trade in Services', (1995) 32 CMLRev. 5, pp. 1177–1225, at 1190.

128. Paragraph 1 of the Annex on Movement of Natural Persons Supplying Services under the Agreement stipulates that "this Annex applies to measures affecting natural persons

supply of a service is particularly hampered by many types of bureaucratic obstacles, such as visas and work permits and restrictions on families, which effectively operate as non-tariff barriers to trade in services. These barriers to the movement of key personnel with specialist, technical or managerial skills can significantly increase costs, prevent the effective distribution and use of corporate human resources including the transfer of technology to locally based personnel, and delay and impede the delivery of services to customers. Indeed, the movement of natural persons has only been liberalised to an extremely limited extent, mainly restricted to intra-company personnel movements and to highly skilled and top-level executives mostly deployed in conjunction with commercial presence (supply mode three), with little progress in the provision of professional services.

(3) Specific commitments of the EC and its Member States

However, the European Community and its Member States are amongst a small group of WTO members which have made the greatest commitments to movement on natural persons. Thus, the European Union and its Member States guarantee opportunities for foreign professionals without commercial presence to perform temporary assignments in several professional and business sectors.

Article I:2(d) GATS does not define the conditions under which the movement of a service provider may take place. These are left to the schedules of specific commitments of WTO members[129] within the context of the GATS Annex on Movement of Natural Persons Supplying Services under the Agreement. This Annex makes clear that the GATS does

"not apply to measures affecting natural persons seeking access to the employment market of a Member, nor ... to measures regarding citizenship, residence or employment on a permanent basis" (Paragraph 2).

Furthermore, it does

"not prevent a Member from applying measures to regulate the entry of natural persons into, or their temporary stay in, its territory, including those measures necessary to protect the integrity of, and to ensure the orderly movement of natural persons across, its borders, provided that such measures are not applied in such a manner as to nullify or impair the benefits accruing to any Member under the terms of a specific commitment" (Paragraph 4).

In the absence, furthermore, of any agreed definitions regarding employment

---

who are service suppliers of a Member, and natural persons of a Member who are employed by a service supplier of a Member, in respect of the supply of a service.".

129. The schedules of specific commitments require Members to indicate horizontally and sectorally what commitments they are making for mode four with regard to market access (Article XVI), national treatment (Article XVII) and any additional commitments (Article XVIII).

category or function, WTO Members enjoy considerable discretion in defining the extent of liberalisation under this mode of supply of a service. Many of the scheduled commitments do not include specific time limits and are limited mainly by pre-employment criteria, economic needs tests and numerical quotas. In addition to these scheduling, definition and classification problems difficulties in liberalising the movement of natural persons are further compounded by domestic regulatory practices regarding qualification requirements and procedures, technical standards, and licensing requirements which Members are allowed to maintain provided they do not constitute unnecessary barriers to trade in services and conform to the disciplines of Article VI:4 GATS.[130] Domestic regulatory practices are not scheduled unless Members make additional commitments under Article XVIII GATS. Most Members have not made such additional unilateral commitments, presumably preferring to negotiate relevant commitments, such as aspects of immigration and labour market policies, in accordance with the disciplines of Article VI:4 GATS.

The GATS commitments made so far are disappointing to DCs and LDCs who see them as unbalanced in the treatment of capital and labour, depriving them of comparative advantage in this form of service delivery due to lower labour costs. These Members, consequently, are seeking more fourth mode of supply commitments vis-à-vis themselves.[131]

However, such demands are likely to be met with considerable reticence by developed WTO Members as they would necessarily amount to narrowing discretionary powers to regulate the movement of natural persons considered necessary for the flexible management of immigration and labour market development policies.

The European Community does not as yet possess a uniform immigration policy with respect to third country nationals. It would be difficult, therefore, to effectively monitor and measure the impact of the implementation of mode four commitments at the European Community level. Until the Maastricht Treaty competence in the field of immigration was largely retained by national authorities of Member States. However, since the entry into force of the Maastricht Treaty on 1 November 1993, a considerable degree of competence in the field of immigration has been conferred upon the Commnity.[132]

The European Community does not impose quotas in its schedules of specific commitments, but limits the professions in which foreigners may work to 17 and

---

130. These disciplines aim to ensure that domestic regulatory policies and practices are: (a) based on objective and transparent criteria, such as competence and the ability to supply the service; (b) not more burdensome than necessary to ensure the quality of the service; (c) in the case of licensing procedures, not in themselves a restriction on the supply of the service.

131. Such demands are supported by both the preamble to the GATS and Article IV GATS on 'Increasing Participation of Developing Countries'.

132. Part IV of Title III of the EC Treaty; for a more detailed discussion see chapter 9, *supra*.

further uses economic needs tests, especially for the United Kingdom and Italy, without, however, defining applicable criteria. The European Community also provides for a limited temporary period of 3 months for contracted work, but does not otherwise specify duration of stay since this is regulated nationally.

Select Bibliography

PERIODICALS

Bernard, Nicolas, 'Discrimination and free movement in EC Law', (1996) 45
   International and Comparative Law Quarterly 1, pp. 82–108
Closa, Carlos, 'The concept of citizenship in the Treaty on European Union',
   (1992) 29 CML Rev. 6, pp.1137–1169
Costello, Cathryn, 'Case C-348/96, *Donatella Calfa*, Judgment of the Full
   Court of 19 January 1999, n.y.r.', (2000) 37 CML Rev. 3, pp. 817–827
Daniele, Luigi, 'Non-discriminatory restrictions to the free movement of
   persons', (1997) 22 EL Rev. 3, pp. 191–200
Dassesse, Marc, 'The Treaty on European Union: implications for the free
   movement of capital', (1992) 6 *Journal of International Banking* pp. 238–243
Davies, Paul, 'Posted workers: single market in protection of national labour
   law systems?', (1997) 34 CML Rev. 3, pp. 571–602
Edward, D., 'Establishment and services: an analysis of the insurance cases',
   (1987) 12 EL Rev., pp. 231–256
Gormley, Lawrence, 'The application of Community Law in the United
   Kingdom 1976–1985', (1986) 23 CML Rev., pp. 287
Greaves, Rosa, 'Advertising restrictions and the free movement of goods and
   services', (1998) 23 EL Rev. 4, pp. 305–319
Hathaway, James C., 'Harmonising for whom? The devaluation of refugee
   protection in the era of european economic integration', (1993) 26 *Cornell
   International Law Journal* 3, pp. 719–736
Hatzopoulos, Vassilis, 'Recent developments of the case law of the ECJ in the
   field of services', (2000) 37 CML Rev., pp. 43–82
Hillion, Christophe, 'Institutional aspects of the partnership between the
   European Union and the Newly Independent States of the Former Soviet
   Union: Case studies of Russia and Ukraine', (2000) 37 CML Rev.,
   pp. 1211–1235
Inglis, Kirstyn, 'The Europe agreements compared in the light of their pre-
   accession re-orientation', (2000) 37 CML Rev., pp. 1173–1210
Lenaerts, Koen, 'Education in European Community law after Maastricht',
   (1994) 31 CML Rev., pp. 7–41
Marenco, Giuliano, 'The notion of restrictions on the freedom of
   establishment and provision of services in the case law of the court', (1991)
   11 YBEL, pp. 111–150

Monar, Jörg, 'Justice and Home Affairs in the Treaty of Amsterdam: reform at the price of fragmentation', (1998) 23 EL Rev. 4, pp. 320–335

O'Keefe, David, 'The Schengen Convention: a suitable model for european integration', (1991) 11 YBEL, pp. 185–219

— 'Practical difficulties of the application of article 48 of the Treaty', (1982) 19 CML Rev. 1, pp. 35–60

Peers, Steve, 'Indirect rights for third country service providers confirmed', (1995) 20 EL Rev., pp. 303–309

— 'Towards equality: actual and potential rights of third country nationals in the European Union', (1996) 33 EL Rev. 1, pp. 7–50

Penza, 'Le passeport europeén', (1982) *Revue du Marché Commun* p. 489

Pertek, J., 'Free movement of professionals and recognition of higher education diplomas', (1992) 12 YBEL, pp. 293–324

Roth, Wulf-Henning, 'Wettbewerb der Mitgliedstaaten oder Wettbewerb der Hersteller?', (1995) 159 *Zeitschrift für das gesamte Handelsrecht und Wirtschaftsrecht* 1, pp. 78–95

Rudolf, Beate, and Bernard H. Oxman, '*Matthews v. United Kingdom*, Application No. 24833/94 European Court of Human Rights, February 18, 1999', (1999) 93 *American Journal of International Law* 3, p. 668

Shaw, Jo, 'European Union citizenship: the IGC and beyond', (1997) 3 *European Public Law* 3, pp. 413– 439

Sherlock, Ann, 'Deportation of aliens and Article 8 ECHR', (1998) 23 EL Rev., pp. 62–75

Snell, J. and M. Andenas, 'Exploring the outer limits – restrictions on the free movement of goods and services, (1999) 10 EBL Rev. 7–8, pp. 252–283

Stanley, P., 'Case C-107/94, *Asscher v. Staatssecretaris van Financiën*, Judgment of 27 June 1996, Fifth Chamber [1996] ECR I-3089', (1997) 34 CML Rev. 3, pp. 713–726

Tomuschat, Christian, 'Case C-85/96, *Maria Martinez Sala v. Freistaat Bayern*, Judgment of 12 May 1998, Full Court [1998]', (2000) 37 CML Rev. 2, pp. 449–457

Torgersen, O.-A., 'The limitations to the free movement of goods and the freedom to provide services – in search of a common approach', (1999) 10 EBL Rev. 9–10, pp. 371–387

Weatherill, S., 'After Keck: Some thoughts on how to clarify the clarification', (1996) 33 CML Rev. 5, pp. 885–906

Weiss, Friedl, 'The General Agreement on Trade in Services', (1995) 32 CML Rev. pp.1177–1225

BOOKS

Bernitz, Ulf and Hedvig Lokrantz Bernitz, 'Human rights and european identity: The debate about european citizenship', in Philip Alston (ed.), *The European Union and Human Rights*, (Oxford: OUP, 1999)

Craig, Paul and Gráinne de Burca, *EU law: texts, cases and materials*, (2nd edn, Oxford: OUP, 1998)

Cranston, Ross (ed.), *The Single Market and the Law of Banking*, (London: Lloyds of London Press, 1991)

Dassesse, Marc, Stuart Isaacs and Graham Penn, *EC Banking Law*, (2nd rev. edn, London: Lloyds of London Press, 1994)

Evans, Andrew, *A Textbook of European Union Law*, (Oxford: Hart Publishing, 1998)

Guild, Elspeth (ed.), *The Legal Frameworks and Social Consequences of Free Movement of Persons in the European Union*, (The Hague: Kluwer Law International, 1999)

Hailbronner, Kay, *Immigration and Asylum Law and Policy of the European Union*, (The Hague: Kluwer Law International, 2000)

Handoll, John, *Free Movement of Persons in the EU*, (Chichester: John Wiley, 1995)

Kapteyn, Paul J.G. and Pieter Verloren van Themaat, *Introduction to the Law of the European Communities*, (3rd edn, L.W. Gormley (ed.), London: Kluwer Law International, 1998)

O'Keefe, David and Margot Horspool, *European Citizenship and the Free Movement of Persons: Essays in honour of G.J. Hand*, (Sweet and Maxwell, 1996)

Nascimbe, Bruno, *Nationality Laws in the EU*, (Milan: Giuffrè, 1996)

Noll and Vedsted, 'Non-communitarians: refugees and asylum policies', in Philip Alston (ed.), *The European Union and Human Rights*, (Oxford: OUP, 1999)

Plender, Richard, 'An incipient form of European Citizenship', in Francis Geoffrey Jacobs (ed.), *European Law and the Individual*, (Amsterdam: North-Holland Publishing Co., 1976)

— in Vaughan (ed.), *Law of the European Communities*, (North-Holland Publishing Co.)

Steiner, Josephine and Lorna Woods, *Textbook on EC Law*, (7th edn, London: Blackstone Press, 2000)

Usher, John Anthony, *The Law of Money and Financial Services in the EC*, (2nd edn, Oxford: Oxford EC Law Library, 2000)

Weatherill, Stephen and Paul Beaumont, *EU Law*, (3rd (new) edn, London: Penguin Books, 1999)

Index

EUROPEAN MONOGRAPHS

1. Lammy Betten (ed.), *The Future of European Social Policy* (second and revised edition, 1991).

2. J.M.E. Loman, K.J.M. Mortelmans, H.H.G. Post, J.S. Watson, *Culture and Community Law: Before and after Maastricht* (1992).

3. Prof. Dr. J.A.E. Vervaele, *Fraud Against the Community: The Need for European Fraud Legislation* (1992).

4. P. Rawortli, *The Legislative Process in the European Community* (1993).

5. J. Stuyck, *Financial and Monetary Integration in the European Economic Community* (1993).

6. J.H.V. Stuyck, A.J. Vossestein (eds.), *State Entrepreneurship, National Monopolies and European Community Law* (1993).

7. J. Stuyck, A. Looijestijn-Clearie (eds.), *The European Economic Area EC-EFTA* (1994).

8. R.B. Bouterse, *Competition and Integration – What Goals Count?* (1994).

9. R. Barents, *The Agricultural Law of the EC* (1994).

10. Nicholas Emiliou, *The Principle of Proportionality in European Law: A Comparative Study* (1996).

11. Eivind Smith, *National Parliaments as Cornerstones of European Integration* (1996).

12. Jan H. Jans, *European Environmental Law* (1996).

13. Siofra O'Leary, *The Evolving Concept of Community Citizenship: From the Free Movement of Persons to Union Citizenship* (1996).

14. Laurence Gormley (ed.), *Current and Future Perspectives on EC Competition Law* (1997).

15. Simone White, *Protection of the Financial Interests of the European Communities: The Fight against Fraud and Corruption* (1998).

16. Morten P. Broberg, *The European Commission's Jurisdiction to Scrutinise Mergers* (1998).

17. Doris Hildebrand, *The Role of Economic Analysis in the EC Competition Rules* (1998).

18. Christof R.A. Swaak, *European Community Law and the Automobile Industry* (1999).

19. Dorthe Dahlgaard Dingel, *Public Procurement. A Harmonization of the National Judicial Review of the Application of European Community Law* (1999).

20. J.A.E. Vervaele (ed.) *Compliance and Enforcement of European Community Law* (1999).

21. Martin Trybus, *European Defence Procurement Law: International and National Procurement Systems as Models for a Liberalised Defence Procurement Market in Europe* (1999).

22. Helen Staples, *The Legal Status of Third Country Nationals Resident in the European Union* (1999).

23. Damien Geradin (ed.) *The Liberalization of State Monopolies in the European Union and Beyond* (2000).

24. Katja Heede, *European Ombudsman: Redress and Control at Union Level* (2000).

25. Ulf Bernitz, Joakim Nergelius (eds.) *General Principles of European Community Law* (2000).

26. Michaela Drahos, *Convergence of Competition Laws and Policies in the European Community* (2001).

27. Damien Geradin (ed.) *The Liberalization of Electricity and Natural Gas in the European Union* (2001).

28. Gisella Gori, *Towards an EU Right to Education* (2001).

29. Brendan Smith, *Constitution Building in the European Union* (2001).

30. Friedl Weiss and Frank Wooldridge, *Free Movement of Persons within the European Community* (2002).